3B

FOCUS ON GRAMMAR

AN INTEGRATED SKILLS APPROACH

THIRD EDITION

MARJORIE FUCHS

MARGARET BONNER

MIRIAM WESTHEIMER

PEARSON
Longman

To the memory of my parents, Edith and Joseph Fuchs—MF
To my parents, Marie and Joseph Maus, and to my son, Luke Frances—MB
To my husband, Joel Einleger, and my children, Ari and Leora—MW

FOCUS ON GRAMMAR 3B: An Integrated Skills Approach, Third Edition

Copyright © 2006, 2000, 1994 by Pearson Education, Inc.
All rights reserved.
No part of this publication may be reproduced,
stored in a retrieval system, or transmitted
in any form or by any means, electronic, mechanical,
photocopying, recording, or otherwise,
without the prior written permission of the publisher.

Pearson Education, 10 Bank Street, White Plains, NY 10606

Vice president, multimedia and skills: Sherry Preiss
Executive editor: Laura Le Dréan
Senior development editor: Françoise Leffler
Vice president, director of design and production: Rhea Banker
Director of editorial production: Linda Moser
Production supervisor: Christine Edmonds
Senior production editor: Kathleen Silloway
Art director: Ann France
Senior manufacturing buyer: Nancy Flaggman
Photo research: Aerin Csigay
Cover design: Rhea Banker
Cover images: (background) Comstock Images (#comks76622) RF, (background center) Nick
   Koudis (#AA010649) RF; (center) Harald Sund (#200131667-001) RM
Text design: Quorum Creative Services, Rhea Banker
Text composition: ElectraGraphics, Inc.
Illustrators: Steve Attoe pp. 2, 58, 59, 135, 163, 356; Bumar Technical Corporation p. 172; Moffitt Cecil pp. 19,
   21, 240, 406; Ronald Chironna pp. 28, 419; Chi Chung pp. 249, 250; Chris Gash pp. 8, 9, 212, 217; Brian
   Hughes pp. 16, 139, 210, 229, 230, 281, 285; Jock MacRae pp. 42, 103; Tom Newsom pp. 41, 49, 50, 99,
   100, 208; PC&F pp. 259, 261; Dusan Petrici pp. 17, 65, 149, 150, 256; Steve Schulman pp. 226, 352, 354,
   364, 366, 420 (left); Susan Scott p. 34; Gary Torrisi pp. 199, 201, 295, 420 (right); Meryl Treatner pp. 73, 113.
Text credits: See p. viii.
Photo credits: See p. viii.

Library of Congress Cataloging-in-Publication Data

Focus on grammar. An integrated skills approach.— 3rd ed.
   p. cm.
   ISBN 0-13-147466-9 (v. 1 : student book : alk. paper) — ISBN 0-13-189971-6 (v. 2 :
student book : alk. paper) — ISBN 0-13-189984-8 (v. 3 : student book : alk. paper) —
ISBN 0-13-190008-0 (v. 4 : student book : alk. paper) — ISBN 0-13-191273-9 (v. 5 :
student book : alk. paper)
   1. English language—Textbooks for foreign speakers. 2. English language—Grammar—
Problems, exercises, etc.
PE1128.F555 2005
428.2'4—dc22

2005007655

ISBNs: 0-13-189995-3 (Student Book B)
        0-13-193924-6 (Student Book B with Audio CD)

LONGMAN ON THE **WEB**

Longman.com offers online resources for
teachers and students. Access our Companion
Websites, our online catalog, and our local
offices around the world.

Visit us at **longman.com**.

Printed in The United States of America
   2 3 4 5 6 7 8 9 10—WC—12 11 10 09 08 07 06

CONTENTS

PART **VIII** MORE MODALS AND SIMILAR EXPRESSIONS

APPENDICES

ABOUT THE AUTHORS

Marjorie Fuchs has taught ESL at New York City Technical College and LaGuardia Community College of the City University of New York and EFL at the Sprach Studio Lingua Nova in Munich, Germany. She has a master's degree in Applied English Linguistics and a Certificate in TESOL from the University of Wisconsin—Madison. She has authored and co-authored many widely used books and multimedia materials, notably *Crossroads, Top Twenty ESL Word Games: Beginning Vocabulary Development, Families: Ten Card Games for Language Learners, Focus on Grammar 4: An Integrated Skills Approach, Focus on Grammar 3 CD-ROM, Focus on Grammar 4 CD-ROM, Longman English Interactive 3* and *4, Grammar Express Basic, Grammar Express Basic CD-ROM, Grammar Express Intermediate,* and the workbooks to the *Longman Dictionary of American English, the Longman Photo Dictionary, The Oxford Picture Dictionary, Focus on Grammar 3* and *4,* and *Grammar Express Basic.*

Margaret Bonner has taught ESL at Hunter College and the Borough of Manhattan Community College of the City University of New York, at Taiwan National University in Taipei, and at Virginia Commonwealth University in Richmond. She holds a master's degree in Library Science from Columbia University, and she has done work toward a Ph.D. in English Literature at the Graduate Center of the City University of New York. She has authored and co-authored numerous ESL and EFL print and multimedia materials, including textbooks for the national school system of Oman, *Step into Writing: A Basic Writing Text, Focus on Grammar 4: An Integrated Skills Approach, Focus on Grammar 4 Workbook, Grammar Express Basic, Grammar Express Basic CD-ROM, Grammar Express Basic Workbook, Grammar Express Intermediate, Focus on Grammar 3 CD-ROM, Focus on Grammar 4 CD-ROM, Longman English Interactive 4,* and *The Oxford Picture Dictionary Intermediate Workbook.*

Miriam Westheimer taught EFL at all levels of instruction in Haifa, Israel, for a period of six years. She has also taught ESL at Queens College, at LaGuardia Community College, and in the American Language Program of Columbia University. She holds a master's degree in TESOL and a doctorate in Curriculum and Teaching from Teachers College of Columbia University. She is the co-author of a communicative grammar program developed and widely used in Israel.

TEXT AND PHOTO CREDITS

INTRODUCTION

 ## The *Focus on Grammar* series

Written by ELT professionals, *Focus on Grammar: An Integrated Skills Approach* helps students to understand and practice English grammar. The primary aim of the course is for students to gain confidence in their ability to speak and write English accurately and fluently.

The **third edition** retains the series' focus on English grammar through lively listening, speaking, reading, and writing activities. The new *Focus on Grammar* also maintains the same five-level progression as the second edition:

- Level 1 (Beginning, formerly Introductory)
- Level 2 (High-Beginning, formerly Basic)
- Level 3 (Intermediate)
- Level 4 (High-Intermediate)
- Level 5 (Advanced)

 ## What is the *Focus on Grammar* methodology?

Both controlled and communicative practice

While students expect and need to learn the formal rules of a language, it is crucial that they also practice new structures in a variety of contexts in order to internalize and master them. To this end, *Focus on Grammar* provides an abundance of both controlled and communicative exercises so that students can bridge the gap between knowing grammatical structures and using them. The many communicative activities in each Student Book unit provide opportunity for critical thinking while enabling students to personalize what they have learned in order to talk to one another with ease about hundreds of everyday issues.

A unique four-step approach

The series follows a four-step approach:

Step 1: Grammar in Context shows the new structures in natural contexts, such as articles and conversations.

Step 2: Grammar Presentation presents the structures in clear and accessible grammar charts, notes, and examples.

Step 3: Focused Practice of both form and meaning of the new structures is provided in numerous and varied controlled exercises.

Step 4: Communication Practice allows students to use the new structures freely and creatively in motivating, open-ended activities.

Thorough recycling

Underpinning the scope and sequence of the *Focus on Grammar* series is the belief that students need to use target structures many times, in different contexts, and at increasing levels of difficulty. For this reason, new grammar is constantly recycled throughout the book so that students have maximum exposure to the target forms and become comfortable using them in speech and in writing.

A complete classroom text and reference guide

A major goal in the development of *Focus on Grammar* has been to provide students with books that serve not only as vehicles for classroom instruction but also as resources for reference and self-study. In each Student Book, the combination of grammar charts, grammar notes, a glossary of grammar terms, and extensive appendices provides a complete and invaluable reference guide for students.

Ongoing assessment

Review Tests at the end of each part of the Student Book allow for continual self-assessment. In addition, the tests in the new *Focus on Grammar* Assessment Package provide teachers with a valid, reliable, and practical means of determining students' appropriate levels of placement in the course and of assessing students' achievement throughout the course. At Levels 4 (High-Intermediate) and 5 (Advanced), Proficiency Tests give teachers an overview of their students' general grammar knowledge.

What are the components of each level of *Focus on Grammar*?

Student Book

The Student Book is divided into eight or more parts, depending on the level. Each part contains grammatically related units, with each unit focusing on specific grammatical structures; where appropriate, units present contrasting forms. The exercises in each unit are thematically related to one another, and all units have the same clear, easy-to-follow format.

Teacher's Manual

The Teacher's Manual contains a variety of suggestions and information to enrich the material in the Student Book. It includes general teaching suggestions for each section of a typical unit, answers to frequently asked questions, unit-by-unit teaching tips with ideas for further communicative practice, and a supplementary activity section. Answers to the Student Book exercises and audioscripts of the listening activities are found at the back of the Teacher's Manual. Also included in the Teacher's Manual is a CD-ROM of teaching tools, including PowerPoint presentations that offer alternative ways of presenting selected grammar structures.

Workbook

The Workbook accompanying each level of *Focus on Grammar* provides additional exercises appropriate for self-study of the target grammar for each Student Book unit. Tests included in each Workbook provide students with additional opportunities for self-assessment.

Audio Program

All of the listening exercises from the Student Book, as well as the Grammar in Context passages and other appropriate exercises, are included on the program's CDs. In the book, the symbol ∩ appears next to the listening exercises. Another symbol ∩, indicating that listening is optional, appears next to the Grammar in Context passages and some exercises. All of these scripts appear in the Teacher's Manual and may be used as an alternative way of presenting the activities.

Some Student Books are packaged with a separate Student Audio CD. This CD includes the listening exercise from each unit.

CD-ROM

The *Focus on Grammar* CD-ROM provides students with individualized practice and immediate feedback. Fully contextualized and interactive, the activities broaden and extend practice of the grammatical structures in the reading, writing, listening, and speaking skills areas. The CD-ROM includes grammar review, review tests, score-based remedial practice, games, and all relevant reference material from the Student Book. It can also be used in conjunction with the *Longman Interactive American Dictionary* CD-ROM.

Assessment Package (NEW)

An extensive, comprehensive Assessment Package has been developed for each level of the third edition of *Focus on Grammar*. The components of the Assessment Package are:

1. **Placement, Diagnostic, and Achievement Tests**

   - a Placement Test to screen students and place them into the correct level
   - Diagnostic Tests for each part of the Student Book
   - Unit Achievement Tests for each unit of the Student Book
   - Part Achievement Tests for each part of the Student Book

2. **General Proficiency Tests**

   - two Proficiency Tests at Level 4 (High-Intermediate)
   - two Proficiency Tests at Level 5 (Advanced)

   These tests can be administered at any point in the course.

3. **Audio CD**

   The listening portions of the Placement, Diagnostic, and Achievement Tests are recorded on CDs. The scripts appear in the Assessment Package.

4. **Test-Generating Software**

   The test-bank software provides thousands of questions from which teachers can create class-appropriate tests. All items are labeled according to the grammar structure they are testing, so teachers can easily select relevant items; they can also design their own items to add to the tests.

Transparencies (NEW)

Transparencies of all the grammar charts in the Student Book are also available. These transparencies are a classroom visual aid that will help instructors point out important patterns and structures of grammar.

Companion Website

The companion website contains a wealth of information and activities for both teachers and students. In addition to general information about the course pedagogy, the website provides extensive practice exercises for the classroom, a language lab, or at home.

What's new in the third edition of the Student Book?

In response to users' requests, this edition has:

- a new four-color design
- easy-to-read color coding for the four steps
- new and updated reading texts for Grammar in Context
- post-reading activities (in addition to the pre-reading questions)
- more exercise items
- an editing (error analysis) exercise in each unit
- an Internet activity in each unit
- a Glossary of Grammar Terms
- expanded Appendices

References

Alexander, L. G. (1988). *Longman English Grammar.* White Plains: Longman.

Biber, D., S. Conrad, E. Finegan, S. Johansson, and G. Leech (1999). *Longman Grammar of Spoken and Written English.* White Plains: Longman.

Celce-Murcia, M., and D. Freeman (1999). *The Grammar Book.* Boston: Heinle and Heinle.

Celce-Murcia, M., and S. Hilles (1988). *Techniques and Resources in Teaching Grammar.* New York: Oxford University Press.

Firsten, R. (2002). *The ELT Grammar Book.* Burlingame, CA: Alta Book Center Publishers.

Garner, B. (2003). *Garner's Modern American Usage.* New York: Oxford University Press.

Greenbaum, S. (1996). *The Oxford English Grammar.* New York: Oxford University Press.

Leech, G. (2004). *Meaning and the English Verb.* Harlow, UK: Pearson.

Lewis, M. (1997). *Implementing the Lexical Approach.* Hove East Sussex, UK: Language Teaching Publications.

Longman (2002). *Longman Dictionary of English Language and Culture.* Harlow, UK: Longman.

Willis, D. (2003). *Rules, Patterns and Words.* New York: Cambridge University Press.

TOUR OF A UNIT

Each unit in the *Focus on Grammar* Series presents a specific grammar structure (or two, in case of a contrast) and develops a major theme, which is set by the opening text. All units follow the same unique **four-step approach.**

Step 1: Grammar in Context

The **conversation** or **reading** in this section shows the grammar structure in a natural context. The high-interest text presents authentic language in a variety of real-life formats: magazine articles, web pages, questionnaires, and more. Students can listen to the text on an audio CD to get accustomed to the sound of the grammar structure in a natural context.

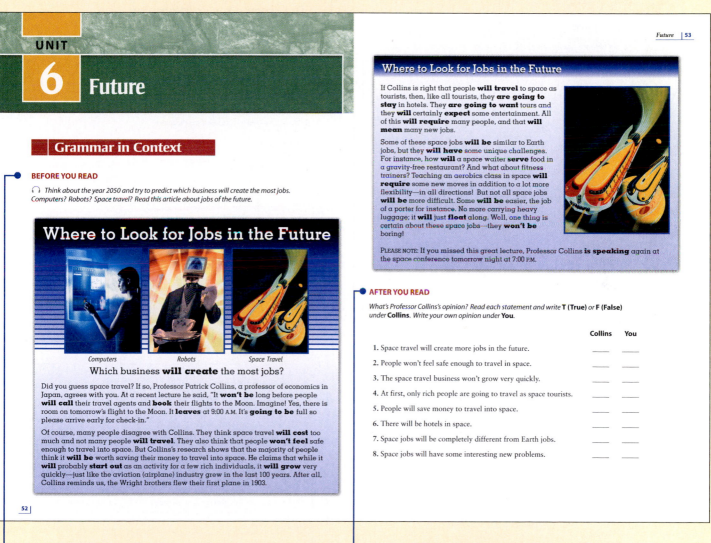

> • *Pre-reading questions* create interest, elicit students' knowledge about the topic, and lead students to make predictions about the text.

> • A *post-reading activity* helps students understand the text and focus on the grammar structure.

Step 2: Grammar Presentation

This section is made up of grammar charts, notes, and examples. The **grammar charts** focus on the forms of the grammar structure. The **grammar notes** and **examples** focus on the meanings and uses of the structure.

*Clear and easy-to-read **grammar charts** present the grammar structure in all its forms and combinations.*

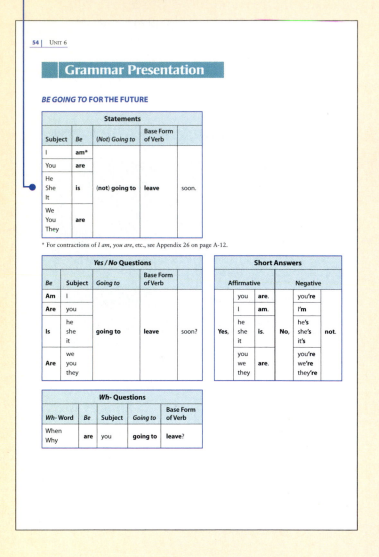

54 | UNIT 6

Grammar Presentation

BE GOING TO FOR THE FUTURE

		Statements		
Subject	Be	(Not) Going to	Base Form of Verb	
I	am*			
You	are			
He She It	is	(not) going to	leave	soon.
We You They	are			

* For contractions of *I am, you are,* etc., see Appendix 26 on page A-12.

	Yes / No Questions			
Be	Subject	Going to	Base Form of Verb	
Am	I			
Are	you			
Is	he she it	going to	leave	soon?
Are	we you they			

Short Answers					
Affirmative			Negative		
	you	are.		you're	
	I	am.		I'm	
Yes,	he she it	is.	No,	he's she's it's	not.
	you we they	are.		you're we're they're	

Wh- Questions				
Wh- Word	Be	Subject	Going to	Base Form of Verb
When Why	are	you	going to	leave?

*Each **grammar note** gives a short, simple explanation of one use of the structure. The accompanying **examples** ensure students' understanding of the point.*

56 | UNIT 6

GRAMMAR NOTES	EXAMPLES

1. There are several ways to talk about the **future**. You can use:
• *be going to*
• *will*
• **present progressive**
• **simple present**
 	
Now
Past ——————————— Future
               — X —
        meeting
 	
USAGE NOTE: Sometimes only one form of the future is appropriate, but in many cases more than one form is possible.
	• They**'re going to have** a meeting.
	• I think I**'ll go.**
	• It**'s taking** place next week.
	• It **starts** at 9:00 A.M. on Monday.

2. To make **predictions** or **guesses** about the future, use:
• *be going to*
    OR
• *will*
▶ BE CAREFUL! Use *be going to* instead of *will* when something in the present helps you make the prediction about the future.
	• People **are going to travel** to space.
	    OR
	• People **will travel** to space.
	
	• Look at those dark clouds! It**'s going to** rain.
	NOT It'll rain.

3. To talk about future **intentions** or **plans**, use:
• *be going to*
    OR
• *will*
    OR
• **present progressive**
 	
We often use *will* when we decide something at the moment of speaking.
 	
We often use the **present progressive** when we talk about future plans that are already arranged.
	• I**'m going to fly** to Mars next week.
	    OR
	• I**'ll fly** to Mars next week.
	    OR
	• I**'m flying** to Mars next week.
	
	A: The show is opening next week.
	B: Sounds interesting. I think I**'ll go.**
	
	• I**'m flying** to Chicago next month. I already have a ticket.

Pronunciation Note
In informal speech, *going to* is often pronounced "gonna" /gənə/.

*• **Be careful! notes** alert students to common errors made by students of English.*

*• **Time lines** clarify the meaning of verb forms.*

Step 3: Focused Practice

This section provides students with a variety of contextualized **controlled exercises** to practice both the forms and the uses of the grammar structure.

Focused Practice *always begins with a "for recognition only" exercise called* **Discover the Grammar**.

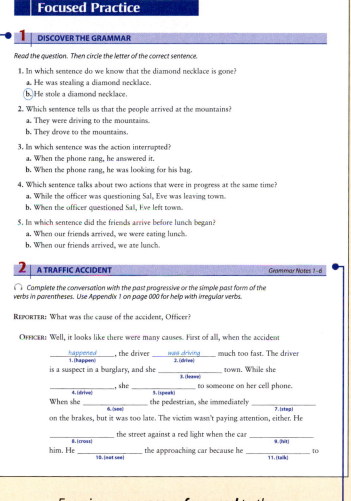

A **variety of exercise types** *guide students from recognition to accurate production of the grammar structure.*

Exercises are **cross-referenced** to the appropriate grammar notes to provide a quick review.

Focused Practice *always ends with an* **editing** *exercise to teach students to find and correct typical mistakes.*

---

38 | UNIT 4

Focused Practice

1 | DISCOVER THE GRAMMAR

Read the question. Then circle the letter of the correct sentence.

1. In which sentence do we know that the diamond necklace is gone?
   a. He was stealing a diamond necklace.
   b. He stole a diamond necklace.

2. Which sentence tells us that the people arrived at the mountains?
   a. They were driving to the mountains.
   b. They drove to the mountains.

3. In which sentence was the action interrupted?
   a. When the phone rang, he answered it.
   b. When the phone rang, he was looking for his bag.

4. Which sentence talks about two actions that were in progress at the same time?
   a. While the officer was questioning Sal, Eve was leaving town.
   b. When the officer questioned Sal, Eve left town.

5. In which sentence did the friends arrive before lunch began?
   a. When our friends arrived, we were eating lunch.
   b. When our friends arrived, we ate lunch.

2 | A TRAFFIC ACCIDENT   *Grammar Notes 1–6*

Complete the conversation with the past progressive or the simple past form of the verbs in parentheses. Use Appendix 1 on page 000 for help with irregular verbs.

REPORTER: What was the cause of the accident, Officer?

OFFICER: Well, it looks like there were many causes. First of all, when the accident
__happened__, the driver __was driving__ much too fast. The driver
   1. (happen)   2. (drive)
is a suspect in a burglary, and she _____ town. While she
                                    3. (leave)
_____, she _____ to someone on her cell phone.
   4. (drive)   5. (speak)
When she _____ the pedestrian, she immediately _____
               6. (see)   7. (step)
on the brakes, but it was too late. The victim wasn't paying attention, either. He
_____ the street against a red light when the car _____
   8. (cross)   9. (hit)
him. He _____ the approaching car because he _____ to
          10. (not see)   11. (talk)

---

40 | UNIT 4

4 | BLIZZARD   *Grammar Notes 1–6*

Combine the pairs of sentences. Use the past progressive or the simple past form of the verb. Remember to use commas when necessary.

1. The blizzard started. Mr. Ligo attended a party.
   When __the blizzard started, Mr. Ligo was attending a party.__

2. The wind began to blow. The electricity went out.
   When _____

3. He drove home. He listened to his car radio.
   While _____

4. He pulled over to the side of the road. He couldn't see anything.
   _____ when _____

5. He listened to the news. He heard about the burglary.
   While _____

6. It stopped snowing. Mr. Ligo went to the police station.
   When _____

5 | EDITING

Read this personal journal entry. There are seven mistakes in the use of the past progressive and the simple past. The first mistake is already corrected. Find and correct six more. Remember to look at punctuation!

> happened
> What was happening to me this morning was so unbelievable! I walked down the
> street while a woman stopped in front of me and asked me for directions to the
> nearest bank. At that moment, I was seeing my friend Bill across the street.
> I called out to him and asked him to wait for me. Luckily for me, he did. Bill
> saw everything. While I talking to the woman, a pickpocket was put his hand
> into my backpack. Bill started to walk away. I thought he didn't want to wait
> for me, but I was wrong. When Bill saw the pickpocket he went to call the
> police. They were arriving immediately. The police arrested the woman and the
> pickpocket. What an experience!

Step 4: Communication Practice

This section provides open-ended **communicative activities** giving students the opportunity to use the grammar structure appropriately and fluently.

A **listening** activity gives students the opportunity to check their aural comprehension.

A **writing** activity allows students to use the grammar structure in a variety of formats.

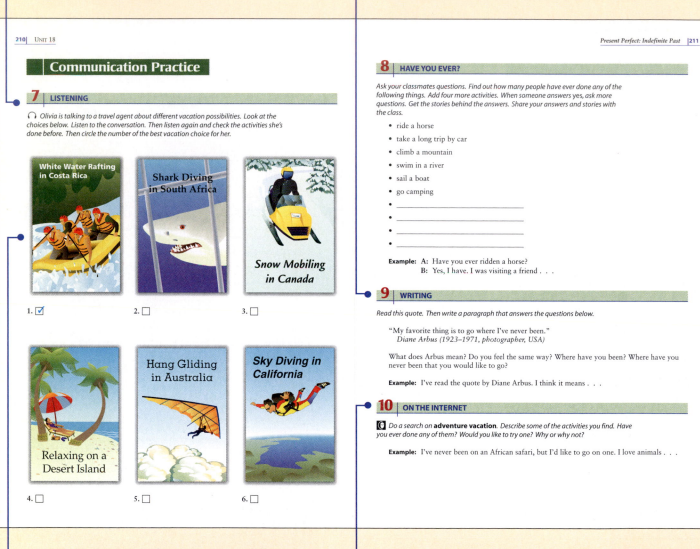

210 | UNIT 18

Communication Practice

7 | LISTENING

🎧 Olivia is talking to a travel agent about different vacation possibilities. Look at the choices below. Listen to the conversation. Then listen again and check the activities she's done before. Then circle the number of the best vacation choice for her.

White Water Rafting in Costa Rica

Shark Diving in South Africa

Snow Mobiling in Canada

1. ☑   2. ☐   3. ☐

Relaxing on a Desert Island

Hang Gliding in Australia

Sky Diving in California

4. ☐   5. ☐   6. ☐

Present Perfect: Indefinite Past **|211**

8 | HAVE YOU EVER?

Ask your classmates questions. Find out how many people have ever done any of the following things. Add four more activities. When someone answers yes, ask more questions. Get the stories behind the answers. Share your answers and stories with the class.

- ride a horse
- take a long trip by car
- climb a mountain
- swim in a river
- sail a boat
- go camping
- _____
- _____
- _____
- _____

Example: A: Have you ever ridden a horse?
B: Yes, I have. I was visiting a friend . . .

9 | WRITING

Read this quote. Then write a paragraph that answers the questions below.

"My favorite thing is to go where I've never been."
Diane Arbus (1923–1971, photographer, USA)

What does Arbus mean? Do you feel the same way? Where have you been? Where have you never been that you would like to go?

Example: I've read the quote by Diane Arbus. I think it means . . .

10 | ON THE INTERNET

💻 Do a search on **adventure vacation**. Describe some of the activities you find. Have you ever done any of them? Would you like to try one? Why or why not?

Example: I've never been on an African safari, but I'd like to go on one. I love animals . . .

Many exercises and activities are **art based** to provide visual cues and an interesting context and springboard for meaningful conversations.

An **Internet** activity gives students the opportunity to expand on the content of the unit and interact with their classmates creatively and fluently.

TOUR BEYOND THE UNIT

In the *Focus on Grammar* series, the grammatically related units are grouped into parts, and each part concludes with a section called **From Grammar to Writing** and a **Review Test** section.

From Grammar to Writing

This section presents a point which applies specifically to writing, for example, using descriptive adjectives to develop a paragraph. Students are guided to practice the point in a **piece of extended writing**.

• An **introduction** relates the grammar point to the writing focus.

• Students practice **pre-writing strategies** such as word-mapping, tree-diagramming, and outlining.

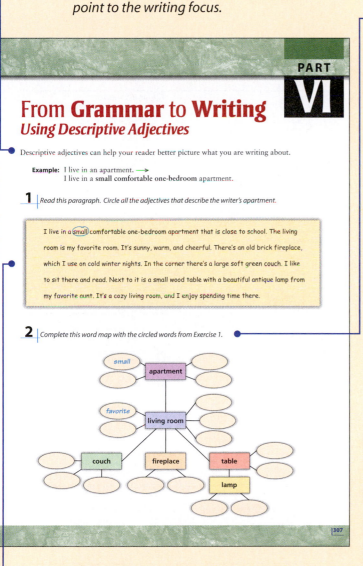

From Grammar to Writing
Using Descriptive Adjectives

PART **VI**

Descriptive adjectives can help your reader better picture what you are writing about.

Example: I live in an apartment. →
I live in a **small comfortable one-bedroom** apartment.

1 | Read this paragraph. Circle all the adjectives that describe the writer's apartment.

> I live in a (small) comfortable one-bedroom apartment that is close to school. The living room is my favorite room. It's sunny, warm, and cheerful. There's an old brick fireplace, which I use on cold winter nights. In the corner there's a large soft green couch. I like to sit there and read. Next to it is a small wood table with a beautiful antique lamp from my favorite aunt. It's a cozy living room, and I enjoy spending time there.

2 | Complete this word map with the circled words from Exercise 1.

307

308 | PART VI

3 | Before you write . . .

1. Work in small groups. Put the adjectives from the box into the correct categories. Brainstorm other adjectives for each category. You can use a dictionary for help.

attractive	coarse	comfortable	cozy	cute	enormous
gorgeous	hard	hideous	huge	large	little
lovely	rough	run-down	soft	tiny	ugly

a. things that are big: _large,_

b. things that are small: _little,_

c. things that look good: _attractive,_

d. things that look bad: _run-down,_

e. things that feel good: _soft,_

f. things that feel bad: _hard,_

2. Think about a room you know. On a separate piece of paper, draw a word map like the one in Exercise 2. Use some of the adjectives in the box above.

3. Discuss your map with a partner. Do you want to add or change any adjectives?

Example: A: How small is the kitchen?
B: Oh, it's tiny.

4 | Write a paragraph about the room from Exercise 3. Use your word map.

5 | Exchange paragraphs with a different partner. Complete the chart.

Did the writer use adjectives that describe how things _____?			
	Yes	**No**	**Example(s)**
look	☐	☐	_____
feel	☐	☐	_____
smell	☐	☐	_____
sound	☐	☐	_____
What would you like more information about?			_____

6 | Work with your partner. Discuss each other's editing questions from Exercise 5. Then rewrite your own paragraph. Answer any questions your partner asked.

• **Writing formats** include business letters, personal letters, notes, instructions, paragraphs, reports, and essays.

• The section includes **peer review** and **editing** of the students' writing.

Review Test

This review section, covering all the grammar structures presented in the part, can be used as a test. An **Answer Key** is provided at the back of the book.

PART VI

Review Test

I *Complete the advertisements by choosing the correct words in parentheses.*

1. FOR RENT. Live _____*comfortably*_____ in this _____ studio
   a. (comfortable / comfortably)   b. (cozy / cozily)

   apartment. _____ rent makes it a _____
   c. (Cheap / Cheaply)   d. (perfect / perfectly)

   home for one student.

2. FOR SALE. Woman's bicycle. I'm asking the _____ low price of $65
   a. (incredible / incredibly)

   for this _____ five-speed bike. I've _____
   b. (new / newly)   c. (hard / hardly)

   used it at all. Don't miss this _____ bargain.
   d. (terrific / terrifically)

3. FREE to a _____ family. Skipper is a _____
   a. (good / well)   b. (beautiful / beautifully)

   and friendly puppy. He behaves _____ with children, and he is very
   c. (good / well)

   _____. We are moving very soon, so if you want Skipper, please act
   d. (obedient / obediently)

   _____.
   e. (quick / quickly)

II *Circle the letter of the correct answer to complete each sentence.*

1. I passed my driver's test. It seemed much _____ this time.   A Ⓑ C D

   (A) easy   (C) easiest

   (B) easier   (D) easily

2. Our team didn't play _____ I expected. I was disappointed.   A B C D

   (A) as well as   (C) as badly as

   (B) well   (D) better

3. The faster Tranh walks, _____.   A B C D

   (A) more tired   (C) the more tired he gets

   (B) he gets tired   (D) he gets more tired

(continued)

309

- The Review Tests *include* **multiple-choice questions** *in standardized test formats, giving students practice in test taking.*

Answer Key (right panel)

(Unit 21)
2. enough
3. a lot of
4. How much
5. a little
6. a few
7. some
8. How many
9. any
10. much
11. a lot of
12. a few

III (Unit 22)
2. a, a, an
3. the
4. The
5. the, the
6. the
7. an
8. a
9. the, an

IV (Unit 22)
3. the
4. Money
5. Travel, Staying
6. The
7. Vegetables

V (Unit 22)
1. b. some
   c. a
   d. an
   e. The
   f. The
2. a. some
   b. some
   c. the
   d. some
   e. The
   f. the

VI (Units 21 and 22)
2. B   4. A   6. C
3. C   5. A   7. A

PART VI

I (Unit 23)
1. b. cozy
   c. Cheap
   d. perfect
2. a. incredibly
   b. new
   c. hardly
   d. terrific
3. a. good
   b. beautiful
   c. well
   d. obedient
   e. quickly

II (Units 25 and 26)
2. A   5. B   8. B   11. D
3. C   6. C   9. A   12. B
4. A   7. D   10. C   13. D

III (Unit 23)
2. C   5. C   8. B   11. C
3. D   6. B   9. B   12. B
4. B   7. A   10. C

IV (Units 25 and 26)
2. faster, more confused
3. later, sillier
4. harder, more fluently
5. more often, bigger
6. louder, faster
7. more frequently, worse

V (Units 24 and 26)
2. is as large as Apartment 22-G.
3. isn't as far (away) as Tony's pizzeria.
4. is as expensive as Tony's pizza.
5. play (OR are playing OR have played) as well as the Shock.
6. doesn't run as fast as (OR isn't as fast as) Jennifer.

VI (Units 25 and 26)
1. b. longest
   c. hardest
   d. the
   e. of
   f. best
2. a. big
   b. than
   c. much
   d. exciting
   e. Sooner
   f. as

VII (Units 23–26)

I think today has been the ~~bad~~ *worst* day of my life. My car broke down on the expressway during rush hour this morning—~~a~~ *the* busiest time of day. I sat there for an hour waiting for a tow truck. The longer I waited, the *more* nervous I became. I was a wreck when I got to work. Of course, this was the day we were closing *the* biggest deal of the year. My boss called me five times about one letter. And *the* more frequently he called, the worse I typed. My next worry is the repair bill for the car. I hope it isn't as high *as* the last time.

I'm going to try to relax now. There's an *interesting* ~~interested~~ movie on cable TV tonight. Jan saw it last week and says it's the *best* ~~better~~ film she's seen in a long time. After the movie, I'll take a ~~hotter~~ *hot* bath and go to bed. I'm looking forward to tomorrow. It can't be as *bad* ~~badly~~ as today!

RT-4

- The Review Tests Answer Key *provides* **cross-references** *to the appropriate unit(s) for easy review.*

ACKNOWLEDGMENTS

Before acknowledging the many people who have contributed to the third edition of *Focus on Grammar*, we wish to express our gratitude to those who worked on the first and second editions, and whose influence is still present in the new work. Our continuing thanks to:

- Joanne Dresner, who initiated the project and helped conceptualize the general approach of *Focus on Grammar*.

- Nancy Perry, Penny Laporte, Louisa Hellegers, and Joan Saslow, our editors for the first edition, and Françoise Leffler, our editor for the second edition, for helping to bring the books to fruition.

- Sharon Hilles, our grammar consultant, for her insight and advice on the first edition.

In the third edition, *Focus on Grammar* has continued to evolve as we update materials and respond to the valuable feedback from teachers and students who have been using the series. We are grateful to the following editors and colleagues:

- Laura Le Dréan, Executive Editor, for her dedication and commitment. In spite of an incredibly full schedule, she looked at every page of manuscript and offered excellent suggestions. In addition, she was always available and responsive to authors' concerns.

- Françoise Leffler, Senior Development Editor, for her continued dedication to the series and to improving *Focus on Grammar* with each new edition. As in the previous edition, we relied on her unflagging attention to detail and her wonderful sense of style.

- Kathleen Silloway, Senior Production Editor, for piloting the book through its many stages of production and for always giving us a heads up when more *FOG* was about to roll in.

- Irene Schoenberg, for generously sharing her experience in teaching our first two editions and for her enthusiastic support.

Finally, we are grateful, as always, to Rick Smith and Luke Frances, for their helpful input and for standing by and supporting us as we navigated our way through our third *FOG*.

We also wish to acknowledge the many reviewers for reading the manuscript and offering many useful suggestions.

Aileen Allison, Golden Gate Language School, Campbell, CA; **Larisa Álvarez Ávila,** Centro Educativo Renacimiento, Mérida, Yucatán, Mexico; **Jaime Bolaños,** Colegio Ker Liber, Guadalajara, Mexico; **Vahania Carvajal García,** Instituto Cultural Regina Teresiano, Hermosillo, Sonora, Mexico; **Julie Charland,** Ateliers de Langues CSCG, Québec City, Québec, Canada; **Amelia Chávez Ruiz,** Lake Forest School, Mexico State, Mexico; **Elisa Laura Chavira,** Instituto Cumbre del Noroeste, Ciudad

Obregón, Mexico; **Ronald Clark,** Boston University, Boston, MA; **Judy Cleek,** University of Tennessee at Martin, Martin, TN; **Elizabeth Clemente,** Instituto Tecnológico de Estudios Superiores de Monterrey, Atizapan, Mexico State, Mexico; **Sharon Cliff,** Richmond College, Richmond, TX; **Marilyn De Liro Álvarez,** Instituto "Las Brisas," Nuevo León, Mexico; **Susanna Eguren,** Instituto Cultural Peruano Norteamericano, Lima, Peru; **Marcia Gethin-Jones,** University of Connecticut, Stamford, CT; **Monica Hilding,** Central Community School, Salt Lake City, UT; **Sue Hynes,** Daley College, Chicago, IL; **Silvia Icela Espinoza Galvez,** Colegio Lux, Hermosillo, Sonora, Mexico; **Elizabeth Kelley,** University of California, San Diego, CA; **Anik Low,** Collège Jean-de-Brébeuf, Montréal, Québec, Canada; **Hank Mantell,** International Education Programs, University of California, Riverside, CA; **Javier Martínez García,** Instituto Las Américas, Mexico City, D. F., Mexico; **Darlene Mitchell,** International English Center, Boulder, CO; **Norma Morales Sánchez,** Instituto Carlos Gracido, Oaxaca, Mexico; **Robin Persiani,** Sierra College, Grass Valley, CA; **Mary Lou Price,** University of Texas at Austin, Austin, TX; **Mary Kay Purcell,** University of Evansville, Evansville, IN; **Graciela Ramírez Hernández,** Instituto Hispano Inglés de México, Mexico City, Mexico; **Mark Rau,** American River College, Sacramento, CA; **Nicholas Renton,** American Culture and Language Program, Los Angeles, CA; **Ernesto Romo,** Lake Forest School, Mexico State, Mexico; **René Sandoval,** Martin Luther King, Jr. School, Guadalajara, Jalisco, Mexico; **Allen Sellers,** Oregon State University, Corvallis, OR; **Nicola Teague,** San Diego State University, San Diego, CA; **Elena O. Torres González,** Instituto Tecnológico de Estudios Superiores de Monterrey, Atizapan, Mexico State, Mexico; **María Elena Vera de la Rosa,** Lake Forest School, Mexico State, Mexico; **Magneli Villanueva Morales,** Universidad Regiomontana, Monterrey, Nuevo León, Mexico; **Elaine Wilson,** Culture Works, London, Ontario, Canada; **Essio Zamora,** Instituto Carlos Gracido, Oaxaca, Mexico; **Ian Zapp,** Colegio México Irlandés, Guadalajara, Jalisco, Mexico.

PART V

Nouns and Articles: Review and Expansion

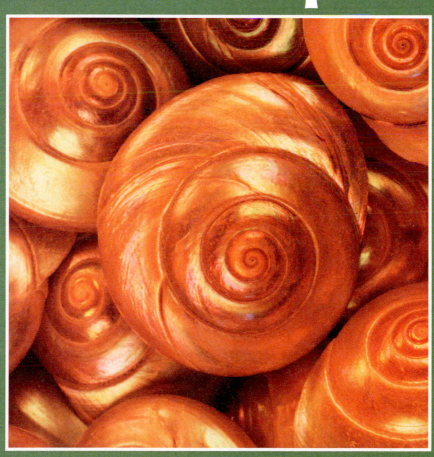

UNIT

21 Nouns and Quantifiers

Grammar in Context

BEFORE YOU READ

🎧 *Look at the map and the photo. Where did each journey start and end? When do you think these journeys took place? Read the history text about a modern explorer's expeditions.*

WHO GOT THERE FIRST?

Was **Christopher Columbus** really the first **explorer** to discover the **Americas**? The great Norwegian **explorer Thor Heyerdahl** didn't think so. He believed that ancient **people** were able to build **boats** that could cross **oceans**.

To test his **ideas**, Heyerdahl decided to build a **copy** of the reed **boats** pictured in ancient Egyptian **paintings** and sail across the **Atlantic Ocean** from **North Africa** to **Barbados**. **Heyerdahl's team** also copied ancient Middle Eastern **pots** and filled them with *enough* **food** for their **journey**—dried **fish**, **honey**, **oil**, *some* **eggs** and **nuts**, and *a little* fresh **fruit**. **Ra**, the **expedition's boat**, carried an international **group** of **sailors** including a **Chadian**, an **Egyptian**, an **Iraqi**, a **Japanese**, a **Mexican**, and a **Norwegian**.

On **May 25, 1969**, **Ra** left **Safi** in **Morocco** and headed across the widest **part** of the **Atlantic**. The **boat** fell apart just before it reached **Barbados**, but all the **men** aboard survived and wanted to try again.

On **May 17, 1970**, **Ra II**, sailing under the **flag** of the **United Nations**, successfully crossed the **Atlantic** in 57 **days**. The **expedition** proved that ancient **civilizations** had *enough* **skill** to reach the **Americas** long before **Columbus** did.

AFTER YOU READ

*Read the statements. Check **True** or **False**.*

	True	False
1. Heyerdahl believed that Columbus was the first explorer to discover the Americas.	☐	☐
2. Heyerdahl's team built a reed boat.	☐	☐
3. The team members were all from Egypt.	☐	☐
4. The first Ra expedition failed.	☐	☐
5. The second Ra expedition crossed the Pacific.	☐	☐

Grammar Presentation

NOUNS AND QUANTIFIERS

Count Nouns			
Article / Number	**Noun**	**Verb**	
A One	**sailor**	is	brave.
The Two	**sailors**	are	

Non-count Nouns		
Noun	**Verb**	
Oil	is	necessary.
Sailing		dangerous.

Quantifiers and Count Nouns		
	Quantifier	**Noun**
I saw	*some* *enough* *a lot of*	sailors. islands. boats.
	a few *several* *many*	
I didn't see	*any* *enough* *a lot of* *many*	

Quantifiers and Non-count Nouns		
	Quantifier	**Noun**
I used	*some* *enough* *a lot of*	oil. salt. honey.
	a little *a great deal of* *much*	
I didn't use	*any* *enough* *a lot of* *much*	

GRAMMAR NOTES

EXAMPLES

1. Proper nouns are the <u>names</u> of particular people, places, or things. They are usually unique (there is only one).

People	Heyerdahl, Africans
Places	Egypt, the Atlantic
Months	September, October
Nationalities	Norwegian, Chinese
Seasons	spring, summer, fall, winter

<u>Capitalize</u> the first letter of proper nouns.

EXCEPTION: We often use *the* before seasons, and we usually don't capitalize the first letter.

- The second **Ra** expedition was successful.

- They arrived in **the spring**.

2. Common nouns refer to people, places, and things, but <u>not by their names</u>. For example, *explorer* is a common noun, but *Heyerdahl* is a proper noun.

People	explorer, sailor, builder
Places	continent, country, city
Things	pots, eggs, fish, honey

<u>Do not capitalize</u> the first letter of a common noun unless the noun is the first word in a sentence.

- Heyerdahl is an **explorer**. NOT Heyerdahl is an ~~Explorer~~.

3. Common nouns can be either count or non-count. **Count nouns** are people, places, or things that you can <u>count separately</u>: *one boat, two boats, three boats . . .*

- **a** sailor, **the** sailor, **two** sailors
- **an** island, **the** island, **three** islands
- **a** map, **the** map, **four** maps

- Count nouns can be <u>singular or plural</u>.
- They take <u>singular or plural verbs</u>.
- You can use *a / an* or *the* before them.

- He saw one **shark**. She saw two **sharks**.
- The **boat** *is* fine, but the **sailors** *are* sick.
- **A sailor** lives alone on **the island**.

4. Non-count nouns are things that you <u>cannot count separately</u>. For example, you can say *gold*, but you cannot say *one gold* or *two golds*.

Abstract words	courage, education, time
Activities	exploring, sailing, farming
Fields of study	geography, history
Foods	corn, chocolate, fish

Some common non-count nouns do not fit into categories.

equipment	homework	news
furniture	information	work

- Non-count nouns have <u>no plural</u> forms.
- They take <u>singular verbs and pronouns</u>.

- We usually do not use *a / an* with them.

- He had a lot of **courage**.
- **Anthropology *is*** an interesting subject. **It *was*** Heyerdahl's favorite subject. NOT ~~An anthropology~~ is an interesting subject.

5. Use the quantifiers *some*, *enough*, *a lot of*, and *any* with both **count nouns** and **non-count nouns**.

                  count   non-count
- We have *some* **eggs** and *some* **honey**.

                  count   non-count
- Are there *enough* **pots** and *enough* **oil**?

                  count
- There were *a lot of* good **days**.

                  non-count
- There was *a lot of* **danger** too.

Use *any* in <u>negative</u> sentences and <u>questions</u>.

                  count
- We didn't see *any* **sharks**.

                  non-count
- Is there *any* **tea** left?

---

6. Use *a few*, *several*, and *many* with **plural count nouns** in <u>affirmative</u> sentences.

- *A few* team **members** got sick.
- They experienced *several* large **storms**.
- *Many* **people** worried about them.

Use *a little*, *a great deal of*, and *much* with **non-count nouns** in <u>affirmative</u> sentences.

- They had *a little* **trouble** with the sail.
- They threw away *a great deal of* **food**.
- *Much* **planning** went into this.

USAGE NOTE: In <u>affirmative</u> sentences, *much* is very formal.

VERY FORMAL: We saw *much* **pollution**.

LESS FORMAL: We saw *a lot of* **pollution**.

▶ **BE CAREFUL!** Don't confuse *a few* and *a little* with *few* and *little*. *Few* and *little* usually mean "not enough."

- I received *a little* **news** during the voyage. *(not a lot, but enough)*
- I received *little* **news** during the voyage. *(not enough news)*

---

7. Use *many* with **count nouns** and *much* with **non-count nouns** in <u>questions</u> and <u>negative</u> sentences.

A: How *many* **ships** did they see?

B: They didn't see *many*.

USAGE NOTE: *Much* isn't formal in questions and negative sentences.

A: How *much* **water** did they carry?

B: They didn't carry *much*.

Reference Notes

For a list of **irregular plural nouns**, see Appendix 6 on page A-4.
For a list of **non-count nouns**, see Appendix 7 on page A-4.
For **categories of proper nouns**, see Appendix 8 on page A-5.
For **spelling rules** for **regular plural nouns**, see Appendix 25 on page A-11.
For **capitalization rules**, see Appendix 27 on page A-13.

Focused Practice

1 | DISCOVER THE GRAMMAR

🎧 *Uta Bremer* **(UB)** *sailed around the world alone on a small boat. Read her interview with Adventure Travel* **(AT)** *magazine. Underline the nouns.*

ADVENTURE TRAVEL

Around the World Alone

AT: It took a lot of <u>courage</u> to make this <u>journey</u>. When did you decide to sail around the world alone?

UB: When I got my boat, *Katya*, for my 19th birthday, I knew right away that I wanted to do this.

AT: When did you start?

UB: I left New York on May 15, two and a half years ago, and I headed for Panama.

AT: How far did you travel?

UB: Thirty thousand miles.

AT: How much equipment were you able to take with you?

UB: I didn't have much money, so I didn't bring many things. I used the stars to navigate by, not electronic technology.

AT: What did you eat?

UB: I bought food in different ports. I loved going to markets and learning about local cooking. And I collected water in a pot when it rained.

AT: How did you spend your time when you were sailing?

UB: At first I listened to the news a lot, but after a while I preferred music. And I did a lot of reading.

AT: What was difficult for you?

UB: The loneliness. I had my cat, Typhoon, but I missed my family.

AT: What did you like best about the trip?

UB: The sight of this harbor. I'm so glad to be back for Thanksgiving.

Write each noun in the correct column.

Proper Nouns	Common Nouns			
	Count Nouns		**Non-count Nouns**	
Katya	journey		courage	

2 | MAKING PLANS

🎧 *Megan and Jason are planning a hiking trip. Complete their conversation with the correct form of the words in parentheses. Use Appendix 7 on page A-4 for help with non-count nouns.*

JASON: There __'s__ still a lot of ___work___ to do this evening. We have
1. (be)   2. (work)
to plan the food for the trip.

MEGAN: I've been reading this book about camping. There _____ some good
3. (be)
_____ about food in it.
4. (advice)

JASON: What does it say?

MEGAN: We should bring a lot of _____ and _____.
5. (bean)   6. (rice)

JASON: _____ _____ good on camping trips too.
7. (potato)   8. (be)

MEGAN: Fresh _____ _____ too heavy to carry. Maybe we can get
9. (vegetable)   10. (be)
some when we pass through a town.

JASON: _____ the _____ ready? We should go over the checklist.
11. (be)   12. (equipment)

MEGAN: I did that. We need some _____ for the radio.
13. (battery)

JASON: Why do we need a radio? I thought we were running away from civilization.

MEGAN: But the _____ never _____. I still want to know what's
14. (news)   15. (stop)
happening.

JASON: That's OK with me. By the way, do we have enough warm _____? It gets
16. (clothing)
chilly in the mountains.

MEGAN: That's true. And the
_____ really
17. (cold)
_____ me at night.
18. (bother)

JASON: But we have warm sleeping
_____.
19. (bag)

3 | HAPPY CAMPERS

Complete these excerpts from a book about family camping. For each paragraph, use the quantifiers in parentheses. You will use some quantifiers more than once.

1. (a little / a few)

Try to get _____*a little*_____ exercise before a long camping trip. It will help you feel better
               a.

on the trip. _____ good stretching exercises every day will help.
           b.

_____ walking or swimming is also useful.
   c.

2. (many / a great deal of)

You will need _____ information for a long trip. Your public library has
             a.

_____ books about family camping. The National Park Service website can also
   b.

provide _____ advice.
       c.

3. (a / some) (much / many)

Making a fire is _____ skill, but it's easy to learn. You won't need
        a.

_____ practice before you can build a roaring campfire. Start with
   b.

_____ paper and leaves. Place the wood on top of these and leave spaces for air.
   c.

Don't use _____ big pieces of wood.
        d.

4. (any / enough) (How much / How many)

"There isn't _____ milk left! Who used it all?" _____ times have
       a.   **b.**

you heard this cry? To avoid this problem, plan your food in advance. _____
               c.

sandwiches are you going to make? _____ bread will you need? Make sure you
          d.

have _____ food and beverages before you leave.
    e.

5. (few / a few) (little / a little)

On our family's first camping trip, we had _____ equipment and almost no
             a.

experience, but we still had a lot of fun. It was a blast. We swam, we hiked, and we made new

friends. Of course, we had _____ problems, but not many. Anyway,
           b.

_____ inconvenience didn't interfere with our fun.
   c.

    Today millions of people enjoy camping. In fact, _____ campsites are
                    d.

available in the summer without a reservation.

4 | EDITING

Read Uta's diary entries. There are seventeen mistakes in the use of nouns and in the use of verb and pronoun agreement. The first three mistakes are already corrected. Find and correct fourteen more.

> ~~*Canary*~~
> October 27. I've been on the ~~canary~~ Islands for three days now. I'll start home when
>
> *weather is*
> the ~~weathers are~~ better. I was so surprised when I picked up my mails today. My
>
> family sent some birthday presents to me. My Birthday is the 31st.
>
> october 29. I think the weather is getting worse. I heard thunders today, but there
>
> wasn't many rain. Typhoon and I stayed in bed. I started reading brave New World.
>
> October 30. I left the Canary Islands today—just like columbus. There's a strong wind
>
> and plenty of sunshine now. I went 250 miles.
>
> October 31. I'm 21 today. To celebrate, I drank little coffee for breakfast and I
>
> opened my presents. I got some perfume and some pretty silver jewelries.
>
> November 1. The electricities are low. I'd better save them until I get near land. I'll
>
> need the radio then. It rained today, so I collected a few waters for cooking.

Communication Practice

5 | LISTENING

🎧 *Megan and Jason are planning to make cookies for their trip. Listen to them talk about the recipe. Then listen again and check the ingredients that they have enough of. Listen a third time and make a shopping list of ingredients that they need to buy.*

Ingredients	
2 cups of butter	1 cup of cornflakes
✓ 3 cups of brown sugar	8 eggs
2 cups of oatmeal (uncooked)	1 cup of raisins
4 cups of flour	2 cups of chocolate chips

Shopping List

butter
_____
_____
_____
_____

6 SHIPWRECKED!

Work with a group. Imagine that you are about to be shipwrecked near a deserted tropical island. You have room in your lifeboat for only five things. Look at the list. Decide what to take and give your reasons. Compare your choices with other groups' choices.

sugar	ax	fireworks
pasta	matches	telescope
beans	fishing equipment	compass
chocolate	radio	maps of the area
fresh water	portable TV set	a book, *Navigating by the Stars*
cooking pot	batteries	a book, *Tropical Plants You Can Eat*

Example: I think we should take a lot of beans. We might not find any food on the island.

7 WRITING

Describe a trip that you have taken. Where did you go, and when? How long did you stay? Who went with you? What did you take along? What did you do there?

Example: Three years ago, I went to Amsterdam with my family. My father was on a short vacation, so we couldn't spend much time there . . .

8 ON THE INTERNET

 Work in groups and choose an explorer from the list below. Then individually do an Internet search for information to answer the questions. Share the information in your group.

Explorers

Ellen Ochoa   Ibn Battuta   Louise Arner Boyd   Jacques Cousteau   Zhang Qian

Questions
- Where was the explorer from?
- When did he or she live?
- What parts of the world did he or she explore?
- How did he or she travel?
- Why did he or she go?
- What were some of his or her achievements?

As a group, present your information to the class. Use maps and pictures from your research.

Example: Ellen Ochoa was the first Hispanic female astronaut.

Articles: Indefinite and Definite

Grammar in Context

BEFORE YOU READ

🎧 *Look at the pictures on this page and the next. Read the title of each story. What kind of a story do you think a fable is? Do you know a fable in your first language? Read the two fables.*

Two Fables

Aesop was **a famous storyteller** in Greece more than 2,000 years ago. **The fables** he told are still famous all over **the world**. Here are two of Aesop's fables.

The Ant and The Dove

An ant lived next to **a river**. One day, **the ant** went to **the river** to drink, and he fell into **the water**. **A dove** was sitting in **a tree** next to **the river**. **The dove** saw **the ant** struggling in **the water**. She picked **a leaf** from **the tree** and dropped it into **the river**. **The ant** climbed onto **the leaf** and floated safely to **the shore**.

An hour later, **a hunter** came to **the river** to catch **birds**. He was **the best hunter** in that part of **the country**, and all **the animals** feared him. When **the ant** saw **the hunter**, he wanted to save his friend, but he thought, "How can **a tiny ant** stop **a big man**?" Then he had **an idea**. He climbed on **the hunter's foot** and bit him hard. **The hunter** shouted in pain, and **the noise** made **the dove** fly away.

Help!

(*continued*)

The Town Mouse and The Country Mouse

A town mouse went to visit his cousin in **the country**. **The country cousin** was poor, but he gladly served his town cousin **the only food** he had—**some beans** and **some bread**. **The town mouse** ate **the bread** and laughed. He said, "What **poor food** you **country mice** eat! Come home with me. I will show you how to live." **The moon** was shining brightly that night, so **the mice** left immediately.

As soon as they arrived at **the town mouse's house**, they went into **the dining room**. There they found **the leftovers** of **a wonderful dinner**, and soon **the mice** were eating **jelly** and **cake** and many nice things. Suddenly, **the door** flew open, and **an enormous dog** ran in. **The mice** ran away quickly. "Good-bye, Cousin," said **the country mouse**. "Are you leaving so soon?" asked **the town mouse**. "Yes," his honest cousin replied. "This has been **a great adventure**, but I'd rather eat **bread** in peace than **cake** in fear."

AFTER YOU READ

Number these sentences from "The Ant and The Dove" in the correct order.

_____ An hour later, a hunter came to the river to catch birds.

_____ She picked a leaf from the tree and dropped it into the river.

_____ The dove saw the ant struggling in the water.

_____ A dove was sitting in a tree next to the river.

_____ The ant climbed onto the leaf and floated safely to the shore.

Now number these sentences from "The Town Mouse and The Country Mouse" in the correct order.

_____ The town mouse ate the bread and laughed.

_____ The mice ran away quickly.

_____ The country cousin was poor, but he gladly served his town cousin the only food he had.

_____ This has been a great adventure.

_____ A town mouse went to visit his cousin in the country.

Grammar Presentation

ARTICLES: INDEFINITE AND DEFINITE

INDEFINITE

Singular Count Nouns		
	A / An	*(Adjective) Noun*
Let's read	a	**story**.
This is	an	**old story**.

Plural Count Nouns / Non-count Nouns		
	(Some)	*(Adjective) Noun*
Let's listen to	*(some)*	**stories** on this CD.
This CD has		**nice music** too.

DEFINITE

Singular Count Nouns		
	The	*(Adjective) Noun*
Let's read	the	**story** by Aesop.
It's	the	**oldest story**.

Plural Count Nouns / Non-count Nouns		
	The	*(Adjective) Noun*
Let's listen to	the	**stories** by Aesop.
I like		**old music** on this CD.

GRAMMAR NOTES

1. We can use **nouns** in two ways:

   a. A noun is **indefinite** when you and your listener do not have a specific person, place, or thing in mind.

   b. A noun is **definite** when you and your listener both know which person, place, or thing you are talking about.

2. Use the **indefinite article** *a / an* with singular count nouns that are **indefinite**.

   • Use *a* before consonant sounds.
   • Use *an* before vowel sounds.

   ► **BE CAREFUL!** It is the sound, not the letter, that determines whether you use *a* or *an*.

   Use **no article** or *some* with plural count nouns and with non-count nouns that are **indefinite**. *Some* means an indefinite number.

EXAMPLES

A: Let's buy **a book**.
B: Good idea. Which one should we buy?
   (A and B are not talking about a specific book.)

A: I bought **the book** yesterday.
B: Good. You've wanted it for a while.
   (A and B are talking about a specific book.)

A: I'm reading *a* **fable**.
B: Oh really? Which one?

   • *a* **r**iver, *a* **t**iny ant
   • *an* **i**dea, *an* **e**xciting story

   • *a* **E**uropean writer (a "Yuropean")
   • *an* **h**onest relative (an "ahnest")

   plural count
   • There are *(some)* **books** on the floor. Are they yours?

   non-count
A: I had to buy *(some)* **food**.
B: Oh. What did you buy?

(continued)

3. Note these uses of *a / an*, **no article**, and *some*:

a. To **identify** (say what someone or something is), use:

- *a / an* with <u>singular count nouns</u>

A: What do you do?
B: I'm *a* **chef**. _(singular count)_

- **no article** with <u>plural count nouns</u> and <u>non-count nouns</u>

A: What are these?
B: They're **beans**. I'm making soup. _(plural count)_
A: And this?
B: It's **bread**. I just baked it. _(non-count)_

b. To make **general statements**, use **no article** with <u>plural count nouns</u> and <u>non-count nouns</u>.

- Ava loves **stories** and **music**. _(plural count)_ _(non-count)_
(stories and music in general)

c. *Some* in general statements means "some, but not all."

- I like *some* **stories**, but a lot of them are boring.

4. Use the **definite article** *the* with most <u>common nouns</u> (count and non-count, singular and plural) that are **definite**. Use *the* when:

a. a person, place, or thing is <u>unique</u>— there is only one

- Aesop is famous all over *the* **world**.
- *The* **moon** was shining brightly.

b. the <u>context</u> makes it clear which person, place, or thing you mean

A: Who is she?
B: She's *the* **teacher**.
(A and B are students in a classroom. A is a new student.)

A: *The* **food** was great.
B: I enjoyed it too.
(A and B are coming out of a restaurant.)

c. the noun is mentioned for the <u>second time</u> (it is often indefinite the first time it is mentioned)

- *An* **ant** lived next to *a* **river**. One day, *the* **ant** went to *the* **river** to drink.
- They ate **cake**. *The* **cake** was delicious.

d. a <u>phrase or adjective</u> such as *first*, *best*, *right*, *wrong*, or *only* identifies the noun

- He was *the* **best** **hunter** in the country.
- He served *the* **only** **food** he had.

5. Adjectives often go <u>directly before a noun</u>. When you use an article or *some*, the adjective goes between the article or *some* and the noun.	• *Old* **fables** are great. • We read **the** *first* **story** in the book. • He has **some** *beautiful old* **books**.

Reference Note
For a list of **non-count nouns,** see Appendix 7 on page A-4.

Focused Practice

 | **DISCOVER THE GRAMMAR**

Read the conversations. Circle the letter of the statement that best describes each conversation.

1. CORA: Dad, could you read me a story?

   DAD: Sure, I'd love to.

   a. Dad knows which story Cora wants him to read.

   (b.) Cora isn't talking about a particular story.

2. FRED: Mom, where's the new book?

   MOM: Sorry, I haven't seen it.

   a. Mom knows that Fred bought a new book.

   b. Mom doesn't know that Fred bought a new book.

3. DAD: I'll bet it's in the hall. You always drop your things there.

   FRED: I'll go look.

   a. There are several halls in the house.

   b. There is only one hall in the house.

4. DAD: Was I right?

   FRED: You weren't even close. It was on a chair in the kitchen.

   a. There is only one chair in the kitchen.

   b. There are several chairs in the kitchen.

5. DAD: Wow! Look at that! The pictures are great.

   FRED: So are the stories.

   a. All books have good pictures and stories.

   b. The book Fred bought has good pictures and stories.

6. FRED: Oh, I forgot . . . I also got a computer game. Do you want to play?

   DAD: Sure. I love computer games.

   a. Dad is talking about computer games in general.

   b. Dad is talking about a particular computer game.

2 | THE LIFE OF AESOP

Grammar Notes 1–5

Circle the correct article to complete this paragraph. Circle Ø if you don't need an article.

People all over (the) / Ø world know a / the fables of Aesop,
            1.   **2.**

but there is very little information about the / Ø life of this
                                            3.

famous Greek storyteller. Scholars agree that Aesop was born

around 620 B.C. In his early years, he was a / the slave, and he
                                                 4.

lived on Samos, an / a island in an / the Aegean Sea. Even as
                5.   **6.**

a / the slave, Aesop had the / Ø wisdom and knowledge. His
7.   **8.**

master respected him so much that he freed him. When Aesop

became a / Ø free man, he traveled to many countries in order to
       9.

learn and to teach. In Lydia, the / Ø king invited him to stay in that country and gave Aesop some
                            10.

difficult jobs in a / the government. In his work, Aesop often used a / Ø fables to convince people
                11.   **12.**

of his ideas. One time, a/ the king sent Aesop to Delphi with a / Ø gold for a / the people of that
                        13.   **14.**   **15.**

city. Aesop became disgusted with the / Ø people's greed, so he sent the / Ø gold back to a / the
                                       16.   **17.**   **18.**

king. A / The people of Delphi were very angry at Aesop for this, and they killed him. After his
     19.

death, a / the famous sculptor made a / the statue of Aesop you see in a / the photo above.
       20.   **21.**   **22.**

3 | FUN AND GAMES

Grammar Notes 1–5

*Complete the conversations with **a**, **an**, or **the**.*

1. **AVA:** I'm sick of this computer game, and I've read all my books.

   DAD: Let's go to ____*the*____ new bookstore on Main Street.

2. **AVA:** Can we buy _____ computer game too?

   DAD: OK. I'm sure they sell games there.

3. **DAD:** Maybe you should turn off _____ computer before we leave.

   AVA: I'll leave it on for Ethan. He likes this game.

4. **DAD:** Do you see the bookstore? I was sure it was on Main Street.

   AVA: I think it's on _____ side street, but I'm not sure which one.

   DAD: I'll try this one.

5. DAD: There it is.

   AVA: You can park right across _____ street.

6. AVA: There's _____ man with drums and a guitar at the back of the store.

   DAD: Maybe he's _____ storyteller. Let's go see.

7. AVA: That was _____ fastest hour I've ever spent.

   DAD: I know. It was _____ excellent performance.

8. AVA: I really enjoyed _____ story about the warrior princess.

   DAD: Me too. It's _____ really exciting story.

9. AVA: We were going to get _____ computer game too, remember?

   DAD: OK. I think the newest games are in _____ front of _____ store.

10. AVA: This is _____ awesome game. Can I get it?

    DAD: Sure. Let's bring everything to _____ cashier. She's right over there.

4 | FAST READERS   Grammar Notes 1, 3–5

Ben went to a bookstore to buy books for his young niece. Complete the sentences with **the** *where necessary. Leave a blank if you don't need an article.*

BEN: I'm looking for _____ books for my 14-year-old niece. What do you recommend?
                        1.

CLERK: Let's go to ___*the*___ young adult section. Does she like _____ mysteries? Doris
                    2.   3.

   Duncan wrote some good ones for teenagers.

BEN: She's read all _____ mysteries by Duncan. She's _____ fastest reader in the family!
                    4.   5.

CLERK: It's hard to keep up with _____ fast readers. Here's a good one by Gillian Cross—
                                6.

   Born of _____ *Sun.* It's about finding a lost Inca city.
             7.

BEN: She'll like that one. She loves _____ books about _____ history—and science too.
                                    8.   9.

CLERK: Then how about *A Short History of* _____ *Universe*? It's in _____ science section.
                                          10.   11.

BEN: This is great! She likes _____ books with beautiful pictures.
                            12.

CLERK: Well, _____ pictures in this one are fantastic. *Nature Magazine* called this book
            13.

   _____ best introduction to this subject.
   14.

BEN: OK, I'll take _____ mystery by Cross and _____ science book. Anything else?
                  15.   16.

CLERK: Well, _____ kids have fun with _____ trivia games. Here's a good one.
            17.   18.

BEN: Great. I'll get _____ trivia game too. Thanks. You've been very helpful.
                    19.

5 | PERSON, PLACE, OR THING?

*This is a trivia game. Complete the clues for each item. Then, using the clues and the appropriate picture, write the answer. Use **a / an** or **the** where necessary. Leave a blank if you don't need an article. The answers to the trivia game are at the end of the exercise.*

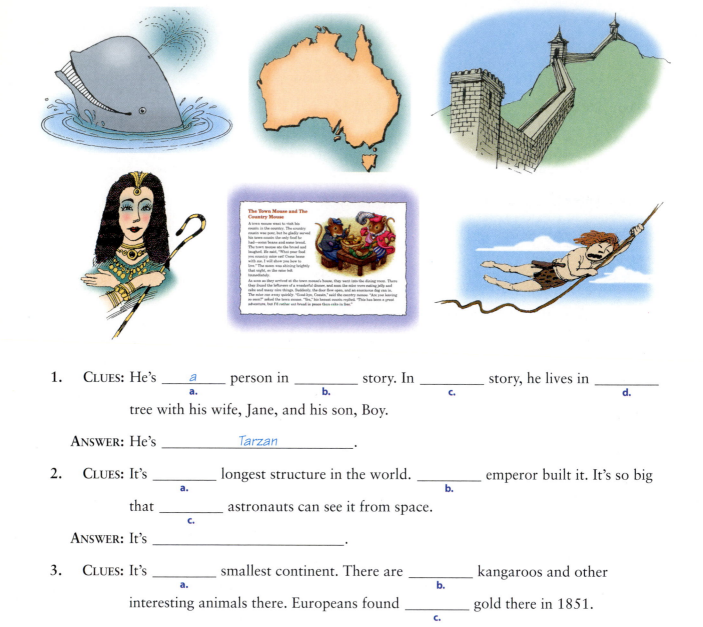

1. CLUES: He's _____*a*_____ person in _____ story. In _____ story, he lives in _____
    a.   b.   c.   d.
    tree with his wife, Jane, and his son, Boy.

    ANSWER: He's _____*Tarzan*_____.

2. CLUES: It's _____ longest structure in the world. _____ emperor built it. It's so big
    a.   b.
    that _____ astronauts can see it from space.
    c.

    ANSWER: It's _____.

3. CLUES: It's _____ smallest continent. There are _____ kangaroos and other
    a.   b.
    interesting animals there. Europeans found _____ gold there in 1851.
    c.

    ANSWER: It's _____.

4. CLUES: They are _____ very short stories. _____ stories are about _____
    a.   b.   c.
    animals, but they teach _____ lessons about how people behave. Aesop wrote
    d.
    _____ most famous ones.
    e.

    ANSWER: They're _____.

5. **Clues:** She was _____ intelligent and beautiful woman. She was _____ most
a.   b.

famous queen of Egypt. She ruled _____ country with her brother.
c.

Answer: She was _____.

6. **Clues:** They are _____ biggest animals that have ever lived. They have _____ fins,
a.   b.

but they aren't _____ fish.
c.

Answer: They're _____.

6 | EDITING

*Read the article about video games. There are thirteen mistakes in the use of **a**, **an**, and
the. The first mistake is already corrected. Find and correct twelve more.*

THE PLUMBER AND THE APE

Once there was a plumber named Mario.
The plumber
~~Plumber~~ had beautiful girlfriend. One

day, a ape fell in love with the girlfriend

and kidnapped her. The plumber chased

ape to rescue his girlfriend. This simple

tale became *Donkey Kong*, a first video

game with a story. It was invented by Sigeru Matsimoto, a artist with Nintendo,

Inc. Matsimoto loved the video games, but he wanted to make them more

interesting. He liked fairy tales, so he invented story similar to a famous fairy tale.

Story was an immediate success, and Nintendo followed it with *The Mario

Brothers* and then with *Super Mario*. The third game became popular all over a

world, and it is still most famous game in video history. Nintendo has continued

to add the new characters to the story, but success does not change Mario. He is

always brave little plumber in a red hat and work clothes.

Communication Practice

7 | LISTENING

🎧 *Listen to the conversations. Then listen again and circle the correct articles.*

1. AMY: What's that?

   BEN: Oh. It's a / (the) new video game. Do you want to try it?

2. AMY: I'm reading the story you recommended now. Who's Angelica? I can't figure it out.

   BEN: She's a / the princess with magic powers.

3. AMY: What about Aesop? Have you read a / the fable?

   BEN: No. I'm going to tonight.

4. AMY: You know, I'd like to buy a / the book of fables for Ava.

   BEN: Good idea. She loves fables.

5. AMY: Let's go to a / the bookstore this weekend.

   BEN: OK. We can go on Sunday after lunch.

6. AMY: Speaking of lunch, I'm hungry.

   BEN: Here. Why don't you have a / the sandwich?

Read your completed conversations. Circle the letter of the statement that best describes each conversation.

1. **a.** Ben and Amy have already spoken about this video game.
   b. Ben has never mentioned this video game before.

2. **a.** The story has several princesses. One of them has magic powers.
   b. The story has just one princess.

3. **a.** Ben and Amy have already spoken about this fable.
   b. Amy has never mentioned this fable before.

4. **a.** Amy has a specific book of fables in mind.
   b. Amy isn't thinking of a particular book of fables.

5. **a.** Amy has a specific bookstore in mind.
   b. Amy isn't thinking of a particular bookstore.

6. **a.** There is only one sandwich.
   b. There are several sandwiches.

8 | INFORMATION GAP: STORY TIME

Work in pairs (A and B). Student A, follow the instructions on this page. Student B, turn to page 261 and follow the instructions there.

1. Look at the picture below. Ask your partner for the information you need to finish labeling the picture.

   Example: A: Who's the man in the black cape?
   B: He's the magician.

2. Answer your partner's questions.

   Example: B: What's the magician holding?
   A: A magic wand.

When you are finished, compare pictures. Are the labels the same?

9 | QUIZ SHOW

Work with a group. Choose five interesting or famous things. Write three clues for each thing. Then join another group. Give your clues and ask the other group to guess what each thing is. Look at Exercise 5 for ideas.

Example: A: It's a planet. It's the closest one to the sun. There might be water there.
B: Does it have rings?

10 | THE MORAL OF THE STORY

Fables often have a moral—*a sentence at the end that explains the lesson of the story. Read the list of morals. What do you think they mean?*

- You can't please everyone.

- It's better to eat bread in peace than cake in fear.

- Sometimes a little friend turns out to be a great friend.

- Slow and steady wins the race.

- Look before you leap.

Example: "It's better to eat bread in peace than cake in fear."
I think this means it's better to have a good life situation with poorer things than a bad life situation with better things. You can't enjoy the better things if you are living in fear.

Which one could be the moral of "The Ant and The Dove" on page 249? Discuss your ideas with a group.

11 | WRITING

Choose one of the morals that you discussed in Exercise 10. Write a paragraph about an experience that you have had or know about that illustrates the meaning of the moral.

Example: "Slow and steady wins the race."
When I was in high school, I was a good student, but I always waited until the night before a test to study. I learned very fast, so I never had trouble. Then I took a class from Mr. Fox, the toughest teacher in the school . . .

12 | ON THE INTERNET

Do a search on **Aesop's fables**. *Choose a fable to read. Then work with a partner. Tell your partner the fable and listen to your partner's fable. Then discuss the answers to these questions about the two fables.*

- What is the title of the fable?

- Who are the characters in the fable?

- Where are they?

- What is the problem?

- How do they solve the problem?

- What is the moral of the fable?

INFORMATION GAP FOR STUDENT B

1. Look at the picture below. Answer your partner's questions.

Example: **A:**   Who's the man in the black cape?
   B: He's the magician.

2. Ask your partner for the information you need to finish labeling the picture.

Example: **B:**   What's the magician holding?
   A: A magic wand.

crescent moon

super hero

castle

sword

cape

magic wand

magician

coffer

medicine

silver coins

When you are finished, compare pictures. Are the labels the same?

From **Grammar** to **Writing**
Developing a Paragraph with Examples

One way to develop a paragraph is to add examples. Examples give your reader a clear idea of what you are writing about. They often give more information about the people, places, and things you are describing. They also make your writing more interesting.

Example: We celebrate with **food.** $\longrightarrow$
We celebrate with **food. For example, we bake loaves of bread we call "souls."**

1 | *Read this paragraph about a holiday. Write the examples from the box in the correct place in the paragraph.*

My family always hires a mariachi band.	For my sister, we offer toys.
~~we bake loaves of bread we call "souls."~~	We also decorate the altar with candy skulls.

In Mexico we celebrate *Los Días de los Muertos* ("The Days of the Dead") on November 1 and 2. On these days, we remember our relatives who have died. We celebrate with food, special gifts for the dead, and music. For example, _____*we bake loaves of bread we call "souls."*_____ They
1.
are shaped like people. _____
2.
In addition, we remember special things our relatives liked, and we buy them gifts. For example, for my grandfather, we always put out a new hat. _____ On the second day,
3.
everyone in my family meets at the cemetery. This sounds sad, but it is really a big party. _____,
4.
and we all sing. Some people think that *Los Días de los Muertos* is like Halloween, but they are wrong. At Halloween, people pretend to be afraid of evil spirits, but during *Los Días de los Muertos*, we invite the friendly spirits of our family to visit us.

2 | *Complete this outline of the paragraph in Exercise 1.*

1. The name of the holiday and when it is celebrated: _____.

2. The purpose of the holiday: _____.

3. How people celebrate the holiday:

    a. _____ *food* _____

    Examples: ___ *loaves of bread called "souls"* ___ and _____

    b. _____

    Examples: ___ *a new hat for my grandfather* ___ and _____

    c. _____

    Examples: _____ and _____

3 | *Before you write . . .*

1. Develop an outline like the one in Exercise 2 for a paragraph about a holiday that is special to you.
2. Work with a partner. Exchange outlines. Ask questions about your partner's holiday. Answer your partner's questions.

4 | *Write a paragraph about a special holiday. Include information your partner asked you about.*

5 | *Exchange paragraphs with a different partner. Complete the chart with information from your partner's paragraph.*

	Yes	No
1. Does the paragraph include examples?	☐	☐
2. Do the examples give more information about people, places, and things?	☐	☐
3. Are there more examples that you would like to see?	☐	☐
4. If yes, what would you like an example of? _____		
5. What else would you like to know about this holiday? _____		

6 | *Work with your partner. Discuss each other's editing questions from Exercise 5. Then rewrite your own paragraph and make any necessary corrections.*

Review Test

I   *Complete each conversation with the correct form of the words in parentheses.*

1. A: We got _____ *a lot of mail* _____ today.
                       a. (many / a lot of) (mail / mails)

    B: How _____ came?
             b. (much / many) (letter / letters)

2. A: Are you still majoring in mathematics?

    B: No, _____ interest me much anymore.
           a. (it / they) (doesn't / don't)

3. A: There _____ some new furniture in the office.
                a. ('s / are)

    B: I know. I saw _____ new _____ too.
              b. (several / a great deal of)   **c. (computer / computers)**

4. A: Do you enjoy reading?

    B: _____ OK, but I prefer listening to music.
          a. (It's / They're)

5. A: I put _____ in the tomato sauce.
            a. (too much / too many) (salt / salts)

    B: No, you didn't. _____ just fine to me.
                b. (It / They) (tastes / taste)

6. A: Did you watch the six o'clock news?

    B: No. I missed _____ today.
             a. (it / them)

7. A: I brought _____ luggage on this trip.
          a. (a lot of / a)

    B: How _____ do you have?
           b. (much / many) (bag / bags)

8. A: Did you find _____ information for your report on explorers?
               a. (much / many)

    B: Yes, I did. I found _____ good articles online.
                b. (any / some)

9. A: I love this music.

    B: I like _____ too.
          a. (it / them)

II   *Complete the conversation with the correct words or phrases in parentheses.*

A: Joe's birthday is tomorrow. Let's surprise him and give a party.

B: That's not _____ *much* _____ time.
            1. (much / many)

A: One day? That's _____. We still have candles and decorations left
2. (enough / too much)

from the last party.

B: Let's just make _____ hamburgers and fries. And I'll bake a cake.
3. (a lot of / a great deal of)

_____ chopped meat do we have?
4. (How much / How many)

A: Only _____. And we only have _____ rolls.
5. (a few / a little)   6. (a few / a little)

B: Put them on the list. I'll also need _____ eggs for the cake.
7. (some / any)

A: _____?
8. (How many / How much)

B: Two. Is there _____ flour and sugar?
9. (any / many)

A: Not _____. I'll get more.
10. (much / many)

B: I think that's it.

A: Not quite. Joe's got _____ friends. We'd better start calling them.
11. (a lot of / much)

B: Why don't you go shopping? I'll call _____ people while you're gone.
12. (a few / a little)

III | *Complete the conversations with* **a**, **an**, *or* **the**.

1. **A:** Did anyone feed ____the____ cat today?

   B: I did. Why?

   A: He's still hungry.

2. **A:** Look at this picture of Boots.

   B: It's really cute. What kind of cat is it?

   A: It's not _____ cat. It's _____ dog.

   B: You're kidding! What _____ unusual animal!

3. **A:** Please shut _____ door. It just blew open.

   B: OK.

4. **A:** It was cold last night.

   B: _____ ground is still frozen.

5. **A:** How's _____ weather in L.A.?

   B: Sunny. How's New York?

   A: You can't even see _____ sun.

6. **A:** Who's that woman in the uniform?

   B: She's _____ captain of this ship.

7. **A:** What does Martha do?

   B: She's _____ engineer. She works for World Cargo.

8. **A:** We need _____ new car.

   B: I know. But we'll have to wait.

9. **A:** I need _____ car today.

   B: OK. Can you drop me off at work?

   A: Sorry, I have _____ early meeting, so I can't help you.

IV *Complete the sentences with **the** where necessary. Capitalize the first letter when you don't use **the**.*

1. _____ *F*riendship is very important to most people.

2. ___*The*___ friendship of my classmates is very important to me.

3. Sue used _____ money in her bank account to pay her tuition.

4. _____ money isn't everything.

5. _____ travel can be educational. _____ staying at home can be educational too.

6. _____ vegetables in our garden aren't ripe yet.

7. _____ vegetables contain a lot of vitamins.

V *Complete the paragraphs with **a**, **an**, **the**, or **some**.*

1. Yesterday, I went to ___*the*___ biggest video store downtown to rent _____ movies.
   a.   b.

   I found _____ comedy and _____ thriller. _____ comedy was very funny. I really
           c.   d.   e.

   enjoyed it. _____ thriller wasn't that good.
               f.

2. We need to buy _____ office supplies soon. We need _____ paper for _____
                   a.   b.   c.

   printer and _____ disks. _____ paper is more important than _____ disks.
               d.   e.   f.

VI *Each sentence has four underlined words or phrases. The four underlined parts of the sentence are marked A, B, C, or D. Circle the letter of the one underlined word or phrase that is NOT CORRECT.*

1. Many popular flavorings come from Native american cultures.   A B C (D)
   A   B   C   D

2. Chili was unknown in an Asia or Europe a few hundred years ago.   A B C D
         A   B   C   D

3. Now it's the most popular spice in a world.   A B C D
       A B   C D

4. It's hard to imagine the Italian or Szechuan food without chili.   A B C D
                        A   B   C   D

5. Do you know that a chocolate also comes from America?   A B C D
                    A   B   C   D

6. For some American cultures, it was the medicine.   A B C D
       A   B   C   D

7. Now People all over the world use chocolate to flavor food.   A B C D
       A   B   C   D

▶ *To check your answers, go to the Answer Key on page RT-3.*

Adjectives and Adverbs

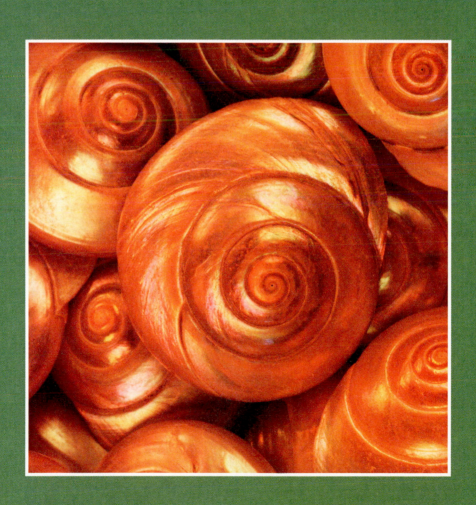

BEFORE YOU READ

🎧 *Look at the house. Is this a good place to live? Why or why not? What do you think is important when looking for a home? Read the ad for two apartments in this house.*

WAKEFIELD HOUSE

Are you looking for a **nice** neighborhood with **safe quiet** streets? Do you love the **big sunny** rooms and **high** ceilings in **old** buildings—but want **modern** appliances too? Apartments in Wakefield House offer that and more. Here's your place to relax **completely** after a **long hard** day at school or work. We are located in a **peaceful residential** area near **famous** Lake Forest Park. And you'll still be a **convenient** drive or bus ride from downtown and the university. **Exciting** nightlife, shopping, and museums are just minutes away.

It sounds **very expensive**, right? But it's not! A **charming one-bedroom** apartment is **surprisingly affordable**. We have two **beautifully furnished** apartments **available** right now. But don't wait! Our apartments rent **very quickly**.
Call 555–1234 now for an appointment.

★ ★

Here's what some of our **satisfied** tenants are saying about life at Wakefield House:

"This neighborhood is like a **small** village. There are some **really friendly** people here."
—Maggie Chang

"This place is **absolutely perfect**. I'll **never** move again!"
—Luis Rivera

"We **often** spend the **whole** weekend here—walking through the **nearby** park or just sitting on the **front** porch."
—Alice Thompson

AFTER YOU READ

Read the statements. Check **True** *or* **False**.

	True	False
1. Wakefield House is in a dangerous neighborhood.	☐	☐
2. The apartments have a lot of light.	☐	☐
3. It's in an exciting area of the city.	☐	☐
4. You'll be surprised that the rent is so low.	☐	☐
5. There are two apartments for rent now.	☐	☐
6. One tenant likes to spend weekends at home.	☐	☐

Grammar Presentation

ADJECTIVES AND ADVERBS

Adjectives
They are **quiet** tenants.
It's a **fast** elevator.
The house looks **nice**.
It's absolutely **perfect**.

Adverbs
They talk **quietly**.
It moves **fast**.
She described it **nicely**.
It's **absolutely** perfect.

Participial Adjectives	
-ing Adjective	*-ed* Adjective
The apartment is **interesting**.	One couple is **interested** in the apartment.
It's an **interesting** one-bedroom apartment.	The **interested** couple called again.
My neighbor is **annoying**.	I'm **annoyed** by his loud music.
He's an **annoying** neighbor.	Another **annoyed** tenant complained.
This street map is **confusing**.	People were **confused** by the street map.
It's a **confusing** street map.	A **confused** driver asked for directions.

GRAMMAR NOTES	EXAMPLES

1. Use **adjectives** to describe or give more information about <u>nouns</u> (people, places, or things).
 	
An adjective usually goes right <u>before the noun</u> it describes.
 	
It can also go <u>after a non-action verb</u> such as *be, look, seem, appear, smell,* or *taste*.
	adjective noun
	• It's a **quiet building**.
	   noun adjective
	• The **building** is **quiet**.
	  (Quiet *tells you more about the building.*)
	
	adjective + noun
	• This is a **small house**.
	
	verb + adjective
	• This house **looks small**.

2. Use **adverbs** to describe or give more information about <u>verbs</u>, <u>adjectives</u>, or other <u>adverbs</u>. An adverb usually goes right <u>after the verb</u> it describes. It usually goes right <u>before the adjective or adverb</u> it describes.	verb + adverb • The apartment **rented quickly**. adverb + adjective • It's an **extremely nice** house. adverb + adverb • They got it **very quickly**.

3. Use **adverbs of manner** to describe or give more information about <u>action verbs</u>. These adverbs often answer "*How?*" questions.
 	
▶ **BE CAREFUL!** Do not put an adverb of manner between the verb and the object.
	A: *How* did they decorate the apartment?
	B: They decorated it **beautifully**!
	
	   verb object adverb
	• She **decorated** the house **beautifully**.
	  NOT She decorated ~~beautifully the house~~.

4. Adverbs of manner are often formed by adding **-ly** to adjectives:
 	
adjective + -ly = adverb
 	
▶ **BE CAREFUL!** Some adjectives also end in *-ly* —for example, *friendly, lonely, lovely,* and *silly*.
 	
Some adverbs of manner have **two forms**: one with *-ly* and one without *-ly*. The form without *-ly* is the same as the adjective.
 	
USAGE NOTE: The form **without -ly** is common in <u>informal</u> speech.
	adjective
	• We need a **quick** decision.
	             adverb
	• You should decide **quickly**.
	adjective
	• It's a **lovely** apartment.
	
	slowly OR **slow**
	quickly OR **quick**
	loudly OR **loud**
	clearly OR **clear**
	• Don't speak so **loudly**.
	       OR
	• Don't speak so **loud**.

5. Some **common adverbs of manner** are not formed by adding -*ly* to adjectives:

   a. The adverb form of ***good*** is ***well***.

                      adjective   adverb
- He's a **good** driver. He drives **well**.

   b. A few **adjectives** and **adverbs** have the <u>same form</u>—for example, *early, fast, hard, late,* and *wrong.*

                      adjective   adverb
- She is a **hard** worker. She works **hard**.

                      adjective   adverb
- The visitor was **late**. He woke up **late**.

▶ **BE CAREFUL!** *Hardly* is not the adverb form of *hard. Hardly* means "almost not."

- There's **hardly** enough room for a bed. *(There's almost not enough room for a bed.)*

   Lately is not the adverb form of *late. Lately* means "recently."

- We haven't seen any nice houses **lately**. We're getting discouraged.

---

6. Use **adverbs of frequency** to say <u>how often</u> something happens.

- She ***usually*** rents to students.

   Adverbs of frequency usually go <u>before</u> the main verb. They usually go <u>after</u> a form of ***be***.

- They ***always*** share a house with friends.
- My neighbors **are** ***always*** home on Sunday.

---

7. **Participial adjectives** are adjectives that end with **-*ing*** or **-*ed***. They come from <u>verbs</u>.

                              verb
- This story **amazes** me.

   Participial adjectives often describe **feelings**.

                      adjective   adjective
- It's an **amazing** story. I'm **amazed**.

   - Use the **-*ing*** form for someone or something that <u>causes</u> a feeling.

- The fly is **disgusting**. *(The fly causes the feeling.)*

   - Use the **-*ed*** form for the person who <u>has</u> the feeling.

- I'm **disgusted**. *(I have the feeling.)*

Reference Notes

For a list of **non-action verbs**, see Appendix 2 on page A-2.
For a discussion of **adverbs of frequency**, see Unit 1 on page 5.
For a list of **participial adjectives**, see Appendix 11 on page A-6.
For the **order of adjectives before a noun**, see Appendix 12 on page A-6.
For **spelling rules** for **base form of verb + -*ing***, see Appendix 21 on page A-10.
For **spelling rules** for **base form of verb + -*ed***, see Appendix 22 on page A-10.
For **spelling rules** for forming -*ly* adverbs, see Appendix 24 on page A-11.

Focused Practice

1 | DISCOVER THE GRAMMAR

Read this notice from a university bulletin board. Underline the adjectives and circle the adverbs. Then draw an arrow from the adjective or adverb to the word it is describing.

APT. FOR RENT
140 Grant Street, Apartment 4B

Are you looking for a place to live? This <u>lovely</u> apartment is in a new building and has two large bedrooms and a sunny kitchen. The building is (very) quiet— absolutely perfect for two serious students. You'll be close to campus. The bus stop is a short walk, and the express bus goes directly into town. You can run or ride your bike safely in nearby parks. The rent is very affordable. Small pets are welcome. Interested students should call Megan at 555-5050. Don't wait! This apartment will rent fast. Nonsmokers, please.

2 | WRITING HOME   *Grammar Notes 1–7*

Circle the correct words to complete Maggie's letter to her brother.

Dear Roger,

    I wasn't sure I'd like living in a (large) / largely city, but I <u>real / really</u> love it! Maybe that's
                1.   **2.**

because my <u>new / newly</u> neighborhood is so <u>beautiful / beautifully</u>. Last Saturday I worked
        3.   **4.**

<u>hard / hardly</u> and unpacked all my stuff. Then I spent Sunday <u>happy / happily</u> exploring the
  5.   **6.**

neighborhood. I couldn't believe the <u>gorgeous / gorgeously</u> houses on these streets.
                            7.

    My apartment is <u>great / greatly</u> and the other tenants are very <u>nice / nicely</u>. My next-door
            8.   **9.**

neighbor, Alice, seemed <u>shy / shyly</u> at first, but I think we're going to become <u>good / well</u>
            10.   **11.**

friends very <u>quick / quickly</u>. She's an art student, and she <u>usual / usually</u> visits museums on
     12.   **13.**

Saturdays. We're going together next week. Life in the city is <u>exciting / excitingly</u>, but I get
                                     14.

<u>terrible / terribly</u> homesick. So I hope you visit me soon!
  15.

                                       Love,
                                       Maggie

3 | DID YOU LIKE IT?   *Grammar Notes 2, 4*

Many different people went to see the apartment described in Exercise 1. Complete their comments about the apartment. Use the correct form of the words in parentheses. See Appendix 24 on page A-11 for help with spelling adverbs ending in -ly.

1. I am very interested. I think the apartment is _____*extremely nice*_____.
   (extreme / nice)

2. I was expecting much bigger rooms. I was _____.
   (terrible / disappointed)

3. I thought it would be hard to find, but it was _____.
   (surprising / easy)

4. This neighborhood is _____.
   (extreme / expensive)

5. This apartment is _____ for this neighborhood.
   (amazing / cheap)

6. I think it's a great place. I'm sure it will rent _____.
   (incredible / fast)

7. The notice said it was a quiet place, but I heard the neighbors _____.
   (very / clear)

8. I heard them too. I thought their voices were _____.
   (awful / loud)

9. The ad described the apartment _____.
   (very / accurate)

10. I like the owner. She's _____.
    (exceptional / friendly)

11. To be honest, this place is _____ for me!
    (absolute / perfect)

12. I'm going to feel _____ if I don't get it.
    (real / upset)

4 | IT'S HARD TO TELL WITH ALICE   *Grammar Note 7*

🎧 *Maggie and Luis are talking about their neighbor. Read their conversation. Complete it with the correct participial adjective form (-ing or -ed) of the verbs in parentheses.*

MAGGIE: What's the matter with Alice?

LUIS: Who knows? She's always _____*annoyed*_____ about something.
      1. (annoy)

MAGGIE I know, but this time I'm really _____.
      2. (confuse)

LUIS: Why? What's so _____ this time?
      3. (confuse)

MAGGIE: Oh, I thought she was happy. She met an _____ man last week.
      4. (interest)

LUIS: Great. Was she _____ in him?
      5. (interest)

MAGGIE: I thought so. She said they saw a _____ movie together. So I thought . . .
      6. (fascinate)

LUIS: Maybe she was _____ by the movie, but she was _____
      7. (fascinate)   **8. (disappoint)**
      with the guy.

MAGGIE: Maybe. It's hard to tell with Alice. Her moods are often very _____.
      9. (surprise)

5 | EDITING

Read the evaluation Luis wrote about his teacher. There are twelve mistakes in the use of adjectives and adverbs. The first mistake is already corrected. Find and correct eleven more.

English 206   **EVALUATION**

Mr. Delgado is an ~~exceptionally~~ *exceptional* teacher. He prepared careful for classes, and his lessons were almost always interested. He explained clearly the material, and he returned always our tests on time. This was not an easy class, but the time always passed fastly because the students were exciting by the material. I studied hardly for this class—more than two hours a night—because Mr. Delgado gave hard tests. His tests were very fairly though. We were never surprising by test questions because they were all from class work or the textbook. I did good in this class, and I'm sure other students will too. I recommend highly his class.

Communication Practice

6 | LISTENING

 A couple is discussing newspaper apartment ads. Read the ads. Then listen to the conversation. Listen again, and number the ads from 1 to 4 to match the order in which the couple discusses them.

Section 6 Real Estate	
CUMBERLAND **Wow! Cute/cozy 2 bed** in quiet area. No pets. $450/month. 555-2343 ext 27	**SMITHFIELD** [1] **Large, lovely 2 bed** in new bldg, nr pub transport. $500/month. 555-3296
LINCOLN **Beautiful 2 bed** in completely renovated bldg. Mod. kitchen & ba. Available immediately $460/month. 555-7859	**FOSTER** **Light and bright 2 bed** on beautifully landscaped street. Newly painted, excel condition. Near shopping and schools. $600/month. 555-7749

7 | WHERE DO YOU LIVE?

Work in small groups. Describe where you live. Tell each other how you found the place.
Explain how you first felt about it (pleased, disappointed, etc.). Describe what it looks like.
Tell how you decorated it. What is special about your place?

> **Example:** I found my apartment last summer when I was walking down the street. I saw an "Apartment for Rent" sign. I knocked on the door. At first, I was disappointed. It's a small apartment . . .

8 | HOME SWEET HOME

Work with a partner. There are many different types of housing. Describe the different
types listed below. How are they similar? How are they different? Use your dictionaries to
help you. Do these types of housing exist in other places you have lived?

- apartment
- boarding house
- dorm (dormitory)
- mansion
- mobile home
- private home
- rented room in someone's house
- studio apartment

> **Example:** A mobile home can be very convenient. You can pull it behind your car.

9 | YOUR IDEAL NEIGHBOR

Work in small groups. Take turns describing your ideal neighbor. Describe the person and
his or her activities. Here are some words you can use.

Adjectives		
cheerful	considerate	gloomy
helpful	loud	messy
neat	reliable	serious

Adverbs		
early	easily	happily
late	loudly	noisily
politely	quietly	seriously

> **Example:** My ideal neighbor isn't loud and doesn't party too late. When we have a problem, we can talk about it politely.

10 | WRITING

Write an ad like the one for Wakefield House on page 268. Describe your ideal home.

Example: Do you want to live in an exciting neighborhood with great stores that stay open late? Do you want a large, modern apartment with a terrific view of all the action in the streets below? The apartments in the Atrium are . . .

11 | ON THE INTERNET

*Do a search on **real estate** or **off-campus housing** in your area or another location that interests you. Print out four ads and discuss them with a partner.*

Example: **A:** Here's an ad for a cozy one-bedroom apartment on a quiet street.
B: Cozy? That probably means small.

Adjectives: Comparisons with *As . . . as* and *Than*

Grammar in Context

BEFORE YOU READ

🎧 *How often do you eat out? What types of restaurant food do you enjoy? Would you like to order the pizza in the photo? Why or why not? Read the newspaper restaurant review.*

A New Place for Pizza

by Pete Tsa

AS FRESH AS IT GETS!

PIZZA PLACE, the chain of popular restaurants, has just opened a new one on Main Street, two blocks from the university. The day I ate there, the service was **not as good as** at the other Pizza Place restaurants in town. The young staff (mostly students) probably needs time to become **more professional**. But the pizza was incredible! It seemed **bigger** and **better than** at the other six locations. As with all food, **the fresher** the ingredients, **the better** the pizza. The ingredients at the new Pizza Place are **as fresh as** you can get (no mushrooms from a can here!), and the choices are much **more varied than** at their other restaurants. We ordered two different types. The one with mashed potatoes and garlic was a lot **more interesting than** the traditional pizza with cheese and tomato sauce, but both were delicious.

Each Pizza Place is different. The one on Main Street is a little **larger** (and **louder**) **than** the others. It's also **more crowded** because students love it. At lunchtime the lines outside this new eatery are getting **longer and longer**. Go early for a **quieter**, **more relaxed** meal.

AFTER YOU READ

*Read the statements about Pizza Place. Check **True** or **False**.*

	True	False
1. The service is great.	☐	☐
2. The pizza is very good.	☐	☐
3. The mushrooms are fresh.	☐	☐
4. They have only two types of pizza.	☐	☐
5. It's crowded because it's small.	☐	☐
6. It's noisy at lunchtime.	☐	☐

Grammar Presentation

ADJECTIVES: COMPARISONS WITH *AS . . . AS* AND *THAN*

Comparisons with *As . . . as*				
	(Not) As	**Adjective**	**As**	
The new restaurant is	**(not) as**	**large** **busy** **good** **interesting** **expensive**	**as**	the other ones.

Comparisons with *Than*		
	Comparative Adjective Form	**Than**	
The new restaurant is	**larger** **busier** **better**	**than**	the other ones.
	more interesting **less expensive**		

GRAMMAR NOTES	EXAMPLES
1. Use *(not) as* + *adjective* + *as* to compare people, places, or things, and show how they are (or aren't) **similar**.	**A:** Pizza Place is **as good as** Joe's. **B:** But Joe's is**n't as expensive as** Pizza Place.
• Use *as* + *adjective* + *as* to show how they are <u>the same or equal</u>. Use *just* to make the comparison stronger.	• The new menu is *just* **as good as** the old. *(The new menu and the old menu are equally good.)*
• Use *not as* + *adjective* + *as* to show how they are <u>not the same or equal</u>.	• The new menu is**n't as varied as** the old. *(The old menu was more varied.)*
REMEMBER: It is not necessary to mention both parts of the comparison when the meaning is clear.	**A:** I liked the old menu. It had more choices. **B:** Too bad the new one is**n't as varied**. *(. . . as the old menu)*

2. Use **comparative adjectives** + *than* to show how people, places, or things are **different**.	• The new restaurant is **bigger than** the old restaurant. • The new waiters are **more professional than** the old waiters.

3. There are several ways of **forming comparative adjectives**.		
a. For **short adjectives** (one-syllable and two-syllable ending in *-y*), use **adjective** + *-er*.	**ADJECTIVE** loud friendly	**COMPARATIVE** loud**er** friendli**er**
There are often **spelling changes** when you add *-er*.	late big early	lat**er** big**ger** earl**ier**
Some adjectives have **irregular** comparative forms.	good bad	**better** **worse**
b. For **long adjectives** (two or more syllables), use *more / less* + **adjective**.	expensive	**more** expensive **less** expensive
c. For **some adjectives**, like *lively, lovely,* or *quiet,* you can use either *-er* or *more*.	• The Inn is **livelier** than Joe's. <div align="center">OR</div>• The Inn is **more lively** than Joe's.	

(continued)

4. Use *than* before the second part of the comparison. **REMEMBER:** It's not necessary to mention both parts of the comparison when the meaning is clear.	• Our table is **smaller than** their table. • The new tables are **smaller**. (*. . . than the old tables*)
5. Comparatives with ***than*** and comparisons with ***as . . . as*** often express the <u>same meaning</u> in different ways. **USAGE NOTE:** With <u>one-syllable adjectives</u>, ***not as . . . as*** is more common than *less . . . than*.	• The Inn is **more expensive than** Joe's. • Joe's is**n't as expensive as** the Inn. • Joe's is **less expensive than** the Inn. • Our server is**n't as fast as** theirs. NOT Our server is ~~less fast than~~ theirs.

6. Repeat the comparative adjective to show how something is <u>increasing or decreasing</u>:
 	
 comparative adjective + *and* + **comparative adjective**
 	
With long adjectives, repeat only ***more*** or ***less***.
	• The lines are getting **longer and longer**.
	  (*Their length is increasing.*)
	
	• It's getting **more and more popular**.
	  (*Its popularity is increasing.*)
	
	• It's **less and less comfortable**.
	  (*The comfort is decreasing.*)

7. Use two comparative adjectives to show <u>cause and effect</u>:
 	
 ***the* + comparative adjective** + ***the* + comparative adjective**
 	
When both comparative adjectives describe the same person, place, or thing, we often <u>leave out the noun</u>.
	• **The more crowded** the restaurant, **the slower** the service.
	  (*The service is slower because the restaurant is more crowded.*)
	
	A: The service is really fast here.
	B: **The faster, the better.**
	  (*The faster the service, the better the service.*)

Reference Notes

For a list of **adjectives** that use **both forms of the comparative**, see Appendix 9 on page A-5.
For a list of **irregular comparative adjectives**, see Appendix 10 on page A-6.
For **spelling rules** for the **comparative form of adjectives**, see Appendix 23 on page A-11.

Focused Practice

1 DISCOVER THE GRAMMAR

Read the information about two brands of frozen pizza. Then decide if each statement is **True (T)** or **False (F)**.

	Maria's Pizza	John's Pizza
Size	12 inches	12 inches
Weight	27 ounces	24 ounces
Price	$5.99	$6.99
Calories*	364	292
Salt content*	731 milligrams	600 milligrams
Baking time	20 minutes	16 minutes
Taste	★ ★ ★	★ ★ ★ ★

* for a five-ounce serving

___F___ 1. Maria's pizza is bigger than John's.

_____ 2. John's pizza is just as big as Maria's.

_____ 3. John's isn't as heavy as Maria's.

_____ 4. Maria's is just as expensive as John's.

_____ 5. John's is more expensive than Maria's.

_____ 6. Maria's is higher in calories than John's.

_____ 7. Maria's is saltier than John's.

_____ 8. The baking time for Maria's isn't as long as the baking time for John's.

_____ 9. John's tastes better than Maria's.

2 CHEESE CHECK

Grammar Note 1

Look at this consumer magazine chart comparing three brands of pizza cheese. Complete the sentences. Use **as . . . as** or **not as . . . as** and the correct form of the words in parentheses.

Brand	Price (per serving)	Taste	Smell
X	5¢	◐	●
Y	3¢	◐	◐
Z	3¢	○	◐

PIZZA CHEESE   ● ◐ ○   Better ←——→ Worse

1. Brand Z ___is as expensive as___ Brand Y.
   (be / expensive)

2. Brand Y _____ Brand X.
   (be / expensive)

3. Brand X _____ Brand Y.
   (taste / good)

4. Brand Z _____ Brand Y.
   (taste / good)

5. Brand Y _____ Brand X.
   (smell / nice)

6. Brand Y _____ Brand Z.
   (smell / nice)

3 | MENU

Look at the menu. Then complete the sentences comparing items on the menu. Use the appropriate comparative form of the adjectives in parentheses and **than**.

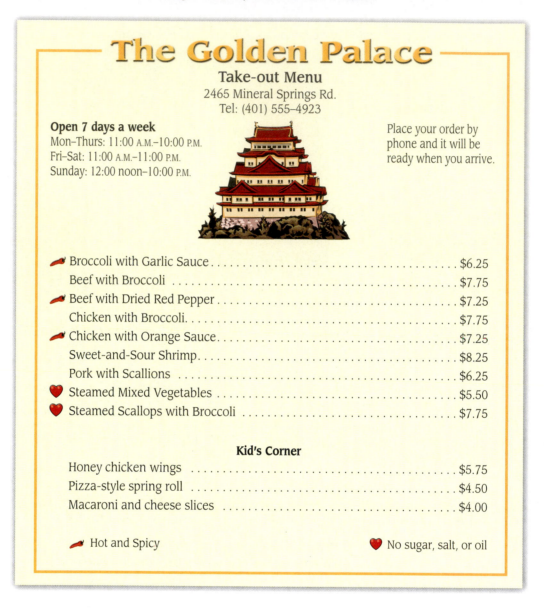

The Golden Palace

Take-out Menu
2465 Mineral Springs Rd.
Tel: (401) 555-4923

Open 7 days a week
Mon–Thurs: 11:00 A.M.–10:00 P.M.
Fri–Sat: 11:00 A.M.–11:00 P.M.
Sunday: 12:00 noon–10:00 P.M.

Place your order by phone and it will be ready when you arrive.

Broccoli with Garlic Sauce $6.25
Beef with Broccoli $7.75
Beef with Dried Red Pepper $7.25
Chicken with Broccoli. $7.75
Chicken with Orange Sauce. $7.25
Sweet-and-Sour Shrimp. $8.25
Pork with Scallions $6.25
Steamed Mixed Vegetables $5.50
Steamed Scallops with Broccoli $7.75

Kid's Corner
Honey chicken wings $5.75
Pizza-style spring roll $4.50
Macaroni and cheese slices $4.00

Hot and Spicy

No sugar, salt, or oil

---

1. The sweet-and-sour shrimp is _____*more expensive than*_____ the steamed scallops.
(expensive)

2. The beef with dried red pepper is _____ the beef with broccoli.
(hot)

3. The pork with scallions is _____ the sweet-and-sour shrimp.
(expensive)

4. The chicken with orange sauce is _____ the scallops with broccoli.
(spicy)

5. The steamed mixed vegetables are _____ the pork with scallions.
(salty)

6. The chicken with broccoli is _____ the chicken with orange sauce.
   (mild)

7. The steamed vegetables are _____ the beef with dried red pepper.
   (healthy)

8. The broccoli with garlic sauce is _____ the chicken with broccoli.
   (cheap)

9. The pork with scallions is _____ the steamed mixed vegetables.
   (oily)

10. The shrimp dish is _____ the scallop dish.
    (sweet)

11. The restaurant's hours on Sunday are _____ they are on Saturday.
    (short)

12. The children's menu is _____ the adult's menu.
    (short)

13. The children's menu is _____ too.
    (expensive)

14. The chicken wings are _____ the macaroni and cheese slices.
    (sweet)

4 | THE MORE, THE MERRIER   *Grammar Notes 6–7*

Complete these conversations. Use the comparative form of the adjectives in parentheses to show an increase/decrease or a cause and effect.

1. **A:** Wow! The lines here are getting _____*longer and longer*_____.
   (long)

   B: I know. And _____*the longer*_____ the wait, _____*the hungrier*_____ I get.
   (long)   (hungry)

2. **A:** It's worth the wait. The food here is getting _____.
   (good)

   B: But _____ the food, _____ the bill!
   (good)   (high)

3. **A:** The lunch crowd is leaving. It's getting _____.
   (crowded)

   B: Great. These books were starting to feel _____.
   (heavy)

4. **A:** There's Professor Lee. You know, his course is getting _____.
   (popular)

   B: It's amazing. _____ it is, _____ it gets.
   (hard)   (popular)

   He's a great teacher.

5. **A:** Is it the hot sauce, or has your cough been getting _____?
   (bad)

   B: It's the hot sauce, but I love it. For my taste, _____,
   (spicy)

   _____.
   (good)

6. **A:** The service used to be slow here, but it's getting _____.
   (fast)

   B: Right. _____ the service, _____ the lines!
   (fast)   (short)

5 | EDITING

*Read this student's essay. There are nine mistakes in the use of **as . . . as** and comparatives with **than**. The first mistake is already corrected. Find and correct eight more.*

When I was a teenager in the Philippines, I was an expert on snacks and

fast foods. I was growing fast, so the more I ate, the ~~hungry~~ *hungrier* I felt. The

street vendors in our town had the better snacks than anyone else. In the

morning, I used to buy rice muffins on the way to school. They are much

sweeter that American muffins. After school, I ate fish balls on a stick or

adidas (chicken feet). Snacks on a stick are small than American hot dogs

and burgers, but they are much varied. My friend thought *banana-cue*

(banana on a stick) was really great. However, they weren't as sweet from

kamote-cue (fried sweet potatoes and brown sugar), my favorite snack.

When I came to the United States, I didn't like American fast food at

first. To me, it was interesting than my native food and less tastier too.

Now I'm getting used to it, and it seems deliciouser and deliciouser.

Does anyone want to go out for a pizza?

Communication Practice

6 | LISTENING

🎧 *A couple is trying to choose between two brands of frozen pizza in the supermarket. Listen to their conversation. Then listen again and check the pizza that is better in each category.*

	Di Roma's	Angela's
1. cheap	✔	☐
2. big	☐	☐
3. healthy	☐	☐
4. tasty	☐	☐
5. fresh	☐	☐

7 | PIZZA AROUND THE WORLD

Look at some of these favorite international pizza toppings. Discuss them with a partner. Make comparisons using some of the adjectives in the box.

delicious	filling	healthy	interesting	spicy	tasty	traditional	unusual

1. Australia

2. Mexico

3. Hong Kong

4. Greece

5. Poland

6. Indonesia

Example: **A:** The pizza from Poland seems more filling than the one from Greece.
B: Yes, and it's not as spicy.

8 | WHAT'S ON THE MENU?

Work in groups. Imagine that you have a restaurant. Give your restaurant a name and decide what to put on the menu. Discuss dishes and prices for each category. Use comparisons in your discussion.

> **Example:** A: We need one more soup. How about chicken noodle?
> B: Too boring! Gazpacho is more interesting.

Soups and Appetizers

_____ . . . . $ _____
_____ . . . . $ _____
_____ . . . . $ _____
_____ . . . . $ _____

Entrées

_____ . . . . $ _____
_____ . . . . $ _____
_____ . . . . $ _____
_____ . . . . $ _____

Salads and Side Dishes

_____ . . . . $ _____
_____ . . . . $ _____
_____ . . . . $ _____
_____ . . . . $ _____

Desserts

_____ . . . . $ _____
_____ . . . . $ _____
_____ . . . . $ _____
_____ . . . . $ _____

Beverages

_____ . . . . $ _____
_____ . . . . $ _____
_____ . . . . $ _____

With your group, role-play ordering from your menu. One person is the server; the others are customers.

> **Example:** CUSTOMER: Is the gazpacho as spicy as the hot-and-sour soup?
> SERVER: No, the hot-and-sour soup is much spicier.

9 | INFORMATION GAP: THICK AND CHUNKY

Work in pairs (A and B). Student A, follow the instructions on this page. Student B, turn to page 288 and follow the instructions there.

1. Look at the charts below comparing two brands of spaghetti sauce.

2. Ask your partner questions to complete the charts.

   Example: A: Which brand is smoother?
   B: Frank's is smoother than Classic's.

3. Draw the following circles:
   ● for the brand that has more of a certain quality
   ⊖ if the brands are equal
   ○ for the brand that has less of a certain quality

4. Answer your partner's questions.

   Example: B: Which brand is thicker?
   A: Frank's is as thick as Classic's.

Spaghetti Sauce

● more   ⊖ equal   ○ less

Quality	Frank's	Classic's
smooth	●	○
thick	⊖	⊖
chunky		
flavorful	○	●
sweet		
salty	●	○

Quality	Frank's	Classic's
spicy		
garlicky	●	○
fresh-tasting		
fattening	○	●
nutritious		
expensive	●	○

When you are finished, compare your charts. Are they the same? Choose a spaghetti sauce to buy. Explain your choice.

10 | WRITING

Write a paragraph comparing your country's food with the food of another country.

   Example: Food in Taiwan is fresher than food in the United States. Taiwan is a small island and there are a lot of farms . . .

11 | ON THE INTERNET

Work with a partner. Find two online menus for the same type of take-out restaurants in your city (for example, pizza places, hamburger places, Chinese restaurants). Print them out and compare them. Which restaurant would you prefer to eat at? Why?

Example: **A:** The food at Mike's Place isn't as cheap as at the Plaza Grill.
B: You're right. But it looks more varied and interesting.

INFORMATION GAP FOR STUDENT B

1. Look at the charts below comparing two brands of spaghetti sauce.

2. Answer your partner's questions.

Example: **A:** Which brand is smoother?
B: Frank's is smoother than Classic's.

3. Ask your partner questions to complete the charts.

Example: **B:** Which brand is thicker.
A: Frank's is as thick as Classic's.

4. Draw the following circles:

● for the brand that has more of a certain quality

◒ if the brands are equal

○ for the brand that has less of a certain quality

Spaghetti Sauce

● more   ◒ equal   ○ less

Quality	Frank's	Classic's	Quality	Frank's	Classic's
smooth	●	○	spicy	○	●
thick	◒	◒	garlicky		
chunky	○	●	fresh-tasting	◒	◒
flavorful			fattening		
sweet	●	○	nutritious	○	●
salty			expensive		

When you are finished, compare your charts. Are they the same? Choose a spaghetti sauce to buy. Explain your choice.

Adjectives: Superlatives

Grammar in Context

BEFORE YOU READ

Look at the photo. Do you recognize this city? Where do you think it is? What are some important features for a city to have? Read the travel brochure.

A Superlative City

TORONTO. It's the capital of the province of Ontario. It's also . . .

* **the largest** city in Canada

* **the most important** economic and financial center of the country

* one of **the most multi-cultural** cities on earth
  (Over 100 languages are spoken!)

* one of **the easiest** towns to get around
  (It has **the second largest** public transportation system in North America.)

* **the safest** city on the continent, and one of **the most peaceful** of all large, international cities

All of these features, and many more, make Toronto one of **the most exciting** cities in the world. Come visit and find out for yourself!

AFTER YOU READ

Read the statements. Check **True** *or* **False**.

	True	False
1. Some Canadian cities are larger than Toronto.	☐	☐
2. Some Canadian cities are more important economically than Toronto.	☐	☐
3. Many cities in the world aren't as diverse and multi-cultural as Toronto.	☐	☐
4. It's easy to get around Toronto.	☐	☐
5. No city in North America is safer than Toronto.	☐	☐

Toronto and the CN Tower seen from Lake Ontario

Grammar Presentation

ADJECTIVES: SUPERLATIVES

Superlatives			
	Superlative Adjective Form		
This is	**the largest** **the busiest** **the best**	city	in the world. of all. I've ever visited.
	the most interesting **the least expensive**		

GRAMMAR NOTES	EXAMPLES

1. Use **superlative adjectives** to compare <u>one</u> person, place, or thing with other people, places, or things in a <u>group</u>.

- The CN Tower is **the tallest** tower in the world.
- Toronto is **the most multi-cultural** city in Canada.

2. There are several ways of **forming superlative adjectives**.

  a. For **short adjectives** (one syllable and two syllables ending in *-y*), use: *the* **+ adjective + *-est*.**

    There are often **spelling changes** when you add *-est*.

    Some adjectives have **irregular** superlative forms.

  b. For **long adjectives** (two or more syllables), use *the most / the least +* **adjective**.

  c. For **some adjectives**, like *lively, lovely,* or *quiet*, you can use either *the . . . -est* or *the most / the least*.

ADJECTIVE	SUPERLATIVE
loud	**the** loud**est**
friendly	**the** friendli**est**
late	**the** lat**est**
big	**the** big**gest**
early	**the** earl**iest**
good	**the best**
bad	**the worst**
expensive	**the most** expensive
	the least expensive

- Rio is **the liveliest** city in the world.

OR

- Rio is **the most lively** city in the world.

3. We often use the superlative with other **words and expressions**:

  a. phrases with *in* and *of*

  b. *one of* or *some of*
    Use a <u>plural noun</u> with these expressions.

  c. *second* (*third, fourth . . .*)

  d. *ever* + present perfect

- This is **the least expensive** hotel *in town*.
- This was **the best** day *of our visit*.
- Toronto is *one of* **the most interesting** *cities* in the world.
  NOT Toronto is one of the most interesting ~~city~~ in the world.
- It has **the** *second* **largest** transportation system.
- This is **the biggest** building *I've ever seen*.

Reference Notes
For a list of **adjectives** that use **both forms of the superlative**, see Appendix 9 on page A-5.
For a list of **irregular superlative adjectives**, see Appendix 10 on page A-6.
For **spelling rules** for the **superlative form of adjectives**, see Appendix 23 on page A-11.

Focused Practice

1 | DISCOVER THE GRAMMAR

Read more information about Toronto. Underline all the superlative adjectives.

What to Do and See in Toronto

 Go to the CN Tower. It's the tallest free-standing structure in the world—even taller than the Petronas Towers in Malaysia. From there you can get the best view of the city and countryside.

 Drive along Yonge Street. At 1,200 miles (1,800 km) it's the longest street in the world. For one weekend in July it's one of the liveliest too. Come and join 1 million others for the exciting Yonge Street Festival.

 Visit PATH, the world's largest underground shopping complex.

 Explore the Old Town of York. It has the most historic buildings in the whole city.

 Take the Yuk Yuk Comedy Tour of the Entertainment District—you'll have a good time on the funniest bus ride in town.

 Visit the Toronto Zoo. There's always something new and fascinating going on. Local people call it the best family outing in Toronto.

2 | CITY STATISTICS

Grammar Notes 1–2

Look at the chart and complete the sentences on the next page. Use the superlative form of the correct adjective.

		ATHENS	MEXICO CITY	SEOUL	TORONTO
	Population	748,110	8,591,309	9,853,972	2,571,400
	Size	428 square km/ 165 square miles	1,479 square km/ 571 square miles	627 square km/ 242 square miles	630 square km/ 243 square miles
	Average January Temperature	10.2°C/ 50.4°F	13.3°C/ 55.9°F	–3.5°C/ 25.7°F	–6.4°C/ 20.5°F
	Average July Temperature	27.9°C/ 82.2°F	16.7°C/ 62.1°F	24.4°C/ 75.9°F	20.7°C/ 69.3°F
	Average Rainfall per Year	394.8 mm/ 15.5 in.	634.3 mm/ 25 in.	1,364.8 mm/ 53.7 in.	877.7 mm/ 32.2 in.
	Cost of a Cup of Coffee ($U.S.)	$4.25	$1.20	$3.00	$3.35

1. Seoul has _____*the largest*_____ population of all four cities, but it isn't
   _____(large / small)_____
   _____ city in size.
   (big / small)

2. Mexico City is _____ city in area.
   (big / small)

3. Athens is _____ city in both population and size.
   (big / small)

4. In winter, _____ cities are Seoul and Toronto.
   (warm / cold)

5. Toronto also has some of _____ July temperatures, but Seoul doesn't.
   (hot / cool)

6. Of all the cities in the chart, Mexico City is _____ in July and
   (hot / cool)
   _____ in January. It has _____ climate of all.
   (warm / cold)   (comfortable / uncomfortable)

7. _____ city is Athens. It's also _____ in July.
   (dry / rainy)   (hot / cold)

8. Seoul is _____ city.
   (dry / rainy)

9. You'll find _____ cup of coffee in Mexico City.
   (cheap / expensive)

10. _____ cup of coffee is in Athens.
    (cheap / expensive)

3 | THE CN TOWER / *LA TOUR CN*   *Grammar Notes 1–3*

Read about the CN Tower. Complete the information. Use the superlative form of the correct adjective from the box.

clear	famous	fast	heavy	long	popular	~~tall~~

1. At 1,815 feet, 5 inches (553.33 m), the CN Tower is _____*the tallest*_____
   free-standing structure in the world.

2. Everyone recognizes the CN Tower. It is _____ building in Canada.

3. At 130,000 tons (117,910 metric tonnes), the CN Tower is one of _____
   buildings in the world.

4. With 2 million visitors every year, it is one of _____ tourist attractions in
   the country.

5. Because of its very high antenna, the tower provides the people of Toronto with some of
   _____ radio and TV reception in North America.

6. Moving at 15 miles (22 km) per hour, the six elevators are among _____
   in the world. The ride to the Look Out Level takes just 58 seconds.

7. If you don't want to take the elevator, you can try the stairs! The CN Tower has
   _____ metal staircase in the world.

4 | WHAT ABOUT YOU?

Write superlative sentences about your own experiences. Use the words in parentheses
*with **the most** and **the least** + the present perfect. Write two sentences for each item.*
Go to Appendix 1, page A-1, for help with the irregular past participles.

Example: Toronto is the most interesting city I've ever visited.
Meadville is the least interesting place I've ever visited.

1. (interesting / city / visit)

_____

_____

2. (comfortable / place / stay)

_____

_____

3. (friendly / people / meet)

_____

_____

4. (expensive / trip / take)

_____

_____

5 | EDITING

Read this postcard. There are seven mistakes in the use of superlative adjectives. The first
mistake is already corrected. Find and correct six more.

most beautiful
Greetings from Toronto — the ~~beautifulest~~ city I've ever visited. Yesterday we went to the CN Tower — the more recognizable structure in all of Canada. From there you get the best view of the city. The restaurant was the most expensivest I've ever seen, so we just enjoyed the view and then went to Kensington Market to eat. This place has the baddest crowds but the cheapest and the goodest food we've had so far. We're staying in East Toronto. It's not the closer place to downtown, but it has some of most historic buildings. In fact, our bed-and-breakfast is called *1871 Historic House*. John Lennon slept here!

Love, Marissa

Communication Practice

6 | LISTENING

🎧 *May and Dan are deciding on a hotel for their vacation in Toronto. Listen to their conversation. Then check the correct hotel for each superlative adjective.*

	Westin Harbour Castle	Hôtel Le Germain	Delta Chelsea
the best view	✔		
the most convenient			
the least convenient			
the most comfortable			
the most expensive			
the least expensive			
the biggest			
the smallest			

7 | IN YOUR COUNTRY

Work in small groups. Discuss cities in your country. You can use these adjectives:

beautiful	interesting
clean	international
crowded	modern
exciting	old
friendly	safe

Example: A: What's the most interesting city in Argentina?

B: I think Buenos Aires is the most interesting city in Argentina. There's so much to do—theater, sports, movies. It's also the most diverse city in the country. People from all over the world live there.

8 | IN THE WORLD

Work in small groups. Discuss your answers to Exercise 4.

Example: A: What's the most interesting city you've ever visited?
B: Barcelona. It has some of the most wonderful buildings in the world. It also has some of the best restaurants . . .

9 | ON THE INTERNET

 Do a search on a city that interests you. Find information about:

- the most famous tourist attractions
- the most historic buildings and areas
- the best restaurants

Discuss the information in small groups.

Example: A: The most famous tourist attraction in Paris is the Eiffel Tower.
B: In Athens, it's the Parthenon.

10 | WRITING

Write a fact sheet with information for tourists about the city you researched for Exercise 9. Include superlatives.

Example: What to Do and See in Meadville
- Go to Joe's for the best pizza in town.
- Ride the number 53 bus for one of the cheapest and best ways to see the major sights.

Adverbs: *As...as,* Comparatives, Superlatives

UNIT
26

Grammar in Context

BEFORE YOU READ

🎧 *Look at the photo. What game are they playing? Which sports do you like to watch? Do you play any sports? Which ones? Why do you like them? Read the transcript of a TV sports program.*

The Halftime Report

CINDY: What a game! Spero, have you ever seen two teams play **more aggressively**?

SPERO: No, I haven't, Cindy. Folks, we're watching the Detroit Shock battle the Los Angeles Sparks. It's halftime, and just listen to that Sparks crowd! I think they cheer **the loudest** of any fans in the game!

CINDY: Well, the court really belonged to the Sparks for the first few minutes of the game, Spero. But the Shock recovered quickly. They've scored almost **as frequently as** the Sparks in the first half. The score is now 30–28, Sparks, and no one can predict a winner at this point.

Tamecka Dixon of the LA Sparks and Ruth Riley of the Detroit Shock

SPERO: I heard that Ruth Riley, the Shock's star player, injured her arm yesterday, but you can't tell from the way she's playing today. She's scored **the most** of her team so far.

CINDY: But Tamecka Dixon of the Sparks isn't far behind. She's playing **more and more intensely**. You can see that she really wants the ball, and she's getting it **more consistently** in every game.

SPERO: You're right, Cindy. **The harder** she plays, **the more** she scores.

CINDY: The Sparks have really been playing a great defense tonight. They've been blocking Riley **more effectively than** any other team this season. But can they stop her?

SPERO: We'll find out now! The second half is ready to begin. See you again after the game.

AFTER YOU READ

Read the statements. Check **True** *or* **False**.

	True	False
1. Both teams are playing aggressively.	☐	☐
2. The Sparks fans cheer louder than the Shock fans.	☐	☐
3. In the first half, the Shock scored as many points as the Sparks.	☐	☐
4. Tamecka Dixon is playing badly.	☐	☐
5. Other Shock players have scored more than Riley.	☐	☐
6. Other teams have blocked Ruth Riley better than the Sparks.	☐	☐

Grammar Presentation

ADVERBS: *AS . . . AS*, COMPARATIVES, SUPERLATIVES

As . . . as					
		As	**Adverb**	**As**	
The Huskies	played didn't play	**as**	**hard well aggressively consistently**	**as**	the Gophers.

Comparatives				
		Comparative Adverb Form	*Than*	
The Huskies	played	**harder better** **more aggressively less consistently**	**than**	the Gophers.

Superlatives			
		Superlative Adverb Form	
The star player	played	**the hardest the best** **the most aggressively the least consistently**	of anyone in the game.

GRAMMAR NOTES	EXAMPLES

1. Use (***not***) ***as*** + **adverb** + ***as*** to compare actions and show how they are (or aren't) **similar**.

- Use ***as*** + **adverb** + ***as*** to show how actions are <u>the same or equal</u>. Use ***just*** to make the comparison stronger.
- Use ***not as*** + **adverb** + ***as*** to show how actions are <u>not the same or equal</u>.

- Riley played ***just* as well as** most players. *(She and the other players played equally well.)*
- Cash did**n't** play **as aggressively as** Ely. *(Cash and Ely didn't play the same. Cash played less aggressively.)*

---

2. Use **comparative adverbs** + ***than*** to show how the actions of two people or things are **different**.

- The Sparks played **better than** the Shock.
- Riley played **more skillfully than** Nolan.
- She played **less aggressively than** Nolan.

---

3. **REMEMBER:** It's not necessary to mention both parts of the comparison when the meaning is clear.

- He played hard. She played just **as hard** (as he did).
- Beard shot **more consistently** (than King).

---

4. Use **superlative adverbs** to compare <u>one</u> action with the actions of other people or things in a <u>group</u>.

We often use the superlative with **expressions** beginning with ***of***.

- All the players worked hard, but Robins worked **the hardest**.

- Villaneuva scored **the most frequently** *of any player* on the team.

---

5. There are several ways of **forming comparative and superlative adverbs**.

a. For **short adverbs** (one syllable), use **adverb** + ***-er*** or ***the*** + **adverb** + ***-est***.

Some adverbs have **irregular** comparative and superlative forms.

b. For **long adverbs** (two or more syllables), use ***more / less*** + **adverb** or ***the most / the least*** + **adverb**.

c. Note that **some adverbs of manner** have <u>two comparative</u> and <u>two superlative</u> forms.

USAGE NOTE: The ***-er / -est*** forms are <u>informal</u>. Do not use them in formal speech and writing.

ADVERB	COMPARATIVE	SUPERLATIVE
fast	fast**er**	**the** fast**est**
hard	hard**er**	**the** hard**est**
well	**better**	**the best**
badly	**worse**	**the worst**
skillfully	**more / less** skillfully	**the most / the least** skillfully
quickly	**more** quickly	**the most** quickly
	quick**er**	**the** quick**est**
slowly	**more** slowly	**the most** slowly
	slow**er**	**the** slow**est**

(continued)

6. Comparatives with *than* and comparisons with *as . . . as* often express the <u>same meaning</u> in different ways.	• The Sparks played **more aggressively than** the Shock. • The Shock did**n't** play **as aggressively as** the Sparks. • The Shock played **less aggressively than** the Sparks.
USAGE NOTE: With <u>one-syllable adverbs</u>, *not as . . . as* is more common than *less . . . than*.	• The Shock did**n't** play **as hard as** the Sparks. NOT The Shock played ~~less hard than~~ the Sparks.

	verb object adverb
7. REMEMBER: Do not put an adverb of manner between the verb and the object.	• Davis handled *the ball* **more skillfully** than Adams. NOT Davis handled ~~more skillfully the ball~~ than Adams.

8. Repeat the comparative adverb to show how something is <u>increasing or decreasing</u>: **comparative adverb** + *and* + **comparative adverb** With long adverbs, repeat only *more* or *less*.	• Kukoc is playing **better and better** as the season continues. *(His performance keeps getting better.)* • He is playing **more and more aggressively**. • The Gophers play **less and less skillfully**.

9. Use **two comparative adverbs** to show <u>cause and effect</u>: *the* + **comparative adverb** + *the* + **comparative adverb**	• **The harder** he played, **the better** he got. *(When he played harder, he got better.)*

Reference Notes

For a list of **irregular comparative and superlative adverbs** see Appendix 10 on page A-6.
For more information about **adverbs**, see Unit 23 on page 270.

Focused Practice

1 | DISCOVER THE GRAMMAR

Read this story from the sports section of the newspaper. Underline all the comparisons with (not) as + adverb + as, *and all the comparative and superlative adverb forms.*

Comets Beat Lions!

In the first basketball game of the season, the Comets beat the Lions, 90 to 83. The Lions played a truly fantastic game, but their defense is still weak. The Comets defended the ball much <u>more aggressively than</u> the Lions did.

Of course, Ace Hernandez certainly helped win the game for the Comets. The Comets' star player was back on the court today to the delight of his many fans. He was hurt badly at the end of last season, but he has recovered quickly. Although he didn't play as well as people expected, he still handled the ball like the old Ace. He certainly handled it the most skillfully of anyone on the team. He controlled the ball the best, shot the ball the most accurately, and scored the most consistently of any of the players on either team. He played hard and helped the Comets look good. In fact, the harder he played, the better the Comets performed. Watch Ace this season.

And watch the Lions. They have a new coach, and they're training more seriously this year. I think we'll see them play better and better as the season progresses.

2 | PICKS OF THE KICKS
Grammar Notes 1, 6–7

Read this chart comparing several brands of basketball shoes. Complete the sentences. Use (not) as + adverb + as *and the words in parentheses. Change the adjectives to adverbs.*

SHOES	Better ◄——————► Worse			
	●	◑	○	
Brand	Comfort	Support	Protection	Durability*
X	●	◑	●	◑
Y	●	○	●	○
Z	○	○	◑	◑

*how long the product lasts

1. X _____*fits as comfortably as*_____ Y.
   (fit / comfortable)

2. Z _____ X or Y.
   (fit / comfortable)

3. Y _____ Z.
   (support / the ankles / good)

4. Y and Z _____ X.
   (support / the ankles / good)

5. Z _____ X or Y.
   (protect / the feet / effective)

6. X _____ Y.
   (protect / the feet / effective)

7. X _____ Z.
   (last / long)

8. Y _____ X or Z.
   (last / long)

3 | A WHOLE NEW BALL GAME

Grammar Notes 1–6, 8–9

🎧 *Complete the conversation between sports commentator Carla Lobo and player Elena Bard. Use the words in parentheses with* **as . . . as** *or with the comparative or superlative forms. Add* **the** *or* **than**, *and choose between* **more** *or* **less** *where necessary.*

LOBO: Why do people still take female basketball players _____*less seriously than*_____
                                                    1. (seriously)

        male players? Do women really play _____ men?
                                           2. (aggressively)

BARD: Absolutely not! We play just _____. And when we fall,
                                   3. (aggressively)

        we hit the floor just _____ the guys do.
                         4. (hard)

LOBO: You could sure see that in tonight's game. Jackson played _____
                                                           5. (fearlessly)

        of any player I've seen, male or female.

BARD: Yes. And _____ women athletes compete,
                          6. (often)

        _____ audiences are going to see that.
                  7. (soon)

LOBO: Some people say women play _____ men.
                                  8. (cooperatively)

BARD: I agree. I think we have better teamwork—we play _____
                                           9. (well)

        on a team. We also play _____. Women players will
                               10. (patiently)

        wait _____ for a good chance to shoot.
              11. (long)

LOBO: Tickets for women's basketball games cost _____ tickets
                                           12. (little)

        for men's games. Does that bother you?

BARD: Sure, but _____ women players attract fans,
                       13. (fast)

        _____ the women's leagues will make money.
        14. (fast)

LOBO: So as time goes on you'll be paid _____ and

        _____.
        15. (well)

BARD: We certainly hope so.

4 | THE ALL-AROUND ATHLETE

Grammar Notes 2–5

Look at the chart on the next page. Then complete the sentences. Use the comparative or superlative form of the adverbs in the box. You will use some adverbs more than once.

bad	far	fast	good	high	slow

	Broad Jump (distance)	Pole Vaulting (height)	5-mile Run (speed)
Nolan	14.3 feet	7 feet, 3 inches	24 minutes
Smith	14.1 feet	7 feet, 2 inches	28 minutes
Diaz	15.2 feet	7 feet, 8 inches	30 minutes
Wang	15.4 feet	8 feet, 2 inches	22 minutes

1. Nolan jumped _____*farther than*_____ Smith.

2. Wang vaulted _____*the highest*_____ of all.

3. Diaz ran _____.

4. Smith ran _____ Wang.

5. Wang jumped _____.

6. Nolan ran _____ Smith.

7. Wang vaulted _____ Smith.

8. All in all, Wang did _____.

9. All in all, Smith did _____.

5 | EDITING

Read this article in a student newspaper. There are nine mistakes in the use of adverbs. The first mistake is already corrected. Find and correct eight more.

Last night was the last game of the season, and the Lions played the ~~goodest~~ *best* they've played for months. Both the Cubs and Lions play a great offensive game, but this time the Lions really played defense much more effectively as the Cubs. Hernandez, the Cubs' star player, has been shooting more aggressively and more aggressively all season. But in last night's game, the more aggressive he played, the most closely the Lions guarded him. Then, in the last two minutes, "Tiny Tim" O'Connell made the winning shot for the Lions. "He's less than six feet tall, but he runs more fastly than anyone else on the court," the Cubs' coach said. "O'Connell doesn't shoot as often other players, but he's a lot more accurately than the bigger guys." The Cubs played a great game last night too, but they just didn't play as good as the Lions.

Communication Practice

6 | LISTENING

 Listen to the sportscaster describing a horse race. Then listen again and rank the horses from first place (1) to last place (5).

_____ Exuberant King

__1__ Get Packin'

_____ Inspired Winner

_____ Señor Speedy

_____ Wild Whirl

7 | SPORTS AROUND THE WORLD

Work as a class. Name several famous athletes for one sport. Compare their abilities. Use the comparative and superlative forms of adverbs. Use your own ideas or the ideas in the box to help you.

Activities	Adverbs
catch	carefully
hit	defensively
kick	easily
play	powerfully
race	regularly
run	seriously
throw	straight
train	successfully

Example: Fatuma Roba is a runner from Ethiopia. She runs faster and more gracefully than most other runners.

8 | A QUESTIONNAIRE

Answer the questionnaire.

1. How many hours do you work every week? _____

2. How many books have you read this month? _____

3. When did you last watch a sports event? _____

4. How many hours a week do you participate in sports? _____

5. How many trips have you taken in the last year? _____

6. How many countries have you visited? _____

Now add your own questions.

7. _____

8. _____

9. _____

10. _____

Work in groups. Compare your answers to questions 1–6 with those of your classmates. Ask the group your own questions (7–10) and compare the answers.

Find out:

1. Who works the hardest?

2. Who reads the most?

3. Who has watched a sports event the most recently?

4. Who participates in sports the most regularly?

5. Who has traveled the most frequently?

6. Who has traveled the most extensively?

Example: Sharif works the hardest. He works 45 hours every week.

9 | WRITING

Write a paragraph comparing two sports figures. Choose either two people that you know or two famous athletes. You can use the ideas from the box in Exercise 7.

Example: My friends Paul and Nick are both good soccer players, but they have different styles. Nick plays more aggressively than Paul, but Paul runs faster and passes more frequently. Nick scores more often, but Paul plays more cooperatively . . .

10 | ON THE INTERNET

Work in teams. Do a search on **Olympics 2004 results** *to find the answers to the questions in this Olympics quiz. The first team to get all the correct answers wins!*

1. Who ran the fastest in the women's marathon?

   a. Deena Kastor   **b.** Mizuki Noguchi   **c.** Catherine Ndereba

2. In the men's 100-meter race, who ran faster than Francis Obikwelu?

   a. Justin Gatlin   **b.** Maurice Green

3. Did Italy score as high as Argentina in men's basketball in the championship game?

   a. Yes   **b.** No

4. Which woman jumped the highest in the women's high jump?

   a. Yelena Isinbayeva   **b.** Viktoriya Styopina   **c.** Hestrie Cloete

From **Grammar** to **Writing**
Using Descriptive Adjectives

Descriptive adjectives can help your reader better picture what you are writing about.

> **Example:** I live in an apartment. ⟶
> I live in a **small comfortable one-bedroom** apartment.

1 | *Read this paragraph. Circle all the adjectives that describe the writer's apartment.*

I live in a (small) comfortable one-bedroom apartment that is close to school. The living

room is my favorite room. It's sunny, warm, and cheerful. There's an old brick fireplace,

which I use on cold winter nights. In the corner there's a large soft green couch. I like

to sit there and read. Next to it is a small wood table with a beautiful antique lamp from

my favorite aunt. It's a cozy living room, and I enjoy spending time there.

2 | *Complete this word map with the circled words from Exercise 1.*

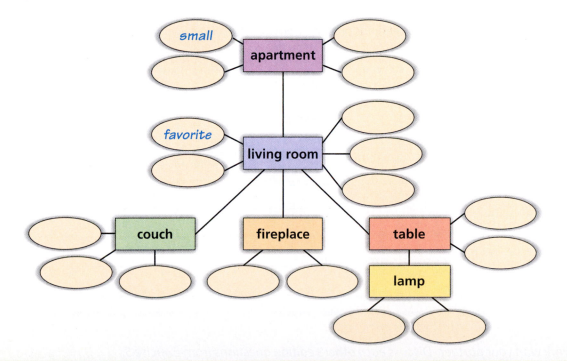

3 | *Before you write . . .*

1. Work in small groups. Put the adjectives from the box into the correct categories. Brainstorm other adjectives for each category. You can use a dictionary for help.

attractive	coarse	comfortable	cozy	cute	enormous
gorgeous	~~hard~~	hideous	huge	~~large~~	~~little~~
lovely	rough	~~run-down~~	~~soft~~	tiny	ugly

a. things that are big: *large,* _____

b. things that are small: *little,* _____

c. things that look good: *attractive,* _____

d. things that look bad: *run-down,* _____

e. things that feel good: *soft,* _____

f. things that feel bad: *hard,* _____

2. Think about a room you know. On a separate piece of paper, draw a word map like the one in Exercise 2. Use some of the adjectives in the box above.

3. Discuss your map with a partner. Do you want to add or change any adjectives?

> **Example:** A: How small is the kitchen?
> B: Oh, it's tiny.

4 | *Write a paragraph about the room from Exercise 3. Use your word map.*

5 | *Exchange paragraphs with a different partner. Complete the chart.*

Did the writer use adjectives that describe how things _____?

	Yes	No	Example(s)
look	☐	☐	_____
feel	☐	☐	_____
smell	☐	☐	_____
sound	☐	☐	_____

What would you like more information about? _____

_____

6 | *Work with your partner. Discuss each other's editing questions from Exercise 5. Then rewrite your own paragraph. Answer any questions your partner asked.*

Review Test

I *Complete the advertisements by choosing the correct words in parentheses.*

1. FOR RENT. Live _____comfortably_____ in this _____ studio
   a. (comfortable / comfortably)   **b. (cozy / cozily)**
   apartment. _____ rent makes it a _____
                c. (Cheap / Cheaply)   **d. (perfect / perfectly)**
   home for one student.

2. FOR SALE. Woman's bicycle. I'm asking the _____ low price of $65
                                               a. (incredible / incredibly)
   for this _____ five-speed bike. I've _____
              b. (new / newly)   **c. (hard / hardly)**
   used it at all. Don't miss this _____ bargain.
                                    d. (terrific / terrifically)

3. FREE to a _____ family. Skipper is a _____
               a. (good / well)   **b. (beautiful / beautifully)**
   and friendly puppy. He behaves _____ with children, and he is very
                                    c. (good / well)
   _____. We are moving very soon, so if you want Skipper, please act
   d. (obedient / obediently)
   _____.
   e. (quick / quickly)

II *Circle the letter of the correct answer to complete each sentence.*

1. I passed my driver's test. It seemed much _____ this time.   A **Ⓑ** C D

   (**A**) easy   (**C**) easiest

   (**B**) easier   (**D**) easily

2. Our team didn't play _____ I expected. I was disappointed.   A B C D

   (**A**) as well as   (**C**) as badly as

   (**B**) well   (**D**) better

3. The faster Tranh walks, _____.   A B C D

   (**A**) more tired   (**C**) the more tired he gets

   (**B**) he gets tired   (**D**) he gets more tired

(continued)

4. Could you talk _____? I'm trying to work.   A B C D

    (**A**) more quietly   (**C**) more quiet

    (**B**) quieter   (**D**) quiet

5. Lisa is staying home. Her cold is a lot _____ today.   A B C D

    (**A**) bad   (**C**) worst

    (**B**) worse   (**D**) the worst

6. Sorry we're late. Your house is much _____ than we thought.   A B C D

    (**A**) far   (**C**) farther

    (**B**) the farthest   (**D**) the farther

7. The movie was so _____ that we couldn't sleep last night.   A B C D

    (**A**) excitingly   (**C**) excite

    (**B**) excited   (**D**) exciting

8. Chris is working very _____ these days.   A B C D

    (**A**) hardly   (**C**) harder

    (**B**) hard   (**D**) hardest

9. Write the report. It's more important _____ your other work.   A B C D

    (**A**) than   (**C**) from

    (**B**) as   (**D**) then

10. The lunch menu is short. It's _____ than the dinner menu.   A B C D

    (**A**) varied   (**C**) less varied

    (**B**) more varied   (**D**) the least varied

11. Thank you! That's _____ I've ever received.   A B C D

    (**A**) the nicer gift   (**C**) nicest gift

    (**B**) a nice gift   (**D**) the nicest gift

12. It's getting more _____ to find a cheap apartment.   A B C D

    (**A**) hardly   (**C**) the most difficult

    (**B**) and more difficult   (**D**) and very difficult

13. My history class is _____ my math class.   A B C D

    (**A**) interesting than   (**C**) as interested as

    (**B**) more interesting   (**D**) more interesting than

III   *Each sentence has four underlined words or phrases. The four underlined parts of the sentences are marked A, B, C, or D. Circle the letter of the one underlined word or phrase that is NOT CORRECT.*

1. My Spanish isn't <u>very</u> <u>good</u>, so I make <u>some</u> <u>embarrassed</u> mistakes.   **A**   **B**   **C**   Ⓓ
             A   B   C   D

2. <u>The harder</u> Sylvia <u>tries,</u> <u>less</u> she <u>succeeds</u>.   **A**   **B**   **C**   **D**
    A   B   C   D

3. This <u>has</u> been <u>the best</u> day <u>than</u> my whole life!   **A**   **B**   **C**   **D**
     A   B   C   D

4. We're <u>always</u> <u>amazing</u> <u>by</u> John's <u>incredible</u> travel stories.   **A**   **B**   **C**   **D**
      A   B   C   D

5. We took <u>a lot of</u> photos because she was <u>such</u> a <u>cutely</u> <u>little</u> baby.   **A**   **B**   **C**   **D**
         A   B   C   D

6. Our <u>new</u> car is <u>hard</u> to drive <u>than</u> our <u>old</u> one.   **A**   **B**   **C**   **D**
     A   B   C   D

7. Patrick doesn't <u>run quickly</u> <u>as</u> Lee, <u>but</u> he can run <u>farther</u>.   **A**   **B**   **C**   **D**
           A   B   C   D

8. You did <u>much</u> <u>more</u> <u>better</u> on the last test <u>than</u> on this one.   **A**   **B**   **C**   **D**
       A   B   C   D

9. What's <u>the</u> <u>more</u> <u>popular</u> of all the <u>new</u> TV shows?   **A**   **B**   **C**   **D**
       A   B   C   D

10. <u>The</u> <u>more</u> I practice my English, the <u>most</u> <u>fluent</u> I get.   **A**   **B**   **C**   **D**
      A   B   C   D

11. The garbage in the street <u>is</u> <u>more</u> <u>disgusted</u> <u>than</u> the potholes.   **A**   **B**   **C**   **D**
                    A   B   C   D

12. Today seems <u>as</u> <u>hotter</u> <u>as</u> yesterday, but the humidity is <u>lower</u>.   **A**   **B**   **C**   **D**
         A   B   C   D

IV   *Complete the sentences with the comparative form of the adjectives and adverbs. Use the information in parentheses to help you.*

1. Ann's criticism was very unfair. I was convinced of that.

   (I thought about it thoroughly. I became angry.)

   The _____*more thoroughly*_____ I thought about it, the _____*angrier*_____ I became.

2. My teacher tried to explain the lesson, but she talked very fast.

   (She talked fast. I felt confused.)

   The _____ she talked, the _____ I felt.

(continued)

3. Bruce gets really silly when he's tired. Last night he studied until midnight.

(It got late. He became silly.)

The _____ it got, the _____ he became.

4. Sylvia studied hard for her French course last semester.

(She studied hard. She spoke fluently.)

The _____ she studied, the _____ she spoke.

5. Greg takes good care of his garden.

(He often waters his tomatoes. They get big.)

The _____ he waters his tomatoes, the _____ they get.

6. My neighbors' dog always barks at me when I run near their house.

(He barks loud. I run fast.)

The _____ he barks, the _____ I run.

7. Eric is frequently late to basketball practice, so he performs badly in games.

(He frequently comes late. He performs badly.)

The _____ he comes late, the _____ he performs.

V *Read the sentences. Complete the summary sentence with the word in parentheses
and **as . . . as** or **not as . . . as**. Use an appropriate verb.*

1. The rent for Apartment 5-G is $550.

The rent for Apartment 22-G is $720.

(expensive) Apartment 5-G *isn't as expensive as Apartment 22-G.* _____

2. Apartment 5-G has five rooms.

Apartment 22-G has five rooms.

(large) Apartment 5-G _____

3. Tony's pizzeria is two blocks away.

Sal's pizzeria is around the corner.

(far) Sal's pizzeria _____

4. A slice of Tony's pizza costs $5.00.

A slice of Sal's pizza also costs $5.00.

(expensive) Sal's pizza _____

5. The Sparks have won six games. They've played very well.

The Shock have won six games too. They've played very well also.

(well) The Sparks _____

6. Amanda runs a six-minute mile.

Jennifer runs a five-and-a-half-minute mile.

(fast) Amanda _____

VI *Complete each paragraph with the words from the box. Use each word once.*

best	hardest	longest	of	~~successful~~	the

1. Pat's the most ____*successful*____ salesperson in her office, and she deserves to be. She works
    _{a.}

the _____ hours. Sometimes she works until 10:00 at night. She also works the
        _{b.}

_____. When she works with a client, she talks _____ most
    _{c.}   _{d.}

persuasively _____ all our people. She's really the _____.
            _{e.}   _{f.}

as	big	exciting	much	sooner	than

2. Communications equipment used to be only for _____ companies, but today,
                                                        _{a.}

even small offices have the latest equipment. Scanners are cheaper _____ they
                                                                        _{b.}

used to be, so they're common in home offices now. Cell phones are everywhere, and they're

_____ more useful—many include e-mail, cameras, and personal planners. The
    _{c.}

most _____ new development is the computer with wireless Internet connection.
        _{d.}

_____ than you think, "Wi-Fi" (Wireless Fidelity) will be _____
    _{e.}   _{f.}

common as the cell phone.

VII *Read this diary entry. There are ten mistakes in the use of adjectives and adverbs. The first mistake is already corrected. Find and correct nine more.*

Wednesday

I think today has been the ~~bad~~ *worst* day of my life. My car broke down on the expressway during rush hour this morning — a busiest time of day. I sat there for an hour waiting for a tow truck. The longer I waited, the nervous I became. I was a wreck when I got to work. Of course, this was the day we were closing biggest deal of the year. My boss called me five times about one letter. And more frequently he called, the worse I typed. My next worry is the repair bill for the car. I hope it isn't as high the last time.

I'm going to try to relax now. There's an interested movie on cable TV tonight. Jan saw it last week and says it's the better film she's seen in a long time. After the movie, I'll take a hotter bath and go to bed. I'm looking forward to tomorrow. It can't be as badly as today!

▶ *To check your answers, go to the Answer Key on page RT-4.*

VII

Gerunds and Infinitives

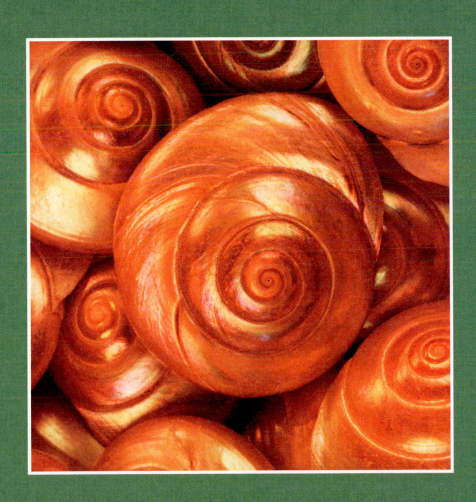

Grammar in Context

BEFORE YOU READ

🎧 *Where can you find posters or signs like these? How do you feel about them?*

Read the online bulletin board about smoking.

Re: Can't Stand Seeing Those Signs!

Posted by Grofumeur on February 16, 2005, at 15:30:03
I **can't stand seeing** all the new No Smoking signs. **Eating** in a restaurant or **having** an espresso in a café is no fun anymore! Junk food is worse than **smoking**. But I bet the government won't **prohibit ordering** burgers and fries for lunch!

Reply posted by Nuffsed on February 17, 12:15:22
Hey, Grofumeur—I don't get sick when my boyfriend has a Big Mac, but **sitting** in a room full of his cigarette smoke makes my hair and clothing stink.

Reply posted by Swissfriend on February 17, 20:53:11
Hi, Smokers! I am a member of Freunde der Tabak, a Swiss group of smokers and non-smokers. We **suggest practicing** courtesy to non-smokers and tolerance of smokers. I **enjoy smoking**, but I **understand not wanting** to inhale second-hand smoke.

Reply posted by Cleanaire on February 18, 9:53:11
Friend—Have you ever tried to **stop smoking**? If so, then you know you are addicted to nicotine. The younger you **start smoking**, the harder it is to quit.

AFTER YOU READ

Check the correct answer(s).

Who _____?	Grofumeur	Nuffsed	Swissfriend	Cleanaire
1. smokes	☐	☐	☐	☐
2. thinks it's difficult to quit smoking	☐	☐	☐	☐
3. doesn't want to see No Smoking signs	☐	☐	☐	☐
4. hates secondhand smoke	☐	☐	☐	☐
5. thinks smokers and non-smokers should be polite	☐	☐	☐	☐

Grammar Presentation

GERUNDS: AS SUBJECTS AND OBJECTS

Gerund as Subject		
Gerund (Subject)	**Verb**	
Smoking	causes	health problems.
Not smoking	is	healthier.

Gerund as Object		
Subject	**Verb**	**Gerund (Object)**
You	should quit	**smoking.**
We	suggest	**not smoking.**

GRAMMAR NOTES	EXAMPLES
1. A **gerund** (**base form of verb + -ing**) is a verb that we use like a <u>noun</u>.	• **Smoking** is bad for your health. • **Swimming** is a good exercise. • I enjoy **running** in the park.

BASE FORM	GERUND
smoke	smok**ing**
swim	swim**ming**

► **BE CAREFUL!** There are often <u>spelling changes</u> when you add -*ing*. Form the **negative** by placing *not* before the gerund.	• **Not exercising** is bad for you. • The doctor suggested **not drinking** coffee for a while.

2. A gerund can be the **subject** of a sentence. It is always <u>singular</u>. Use the third-person-singular form of the verb after gerunds.
 	
► **BE CAREFUL!** Don't confuse a gerund with the progressive form of the verb.
	• **Eating** junk food *makes* me sick.
	• **Inhaling** smoke *gives* me bronchitis.
	
	    gerund
	• **Drinking** a lot of coffee is unhealthy.
	    progressive form
	• He **is drinking** coffee right now.

3. A gerund can also be the **object** of certain verbs. Use a gerund **after these verbs:**	• Jiang *avoids* **hanging out** with smokers. • Have you ever *considered* **quitting**? • I *dislike* **sitting** near smokers in cafés. • We *finished* **studying** and went out. • Did you *miss* **smoking** after you quit? • Dr. Ho *suggested* **not staying up** late.

admit	avoid	consider	deny
dislike	enjoy	finish	miss
practice	quit	suggest	understand

4. We often use *go* + gerund to describe <u>activities</u> such as shopping, fishing, skiing, swimming, and camping.	• Let's *go* **swimming** in the lake. • I *went* **shopping** for running shoes yesterday.

Reference Notes

For a more complete list of **verbs** that can be **followed by gerunds,** see Appendix 13 on page A-7.
For **spelling rules for verb + -*ing*,** see Appendix 21 on page A-10.

Focused Practice

1 DISCOVER THE GRAMMAR

Read part of an article from a health newsletter. Underline the gerunds.

YOUR HEALTH

SWIMMING is a great exercise. It's healthy, fun, and relaxing. Because swimming is a low-impact sport, people can enjoy participating in this activity without fear of injury to bones or muscles.

Jogging, a high-impact activity, can be harmful for some people. I know this from personal experience.

Last year while I was jogging, I injured my right knee. I don't go jogging anymore.

After a painful month of recovery, I stopped running and switched to water sports. I'm now considering joining the swimming team at my health club and competing in races. Staying fit should be fun!

2 HEALTH ISSUES   *Grammar Notes 1–3*

Complete this article with gerunds. Use the verbs in the box. You will use one verb more than once. Choose between affirmative and negative.

| eat | exercise | go | increase | ~~pay~~ | smoke | start | stay |

_____Not paying_____ attention to their health is a mistake a lot of college students make.
                  1.

_____ healthy will help you do well in school and enjoy your college experience.
          2.
Here are some tips:

• Smokers have more colds and less energy. Quit _____ now or don't start.
                                                              3.

• _____ regularly reduces stress and brings more oxygen to your brain. If you
        4.

  don't exercise, consider _____ a program now.
                                    5.

• _____ breakfast is a common mistake. It's the most important meal of the day.
        6.

• Avoid _____ foods with a lot of fat and sugar. Your brain will thank you!
              7.

• Health experts advise _____ the fruits and vegetables in your diet. You need at
                                8.

  least four and a half cups a day, but more is better.

• _____ to the doctor when you're sick is another common mistake. Know where
        9.

  your school Health Service is, and use it when you need it.

3 | A QUESTION OF HEALTH

Grammar Notes 1–4

Write a summary sentence for each conversation. Use the correct form of a verb from the box and the gerund form of the verb in parentheses.

admit	avoid	consider	~~deny~~	enjoy	go	mind	quit

1.   BRIAN: Where are the cookies I bought? You ate them, didn't you?

ELLEN: No, I didn't.

SUMMARY: Ellen _____*denied eating*_____ the cookies.
                    (eat)

2.   ANN: Do you want to go running with me before work?

TOM: Running? Are you kidding? I hate it!

SUMMARY: Tom doesn't _____.
                              (run)

3.   RALPH: Would you like a cigarette?

MARTA: Oh, no, thanks. I don't smoke anymore.

SUMMARY: Marta _____.
                         (smoke)

4.   CHEN: What are you doing after work?

AN-LING: I'm going to that new swimming pool. Would you like to go with me?

SUMMARY: An-ling is going to _____.
                                       (swim)

5.   IRENE: You're lazy. You really need to exercise more.

MIKE: You're right. I *am* lazy.

SUMMARY: Mike _____ lazy.
                         (be)

6.   MONICA: Would you like a piece of chocolate cake?

PAULO: No, thanks. I try to stay away from sweets.

SUMMARY: Paulo _____ sweets.
                         (eat)

7.   CRAIG: I know exercise is important, but I hate it. What about you?

VILMA: Well, I don't *love* it, but it's OK.

SUMMARY: Vilma doesn't _____.
                                (exercise)

8.   ALICE: We've been working too hard. Maybe we need a vacation.

ERIK: A vacation? Hmmm. That's an interesting idea. Do you think we can afford it?

SUMMARY: Erik and Alice _____ a vacation.
                                   (take)

4 | EDITING

Read part of an ex-smoker's journal. There are fourteen mistakes in the use of gerunds as subject and object. The first mistake is already corrected. Find and correct thirteen more. Remember to check for spelling mistakes.

> **smoking**
> DAY 1 I quit ~~to smoke~~! This was the first day of the rest of my life as a non-smoker. Get
>
> through the day wasn't too difficult. I quit drinking coffee today too, and I think that helped.
>
> I used to enjoy had a cigarette with a cup of coffee in the morning.
>
> DAY 3 Today was harder. I called Dinah and admitted wanted to smoke. She advised takeing
>
> deep breaths and staying busy. That worked. I have to resist eat too much. Gaining five pounds
>
> aren't a big deal, but I don't want to gain more than that.
>
> DAY 5 I got through the workweek smoke free. My boss keeps tells me, "You can do it." I really
>
> appreciate to have her support. I miss smoking, but I <u>don't</u> miss to standing outside in the cold
>
> just to smoke. I also don't mind don't burning holes in my clothes!
>
> DAY 7 Dinah suggested to go out to dinner, but I can't risk be around smokers . . . Instead, we
>
> went shoping and I bought a shirt with the money I saved during my first week as a non-smoker.

Communication Practice

5 | LISTENING

🎧 *A doctor is giving advice to a patient. Some things are OK for this patient to do, but other things are not. Listen to the conversation. Then listen again and check the correct column.*

	OK to Do	Not OK to Do
1. smoking	☐	✔
2. drinking coffee	☐	☐
3. losing more weight	☐	☐
4. eating more complex carbohydrates	☐	☐
5. running every day	☐	☐
6. riding a bike every day	☐	☐
7. working eight hours a day	☐	☐

6 | AN OPINION SURVEY

Take a class survey. How many students agree with the statements below? Write the numbers in the appropriate column.

	Agree	Disagree	No Opinion or Don't Know
Seeing someone with a cigarette turns me off.*			
I'd rather hang out with** people who don't smoke.			
It's safe to smoke for only a year or two.			
Smoking can help you when you're bored.			
Smoking helps reduce stress.			
Smoking helps keep your weight down.			
I quit, but sometimes I miss smoking.			

* *turns me off* = disgusts me
** *hang out with* = spend a lot of time with

Discuss your survey results.

   Example: Ten people say that seeing someone smoke turns them off.

7 | POSTER TALK

Work in small groups. Discuss this poster. Complete some of the sentences below to help you in the discussion.

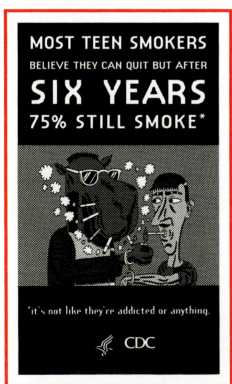

The message of this poster is . . .

The man wants / doesn't want to quit . . .

The camel enjoys . . .

The camel keeps . . .

Lighting up a cigarette . . .

After six years, most people can't resist . . .

I can't imagine . . .

I can't stand . . .

This poster makes me feel like . . .

Smoking is . . .

   Example: The message of this poster is:
   Smoking is an addiction.

8 | NO SMOKING?

Many people agree with laws that prohibit smoking in all public places. What is your opinion? Work in small groups. Think of arguments for and against allowing smoking in public places. Take notes.

Example: Going outside to smoke wastes a lot of time at work.

9 | ON THE INTERNET

Do a search on **how to quit smoking**. *Discuss the tips with the rest of the class.*

Example: A: Many websites advise setting a "quit" date.
B: Yes. Setting a date is important. Getting support from your friends and family is also very important.

10 | WRITING

Write a letter to a friend who wants to stop smoking. Give your friend tips on how to quit. Use gerunds.

Example: Avoid being around people who smoke.

Grammar in Context

BEFORE YOU READ

Look at the website. What does the Student Council do? Does your school have a Student Council? Is student government useful? Have you ever been a member of a student government? Read the information on the website.

Student Council
"Responsible **for improving** school life at Taylor for 50 years."

| The Banner Newspaper | Campus Safety | Course Outlines | Events | Faculty Evaluations | Food Services | Transportation |

Welcome!

Thank you **for visiting** the Student Council webpage. The Council represents all students at Taylor. If you are a Taylor College student, you are already a member! Now is the time to think **about getting** involved and **making** a difference.

What does the Student Council do?

The Council is responsible **for**
• **developing** communication between the students and the administration
• **helping** to improve student-faculty relationships
• **organizing** social events
• **providing** ways (such as this website) for students to share information
• **creating** committees **for improving** services

Why should you get active?

Because you
• have ideas **for solving** important issues
• are good **at communicating** (and love to do it)
• are sick **of sitting** around and **complaining**
• are interested **in meeting** other students, speakers, and faculty

Check out the links.

Then come to the meeting on October 23rd in Buford Hall.
We look forward **to seeing** you there!

TAYLOR COLLEGE SINCE 1958

The Banner Newspaper
Campus Safety
Course Outlines
Events
Faculty Evaluations
Food Services
Transportation

AFTER YOU READ

Check the things that Student Council members can do.

☐ **1.** plan a party for new students

☐ **2.** work on the Student Council website

☐ **3.** accept or reject tuition increases

☐ **4.** make new friends and meet teachers

☐ **5.** hire new employees for the school

☐ **6.** start a new committee

☐ **7.** talk to the administration

Grammar Presentation

GERUNDS AFTER PREPOSITIONS

Preposition + Gerund			
Do you have ideas	**about**	**improving**	life at school?
Are the teachers	**against**	**increasing**	tuition?
The students are	**for**	**having**	online courses.
My roommate left	**before**	**finishing**	the test.

Verb + Preposition + Gerund				
I	**plan**	**on**	**joining**	the Student Council.
We'll	**succeed**	**in**	**improving**	the school.
They	**object**	**to**	**paying**	higher fees.
Please	**think**	**about**	**voting**	for Latoya.

Adjective + Preposition + Gerund				
I'm	**interested**	**in**	**studying**	math.
Are you	**tired**	**of**	**hearing**	complaints?
They are	**happy**	**about**	**not missing**	the meeting.
She is	**used**	**to**	**organizing**	large groups.

GRAMMAR NOTES   **EXAMPLES**

1. Prepositions are words such as: about against at before by for in of on to with without	• Sam is thinking **about** college. • He's not **against** it. • **Before** applying, he'll talk **to** a counselor.
After prepositions, use <u>nouns</u> and <u>pronouns</u>.	• I thanked him **for the book**. • I thanked him **for it**.
Because **gerunds** (base form of verb + *-ing*) are nouns, they can also follow prepositions.	• I thanked him **for giving** me the book.
REMEMBER: Form the **negative** by placing *not* before the gerund.	• She's happy **about not working** today.

2. Many common **expressions** have the forms: • **verb + preposition** OR • **adjective + preposition** You can use a **gerund** after these expressions.	**VERB + PREPOSITION** **ADJECTIVE + PREPOSITION** advise **against** be afraid **of** believe **in** be bored **with** count **on** be excited **about** • She **believes in working** hard. • He **is bored with working** in a store.

3. Do not confuse the **preposition** *to* with part of the infinitive (*to* + base form of verb).	**EXPRESSIONS WITH PREPOSITION *TO*** look forward **to** be opposed **to** object **to** be used **to** resort **to** get used **to**
Use a **gerund**, not an infinitive, <u>after</u> expressions with the preposition *to*.	• I**'m looking forward to seeing** you. NOT I'm looking forward to ~~see~~ you.
▶ **BE CAREFUL!** Notice the difference in meanings: **a.** Use **be / get used to** + **gerund** to mean *be / become accustomed to*.	• I**'m used to driving** to work because I drove to work for years. • Now I have to **get used to taking** the train.
b. Use **used to** + **base form of verb** for <u>past habits</u> or <u>past situations</u> that no longer exist in the present.	• I **used to drive** to work, but now I take the train.

Reference Notes

For a list of **adjectives followed by prepositions**, see Appendix 17 on page A-7.
For a list of **verbs followed by prepositions**, see Appendix 18 on page A-8.
For more on the meanings of *used to*, *be used to*, and *get used to*, see Unit 5 on page 46.

Focused Practice

1 | DISCOVER THE GRAMMAR

Read the Student Council petition to the president of Taylor College. Underline all the preposition + gerund combinations.

Student Council
Please sign this petition
TAYLOR COLLEGE NEEDS BETTER INTERNET ACCESS

To President Hacking:

We are concerned <u>about improving</u> Internet access at Taylor College. Times are changing. With Wi-Fi (for Wireless Fidelity, or a wireless Internet connection), students can get on the Internet anywhere on campus. Many schools have succeeded in making their campuses completely wireless. Taylor College has been slow at developing this technology, but it is becoming more necessary. Taylor College instructors are putting more and more course material online. With only a few Wi-Fi areas, busy students cannot count on finding a place to connect when they have the time to work on course material. By having more Wi-Fi areas, the college will make education more efficient. We are asking the administration to consider increasing the number of "hotspots" for wireless connections. We look forward to having a completely wireless campus in the next few years.

Sincerely,
The Undersigned

Print Name	Signature	Class
LEE RAND	*Lee Rand*	2010
ANTONIO RIVERA	*Antonio Rivera*	2008
MAGGIE CHANG	*Maggie Chang*	2009
RICARDO DA SILVA	*Ricardo da Silva*	2010

2 | SPRING BREAK

Grammar Notes 2–3

Complete the students' statements. Choose the appropriate preposition from the box. *(You will use some prepositions more than once.)* Add the gerund form of the verb in parentheses.

about	for	in	on	to

THE BANNER

Vol. 5, Issue 24   **March 1, 2006**

It's almost time for spring break! We asked students: *"What are your plans for spring break?"* Here are some of their answers:

I'm always very interested

___*in listening*___ to jazz,
    1. (listen)

so I'm going to attend the

Spring Jazz Festival.

Lisa Suarez

We're driving to Quebec City

next weekend. It's famous

_____ great
    7. (have)

food.

Omar Sisane

Jim Hsu

I don't have any plans, but I'm

not concerned _____
                2. (get)

bored. I can always take a walk

or something.

Claire Kaplan

I'm really very worried

_____ well in my
    8. (not do)

Japanese class, so I'm studying

over the break.

My friends and I are driving to

New Orleans. I'm excited

_____ , but I'm
    3. (go)

nervous _____.
          4. (drive)

Emilia Leale

My friends and I are going

camping, and, as usual, my

adorable little brother insists

_____ with us!
    9. (come)

Eun Ko

Don Pitt

I'm really looking forward

_____ at home
    5. (stay)

and _____.
        6. (relax)

Tim Riley

My girlfriend plans

_____ to the
    10. (go)

movies a lot, so I guess I'll see

a lot of movies.

3 | SCHOOL ISSUES

Combine the following pairs of sentences to make statements about school life. Use the prepositions in parentheses.

1. You can't walk on campus late at night. You have to worry about your safety.

   You can't walk on campus late at night without worrying about your safety.
   (without)

2. We can make changes. We can tell the administration about our concerns.

   _____
   (by)

3. The administration can help. It can listen to our concerns.

   _____
   (by)

4. In some cases, students just complain. They don't make suggestions for improvements.

   _____
   (instead of)

5. Students get annoyed with some teachers. Some teachers don't come to class on time.

   _____
   (for)

6. You can improve your grades. Study regularly.

   _____
   (by)

7. We're proud of our school. It has the latest computer technology.

   _____
   (for)

8. Students should learn about issues. Then they'll vote for the next Student Council president.

   _____
   (before)

9. You have great ideas. Those ideas could solve some problems on campus.

   _____
   (for)

10. Our school has been slow. It hasn't improved food services.

    _____
    (at)

11. Latoya is happy. She's running for Student Council.

    _____
    (about)

4 | MAKING CHANGES

Larry Jones quit school after high school and had various jobs. Then he decided to go to college. That was a big change for him. Complete the sentences about Larry. Use the appropriate form of the verbs in parentheses.

1. Larry used to _____*be*_____ a student, but he quit after high school.
   (be)

2. He used to _____ a job.
   (have)

3. In fact, he used to _____ a lot of different jobs.
   (have)

4. When he went back to college, he had to get used to _____ a student again.
   (be)

5. He wasn't used to _____ to school every day and _____.
   (go) **(study)**

6. He had to get used to _____ homework again.
   (do)

7. When Larry was working, he used to _____ quite a bit of money. He used to
   (earn)
   _____ everything too. Now he has to get used to _____ less.
   (spend) **(spend)**

8. It hasn't been easy, but Larry has gotten used to _____ a student's life again.
   (live)

5 | EDITING

Read this post to a student council website. There are seven mistakes in the use of gerunds after prepositions. The first mistake is already corrected. Find and correct six more.

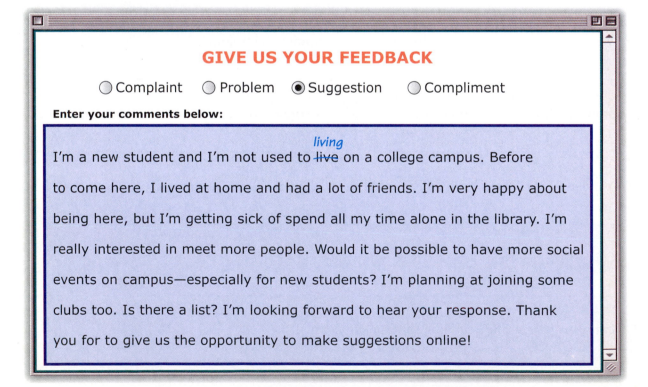

GIVE US YOUR FEEDBACK

○ Complaint   ○ Problem   ◉ Suggestion   ○ Compliment

Enter your comments below:

                                                living
I'm a new student and I'm not used to ~~live~~ on a college campus. Before

to come here, I lived at home and had a lot of friends. I'm very happy about

being here, but I'm getting sick of spend all my time alone in the library. I'm

really interested in meet more people. Would it be possible to have more social

events on campus—especially for new students? I'm planning at joining some

clubs too. Is there a list? I'm looking forward to hear your response. Thank

you for to give us the opportunity to make suggestions online!

Communication Practice

6 | LISTENING

🎧 *Listen to this speech by a candidate for the office of Student Council president. Then listen again and mark the following statements True (T) or False (F).*

__T__ 1. Latoya has experience in working for student government.

_____ 2. She believes in raising student activity fees.

_____ 3. There are only two kinds of food on campus.

_____ 4. The computer labs and libraries close early.

_____ 5. Students feel safe on the campus at night.

_____ 6. Latoya is most interested in improving campus safety.

7 | VOTE FOR ME

Pretend you are running for president of the Student Council. Prepare your campaign speech and read it to the class. Answer some of these questions.

- What are you most interested in?
- What do you believe in?
- What will you insist on?
- What are you opposed to?
- What are you excited about?
- What are you good at?

Example: Vote for me. I'm interested in making our lives better by improving . . .

Now have an election.

8 | STRESS

Below are some life events, both positive and negative, that can lead to stress. Work by yourself and rank them from most stressful (1) to least stressful (8). Then in small groups compare and discuss your lists. Use be used to and get used to to explain your choices.

_____ starting college

_____ moving to a new city

_____ changing jobs or schools

_____ getting married

_____ getting divorced

_____ having or adopting a baby

_____ death of a close family member

_____ getting fired at work

Example: I think getting married is the third most stressful life event on the list. You have to get used to living with another person.

9 | WRITING

Read this letter to the editor of a school newspaper.

To the Editor . . .

I have been attending Longtree College for a year. I am an international student in the Chemistry Department. I am very happy about studying here. However, I have had some problems with academic advisers. The academic advisers are not used to talking to international students, so they get nervous about understanding us.

In addition, the school delays looking at the records of transfer students. I attended a university in Ukraine for two years, and I took several chemistry courses. The Chemistry Department has not yet looked at my records. My adviser recommends taking basic courses, but I am afraid of repeating courses and wasting my time.

I suggest giving a workshop for advisers. In the workshop they can practice talking clearly and organizing their information for international students. I also recommend looking at student records as soon as possible.

Respectfully,
Galina Terela

---

*Now mark the following statements **True (T)** or **False (F)**.*

__F__ 1. Galina is complaining about being a chemistry student.

_____ 2. The advisers have a lot of experience in talking to international students.

_____ 3. They feel confident about communicating with international students.

_____ 4. Galina is a first-year college student.

_____ 5. The Chemistry Department has been slow in reviewing Galina's records.

_____ 6. Galina objects to taking basic chemistry courses.

_____ 7. Galina thinks that advisers should learn about dealing with international students.

Write a letter to the editor of your school newspaper. Write about the things you like and dislike about your school. Use Galina's letter as a model.

10 | ON THE INTERNET

*Do a search on **student council candidates**. Take notes about one candidate's ideas and experience. Discuss your candidate with a small group. Which candidates do you think are the best? Why?*

> **Example:** Natasha Gailes at Louisiana State University talks about a lot of issues. She's interested in improving communication between students and faculty.

Infinitives after Certain Verbs

BEFORE YOU READ

🎧 *What kind of questions do you think Annie answers? Do you think this is a good place to get advice? Read the letter to the newspaper advice column,* Ask Annie.

Lifestyles   **Section 4**

ASK ANNIE

Dear Annie,

I've just moved to Seattle and started going to a new school. I **try to meet** people but nothing **seems to work**. A few weeks ago, I **agreed to have** dinner with someone from my English class. Bad idea. Right after we got to the restaurant, he **asked to borrow** money from me for the check. And he also **wanted to correct** my pronunciation (I'm from Louisiana). Obviously, I **decided not to see** him again. Now my roommate **would like** me **to go out** with her boyfriend's brother. I **asked** her **not to arrange** anything because I really **don't want to date** anyone right now. First, I'd just **like to find** some friends to hang out with. Do you have any suggestions?

Lonely in Seattle

Dear Lonely,

You **seem to have** the right idea about making new friends. A lot of people **try to solve** the problem of loneliness by falling in love. I usually **advise** them **to make** friends first. Perhaps you just **need to relax** a bit. Don't **expect to develop** friendships overnight because that takes time. Instead, do things that you**'d like to do** anyway. Join a sports club. **Learn to dance**. **Try not to focus** so much on your problem, and just **remember to have** fun with your new activities. You'll come into contact with people who have similar interests. Even if you **fail to meet** your new best friends immediately, you will at least have a good time! Don't give up!

Annie

AFTER YOU READ

Read the statements. Check **True** *or* **False**.

	True	False
1. "Lonely" has been successful in meeting people.	☐	☐
2. She isn't asking for advice about dating.	☐	☐
3. Annie thinks making friends is a good idea.	☐	☐
4. She says that friendships develop quickly.	☐	☐
5. Annie thinks that "Lonely" ought to have some fun.	☐	☐

Grammar Presentation

INFINITIVES AFTER CERTAIN VERBS

Statements			
Subject	Verb	(Object)	Infinitive	
I	**decided**		**(not) to write**	to Annie.
You	**urged**	John	**(not) to take**	her advice.
He	**wanted**	(her)	**to advise**	John.

GRAMMAR NOTES	EXAMPLES
1. An **infinitive** is *to* + **base form of the verb**. Form the **negative** by placing *not* before the infinitive.	• She asked me **to call** after 5:00 P.M. • She asked me **not to call** before 5:00 P.M.
2. Certain **verbs** can be **followed by an infinitive**.	• I *want* **to make** some new friends. • I *asked* Annie **to help** me. • She *advised* me **to relax**. • She *told* me **not to worry**.

3. Some verbs, like the ones below, can be **followed directly by an infinitive**.

begin	decide	fail
hope	learn	plan
promise	refuse	try

verb + infinitive
- He *decided* **to join** a health club.
- He *hoped* **to meet** new people.
- She *promised* **to go out** with him.
- She *tried* **not to be** late.

4. Some verbs, like the ones below, need an **object** (noun or pronoun) **before the infinitive**.

advise	allow	encourage
force	invite	order
remind	tell	warn

verb + object + infinitive
- I *invited* Mary **to eat** with us.
- I *reminded* her **to come**.
- She *told* me **to call** her.
- They *warned* us **not to forget**.

5. Some verbs, like the ones below, can be followed by:

• **an infinitive**

    OR

• **an object + infinitive**

ask	expect	help
need	want	would like

infinitive
- I *asked* **to join** the club.

object + infinitive
- I *asked* them **to join** the club.

Reference Notes

For a list of **verbs** that are **followed by infinitives**, see Appendix 14 on page A-7.
For a more complete list of **verbs** that need an **object before the infinitive**, see Appendix 16 on page A-7.

Focused Practice

1 | DISCOVER THE GRAMMAR

Read this entry in a personal diary. Underline all the verb + infinitive and the verb + object + infinitive combinations.

> Annie <u>advised me to join</u> a club or take a class, and I finally did it! I decided to join the
> school's Outdoor Adventure Club, and I went to my first meeting last night. I'm really
> excited about this. The club is planning a hiking trip next weekend. I definitely want to
> go. I hope it won't be too hard for my first adventure. Last night they also decided to
> go rafting in the spring. At first I didn't want to sign up, but the leader was so nice.
> He urged me not to miss this trip, so I put my name on the list. After the meeting, a
> group of people asked me to go out with them. We went to a coffee shop and talked
> for hours. Well, I hoped to make some new friends when I joined this club, but I didn't
> expect everyone to be so friendly. I'm glad Annie persuaded me not to give up.

2 | PLAN TO SUCCEED

Grammar Notes 1–5

Complete the article with the correct form of the verbs in parentheses. Use the
simple present or the imperative form for the first verb.

Most people make careful plans when they _____*decide to take*_____ a vacation. Yet when
                                             1. (decide / take)

they _____ a mate, they depend on luck.
         2. (attempt / find)

    Edward A. Dreyfus, Ph.D., _____ love to chance.
                              3. (warn / single people / not leave)

He _____ his relationship plan when they search for a life partner.
     4. (urge / them / use)

Remember: when you _____, you _____.
                   5. (fail / plan)   **6. (plan / fail)**

STEP ONE: Make a list. What kind of person do you _____?
                                                  7. (wish / meet)

Someone intelligent? Someone who loves sports? List everything.

STEP TWO: Make another list. What kind of person are *you*? List all your characteristics.

_____ this list and comment on it.
    8. (Ask / two friends / read)

_____ about hurting your feelings. The two lists should match.
    9. (Tell / them / not worry)

STEP THREE: Increase your chances. _____ in activities you like.
10. (Choose / participate)

STEP FOUR: Ask for introductions. Dr. Dreyfus _____ embarrassed.
11. (advise / people / not feel)

Everyone _____ a matchmaker!
12. (want / be)

3 | IN OTHER WORDS

Grammar Notes 3–5

For each conversation, use the correct form of a verb from the box followed by an infinitive or an object + infinitive.

agree	encourage	forget	invite	need	remind	~~would like~~

1. **KAREN:** (*yawn*) Don't you have a meeting tomorrow? Maybe you should go home now.

    TOM: It's only eleven o'clock. And *Star Wars* is on in five minutes!

    SUMMARY: Karen *would like Tom to go home.* _____

2. **KURT:** Hey, honey, did you get any stamps?

    LILY: Oh, I forgot. I'll stop at the post office on the way home.

    SUMMARY: Kurt _____

3. **JOHN:** We're going out for coffee. Would you like to join us?

    MARY: I'd love to.

    SUMMARY: John _____

4. **DAD:** I expect you to come home by 10:30. Do you understand? If you don't, I'm grounding you for two weeks.

    JASON: OK, OK. Take it easy, Dad.

    SUMMARY: Jason _____

5. **DON:** You didn't go to the staff meeting. We missed you.

    JEFF: Oh, no! The staff meeting!

    SUMMARY: Jeff _____

6. **MOM:** Don't be scared, sweetie. Just try once more. You'll love it.

    LISA: I hate to ice skate. I always fall down.

    SUMMARY: Lisa's mom _____

7. **BRAD:** Are you using the car tonight?

    TERRY: Well, I have a lot of shopping to do. And I promised Susan I'd give her a ride.

    SUMMARY: Terry _____

4 | EDITING

Read this magazine article. There are nine mistakes in the use of infinitives. The first mistake is already corrected. Find and correct eight more.

> *make*
> You'd like to ~~making~~ some new friends. Maybe you're at a new school or job, or, possibly, you have changed and the "new you" wants meet new people. First, I strongly advise to turn off the TV. Those people on *Friends* are not YOUR friends. You need go out with real people. Decide right now to don't refuse invitations. When a classmate or co-worker invites you for coffee, just say "Yes." Join a club and volunteer to doing something. That responsibility will force you to attend the meetings. By doing these things, you will manage meeting a lot of new people. But don't rush to become close friends with someone right away. Learn to listen. Encourage the person to talks by asking questions. Allow relationships develops naturally, and soon you'll have a group of people you're really comfortable with.

Communication Practice

5 | LISTENING

🎧 *Listen to a couple talk about their family. Then listen again and circle the letter of the sentences that you hear.*

1. **a.** I really wanted to discuss their problems.
   (b.) I really wanted them to discuss their problems.

2. **a.** I finally learned to argue with my stepdaughter.
   b. I finally learned not to argue with my stepdaughter.

3. **a.** I expected to have problems with my daughter.
   b. I expected you to have problems with my daughter.

4. **a.** Sometimes I just wanted to leave the house for a few hours.
   b. Sometimes I just wanted her to leave the house for a few hours.

5. **a.** After all, she didn't choose to live with us.
   b. After all, she chose not to live with us.

6. **a.** Then one day, she asked to go on a family vacation.

   b. Then one day, she asked me to go on a family vacation.

7. **a.** I didn't expect to have a good time.

   b. I didn't expect her to have a good time.

8. **a.** In fact, sometimes I'd like to stop talking for a few minutes.

   b. In fact, sometimes I'd like her to stop talking for a few minutes.

6 | DESCRIBE YOUR PARENTS

Work in pairs. Tell each other about your relationship with your parents.

- What did they encourage you to do?
- How did they encourage you to do that?
- What didn't they allow you to do?
- What did they force you to do?
- What would they like you to do?

- What did they advise you to do?
- Why did they advise you to do that?
- What do they expect you to do?
- What would you prefer to do?
- Why would you prefer to do that?

Example: My parents encouraged me to learn other languages.

Add your own questions.

_____

_____

_____

7 | SOCIALIZING AROUND THE WORLD

Discuss how people in your culture socialize. Do young men and women go out together? If so, do they go out in couples or in groups? What are some ways people meet their future husbands or wives?

Example: **A:** In Brazil, young people usually prefer to go out together in groups. They like to go to clubs or to the movies.

          B: In Germany, families allow young people to go out on dates.

8 | ON THE INTERNET

Do a search on **events** *in your town or city. Make a list of events that interest you. Include the date and time of each event. Discuss the events in a small group and plan to do something together.*

Example: A: I'd like to go to the outdoor concert in River Park on Sunday. It starts at 3:00 P.M.

B: That sounds great, but I promised to help my brother move on Sunday. How about . . .

9 | WRITING

Write e-mails to two or three friends and invite them to join you for the event your group chose for Exercise 8. Remember to use infinitives.

Example: Hi Ari,

Some classmates and I plan to see *Hero* at the Regis Cineplex on Saturday. Can you come with us? We want to go to the 7:00 P.M. show. After the movie, we'll probably go out for pizza. I hope to see you Saturday. It's going to be fun!

Liv

Infinitives of Purpose

Grammar in Context

BEFORE YOU READ

What do you think multi-use *means? What can you use a camera phone for? Read the magazine article.*

Multi-Use Technology: When 1 + 1 = more than 2

You can use it **to send** instant pictures home to your family. You can use it **to call** your friends. But a camera phone is so much more than just a camera plus phone! When the first model came out in 2000, some people (like me) thought, "Why do I need it?" Now, millions of people around the world ask, "How did I live without one?"

Megan uses hers **to get** instant advice on shopping trips. "If I'm shopping for a new sweater, and my friends aren't with me, I take a few pictures, send them, and ask, 'Which one?'"

Carlos, a student, uses his **to organize** everything in his busy life. "I use the calendar **to plan** my week, and I use

the address book **to store** phone numbers and e-mail addresses." In school he uses it **to take** pictures of the teacher's notes on the board.

Marie-Catherine is a TV journalist. "Sometimes I see something interesting, but I don't have a camera or video crew with me. But I

always have my camera phone. I can instantly send my story with a photo or video **in order to meet** my deadline—and **to get** the story before the competition, of course!"

Many people, like Omar, use the camera phone just **to have** fun. "I use it **to surf** the Internet, **e-mail** my friends, **listen** to music, **watch** videos, and **play** games."

For work or for play, camera phones have changed our lives. What will the newest technology bring? It's hard to predict. But one thing is certain: It will be faster and smaller. And, as always, people will find uses for it that are difficult to imagine today.

AFTER YOU READ

Complete the sentence. Check the correct answers.

According to the article, with a camera phone you can _____.

☐ **1.** pay bills   ☐ **3.** watch TV   ☐ **5.** make a weekly schedule

☐ **2.** listen to music ☐ **4.** order clothes ☐ **6.** have a good time

Grammar Presentation

INFINITIVES OF PURPOSE

Affirmative
I left at 9:00 **(in order) to be** on time.

Negative
I left at 9:00 **in order not to be** late.

GRAMMAR NOTES

EXAMPLES

---

1. Use an **infinitive** (*to* + **base form of verb**) to explain the **purpose** of an action. It often answers the question *Why?*

  USAGE NOTES:
  a. In conversation, you can answer the question *Why?* with an incomplete sentence beginning with *to*.

  b. We usually <u>do not repeat</u> *to* when we give more than one purpose.

A: *Why* did you go to the mall?
B: I went there **to buy** a new camera phone.

A: *Why* did you go to the mall?
B: **To buy** a new camera phone.

• I went to the mall **to buy** a sweater, **eat** lunch, and **see** a movie.
  NOT I went to the mall to buy a sweater, ~~to~~ eat lunch, and ~~to~~ see a movie.

---

2. You can also use the longer form *in order to* + **base form of verb** to explain a purpose.

  USAGE NOTE: *To* + base form of verb is much more common in <u>informal</u> speech and writing.

• I bought my first camera phone **in order to send** instant photos.

• I bought my first camera phone **to send** instant photos to friends.

---

3. Use *in order not to* + **base form of verb** to explain a <u>negative purpose</u>.

  USAGE NOTE: *In order not to* is formal. In everyday <u>spoken English</u>, we often express a negative purpose with *because* + **a reason**.

• Reporters use camera phones **in order not to miss** deadlines.

• Reporters use camera phones *because they don't want to miss deadlines*.

Focused Practice

1 | DISCOVER THE GRAMMAR

Read more about camera phones. Underline all the infinitives that express a purpose.

No Camera Phnes Allowed!

New technology is great, but it often brings new problems. Most people use camera phones for good things, for example, <u>to take</u> pictures of their family and friends. But some people use them to play mean jokes on other people or even to steal. When camera phones first came out, some places had to prohibit their use. People were using them to take secret pictures in health clubs and other private places! Not very nice! And what about "digital shoplifting"? Here is an example: My friend Ned (not his real name) often goes to bookstores to look at magazines. Sometimes he sees an interesting article, but he doesn't want to buy the magazine. In order not to pay for the article, he secretly photographs it with his camera phone. Then he goes home to read it! Did Ned steal the article? Should stores ban camera phones in order to prevent digital shoplifting?

2 | THE REASON IS . . .   *Grammar Notes 1, 3*

Match each action with its purpose.

Action	Purpose
_b_ 1. She bought a camera phone because she	a. didn't want to get calls.
____ 2. He took the bus because he	b. wanted to send instant photos.
____ 3. We turned our phone off because we	c. wanted to buy a new camera phone.
____ 4. She taped her favorite TV show because she	d. didn't want to be late.
____ 5. He enrolled in French 101 because he	e. didn't want to miss it.
____ 6. She went to the electronics store because she	f. wanted to learn the language.

Now combine the sentences. Use the infinitive of purpose.

1. *She bought a camera phone to send instant photos.* _____

2. _____

3. _____

4. _____

5. _____

6. _____

3 | PICTURE THIS!

On a moblog, you can post pictures, videos, and text from your camera phone directly to the Web for millions of people to see. Look at this moblog. Complete the sentences with the correct words from the box. Use the infinitive of purpose.

buy fruit and vegetables	communicate with her	drive to Montreal	~~exchange money~~
get more gas	have coffee	pass it	~~take my own picture~~

My Trip to Montreal

1. That's me! I used my camera phone ___*to take my own picture*___.

2. We rented this car _____ _____.

3. This truck was in front of us. We had to drive fast _____.

4. We stopped here _____ _____.

5. We went to the bank _____ _____.

6. We came here _____ _____.

7. We stopped here _____ _____.

8. This is Fabienne. We had to speak French _____.

My Favorites
My Family
My Vacation
My Baby Pics
Home Page

4 | EDITING

Read this online bulletin board about camera phones. There are seven mistakes in the use of the infinitives of purpose. The first mistake is already corrected. Find and correct six more.

> Click here ~~for telling~~ *to tell* us how you've used your camera phone.
>
> ---
>
> I was riding my bike when I saw an accident. A car hit a truck, but it didn't stop. I used my camera phone take a picture of the car and the license plate number. Then I used it to call the police. **Jason Harvey, England**
>
> ---
>
> I was at a great concert in Mexico City. I wanted to share the experience with my best friend back home. I picked up my camera phone and used it to take a photo, record a little bit of a song, and writing a short message. Instantly my friend was "there" with me. Awesome! **Emilia Leale, Italy**
>
> ---
>
> My brother needed a new part for his refrigerator. He called the supply store on his camera phone and tried to describe the broken part. They told him to use his phone to takes a picture. He did it, and the supply store was able to send him the correct part right away. **Min-Soo Kim, Korea**
>
> ---
>
> I sell houses. I always use my camera phone in order no waste my customers' time. When I see an interesting house, I immediately send a photo. Then, if they are interested, I make an appointment for them. **Andrea Cook, USA**
>
> ---
>
> While I was traveling, I got a terrible skin rash. I used my camera phone for calling my doctor and send her a photo of it. She was thousands of miles away, but she used the photo to give me instant advice! **Ana Diaz, Spain**
>
> ---
>
> One of my classmates was sick and had to miss class. I used my camera phone to call him and taking a picture of the teacher's notes on the board. He heard the class fine, but had trouble reading the teacher's handwriting. But that's not the fault of the camera phone! **James Gordon, Australia**

Communication Practice

5 | LISTENING

🎧 *You are calling Lacy's Department Store to get information. Read the list below. Listen to Lacy's automatic telephone message. Then listen again and write the number of the telephone key that you should press for each of the following purposes.*

_____ 1. place an order

_____ 2. find out when the store opens

_____ 3. report a lost or stolen credit card

_____ 4. ask about a bill

_____ 5. ask about a delivery

___1___ 6. speak to a customer service representative

_____ 7. listen to the message again

6 | WHAT'S IT FOR?

Work in groups. Think of uses for the following everyday objects. Use the infinitive of purpose and your imagination! Share your ideas with other groups.

1.   2.   3.

4.   5.   6.

Example: You can use a shell to hold coins, keep soap in, or eat from.

Which item is the most useful? Why?

7 | THE CAMERA PHONE

You've won a camera phone in a contest. What will you use it for? What won't you use it for? Discuss your answers with a partner.

Example: A: I'll use it to send e-mails with photos.
B: I won't use it to copy magazine articles in a bookstore!

8 | REMOTE CONTROL

Read this ad for a remote control.

The SMART Touch 100

You can program this powerful remote to operate up to six video and audio components—your TV, VCR, DVD, CD player, and more. It's easy and convenient to use. So, get smart, get the SMART Touch.

Work in small groups. Imagine that in the future there will be a SMART Touch that will control everything in your house—not only electronic equipment. What will you use it for?

Example: A: I'll use it to turn on the shower.
B: I'll use it to open and close the windows.

9 | WRITING

Write an ad for a new electronic gadget. Describe a real item, or invent one. Use infinitives of purpose.

10 | ON THE INTERNET

*Do a search on **electronic gadgets**. Select one that interests you. What can you use it for? Tell your classmates.*

Example: You can use a Digi Pen to take pictures. It's smaller than a camera phone!

Grammar in Context

BEFORE YOU READ

 Look at the photos. How old do you think each person is? In your opinion, are they old enough to vote? Read the transcript of a radio talk show about voting rights for people under age 18.

 VOICE OF THE PEOPLE

SMITH: Welcome to *Voice of the People*. I'm Ed Smith, and tonight our topic is youth voting rights. Kyle, you're only 16. For someone your age, is getting the vote **important enough to fight** for?

KYLE: Sure. Without it, politicians won't take us **seriously enough to hear** our views.

SMITH: I don't get it. In the 1960s when military service was required, 18-year-olds had an argument: "If we're **old enough to fight** for our country, then we're **old enough to vote**." What's *your* argument?

Kyle

TINA: Well, there are a lot of laws that discriminate against us. We want the vote so that politicians will listen to us and change those laws. We want the same rights adults have.

SMITH: Can you give examples of laws that discriminate against teens?

MICAH: Sure. My parents are divorced. I see my father every weekend. I'd really like to see him more often, but the law says I'm **too young to decide** for myself.

Tina

KYLE: My city has curfew laws. I'm **responsible enough to work** and **pay** taxes, but **too irresponsible to stay out** past 10:00. That's fair?

TINA: Women, ethnic minorities, and people with disabilities have won their civil rights. Now it's our turn.

Micah

AFTER YOU READ

Check the things Kyle can do.

☐ **1.** vote

☐ **2.** work

☐ **3.** pay taxes

☐ **4.** stay out past 10:00

Grammar Presentation

INFINITIVES WITH *TOO* AND *ENOUGH*

Infinitives with *Too*					
	Too	Adjective / Adverb	(*For* + Noun / Object Pronoun)	Infinitive	
We're (not)		**young**		**to vote.**	
They answered	**too**	**quickly**	for Kyle	**to understand**	the issues.
It's (not)		**hard**	(for us)	**to decide.**	

Infinitives with *Enough*					
	Adjective / Adverb	*Enough*	(*For* + Noun / Object Pronoun)	Infinitive	
We're (not)	**old**			**to vote.**	
They have(n't) answered	**clearly**	**enough**	for Kyle	**to understand**	the issues.
It's (not)	**easy**		(for us)	**to decide.**	

GRAMMAR NOTES	EXAMPLES
1. Use the following to give a <u>reason</u>: *too* + **adjective / adverb** + **infinitive**	*adjective* • I'm ***too young*** **to vote**. *(I can't vote.)* • She is**n't** ***too young*** **to vote**. *(She can vote.)* *adverb* • I arrived ***too late*** **to vote**. *(I couldn't vote.)* • She did**n't** arrive ***too late*** **to vote**. *(She could vote.)*
2. You can also use the following to give a <u>reason</u>: **adjective / adverb** + *enough* + **infinitive**	*adjective* • I'm ***old enough*** **to go** into the army. *(I can go into the army.)* • He is**n't** ***old enough*** **to go** into the army. *(He can't go into the army.)* *adverb* • I ran ***fast enough*** **to pass** the physical. *(I passed the physical.)* • She did**n't** run ***fast enough*** **to pass** the physical. *(She didn't pass the physical.)*
3. ***Too*** comes <u>before</u> the adjective or adverb. ***Enough*** comes <u>after</u> the adjective or adverb.	• She's ***too*** old to drive. • I'm not old ***enough*** to drive. NOT I'm not ~~enough old~~.
4. Sometimes we use *for* + **noun / pronoun** <u>before</u> the infinitive.	• It's not too hard ***for people*** **to understand**. *(People understand.)* • It's easy enough ***for them*** **to understand**. *(They understand.)*
5. You **don't need the infinitive** when the meaning is clear.	**A:** Are you going to vote this year? **B:** No, I'm ***too young*** (to vote). OR No, I'm not ***old enough*** (to vote).

Focused Practice

 ## DISCOVER THE GRAMMAR

*People have different opinions about public issues. Read each statement of opinion. Then choose the sentence (**a** or **b**) that summarizes that opinion.*

1. Teenagers are responsible enough to stay out past 10:00 P.M.

   a. Teenagers should have permission to stay out past 10:00 P.M.

   b. Teenagers shouldn't have permission to stay out past 10:00 P.M.

2. Teenagers are too immature to vote.

   a. Teenagers should be able to vote.

   b. Teenagers shouldn't be able to vote.

3. Women are strong enough to be good soldiers.

   a. Women can be good soldiers.

   b. Women can't be good soldiers.

4. Children are mature enough to choose which parent to live with.

   a. Children can choose which parent to live with.

   b. Children can't choose which parent to live with.

5. Teenagers are responsible enough to use the Internet without censorship.

   a. Teenagers can use the Internet without censorship.

   b. Teenagers can't use the Internet without censorship.

6. Adults are too afraid of change to listen to children's ideas.

   a. Adults listen to children's ideas.

   b. Adults don't listen to children's ideas.

7. People with disabilities have worked too hard to give up the fight for equal rights.

   a. People with disabilities can give up the fight for equal rights.

   b. People with disabilities can't give up the fight for equal rights.

8. At age 70, we are not too old to work.

   a. At age 70, we can work.

   b. At age 70, we can't work.

9. Some children's movies are too violent for children to watch.

   a. Kids shouldn't watch some movies for children.

   b. Kids can watch all children's movies.

10. College is too expensive for a lot of people to afford.

    a. Everyone can afford to go to college.

    b. Some people can afford to go to college.

2 | CAN YOU GET BY?

Match the pictures with the sentences below.

1. ___*e*___

2. _____

3. _____

4. _____

5. _____

6. _____

7. _____

8. _____

9. _____

a. The buttons are too high for him to reach.

b. The buttons are low enough.

c. The steps are too steep for him to get up.

d. The box is too heavy.

e. The street is too busy for them to cross.

f. The traffic is light enough for them to cross.

g. She's too old to join the army.

h. She is too young to vote.

i. She is old enough to vote.

3 | CURFEW!   *Grammar Notes 1–4*

*Some teenagers are leaving a concert. Complete their conversations. Use the words in parentheses with the infinitive and **too** or **enough**.*

1. **A:** Hologram is so cool! Did you catch the words in that last song?

   B: No. The guitar was ___*too loud for me to understand*___ the words.
   (loud / me / understand)

2. **A:** They're playing in Hampton Stadium next month.

   B: Let's go. The tickets are _____.
   (cheap / us / afford)

3. **A:** I don't think the stadium has wheelchair access yet.

   B: We'll sit on the grass. This concert is going to be _____.
   (good / you / miss)

4. **A:** It's 9:30. Do we have time to get a slice of pizza?

   B: No. It's _____.
   (late / stop)

5. **A:** I hate this curfew!

   B: Me too! I think we're _____ out past 10:00!
   (old / stay)

6. **A:** Where's Kyle tonight?

   B: Working. He didn't get off _____.
   (early / come)

7. **A:** The new recreation center just opened. Do you want to play basketball tomorrow?

   B: Sure. But I'm still _____ you!
   (slow / beat)

4 | EDITING

*Read this student's journal entry. There are six mistakes in the use of infinitives with **too** or **enough**. The first mistake is already corrected. Find and correct five more.*

> The Hologram concert was awesome! Now I'm too excited ~~for sleeping~~ *to sleep*. That Eve Durkin can really sing. My voice isn't enough good to sing in the shower! After the concert we were really hungry, but it was to late to go for pizza. I HATE this stupid curfew! It's too weird understand. My friend Todd works and has to pay taxes, but the law says he's too young for staying out past 10:00 P.M.! That's really crazy! Well, I'd better try to get some sleep or I'll be too tired too get up in the morning.

Communication Practice

5 | LISTENING

🎧 *A new youth recreation center has been built so that people in wheelchairs can get around easily. Listen to the description of the center. Then listen again and circle the number of the picture that best fits the description.*

1.

2.

3.

4.

6 | YOUTH RIGHTS

Discuss one of these questions as a class. Then vote on your opinions.

- At what age should people start to vote?

- Should towns have curfews for people younger than age 18?

Example: **A:** I think 15 year olds are mature enough to vote. They can read newspapers and understand issues.

B: I disagree. I don't think 15 year olds are concerned enough about politics to vote.

7 | COMMON EXPRESSIONS

What do you think these expressions mean? When would you use them? Discuss your ideas in small groups.

- She's old enough to know better.
- Life is too short to worry about every little thing.
- You're never too old to try.
- It looks good enough to eat.
- It's too hot to handle.
- It's never too late!

8 | WHAT'S YOUR OPINION?

Complete the following sentences. In small groups, compare your opinions.

1. People over age 70 are too . . .

   Example: A: People over age 70 are too old to drive.
   B: Oh, I don't agree. Some elderly people drive better than young people.

2. The leaders of this country are powerful enough . . .

3. Teenagers are too crazy . . .

4. Guns are too dangerous . . .

5. Taxes aren't high enough . . .

6. Women are strong enough . . .

7. Radio and TV broadcasters speak (or don't speak) clearly enough . . .

8. Time goes by too quickly . . .

9 | WRITING

Write a letter to the editor of a newspaper. Choose a topic from Exercise 8.

   Example: To the Editor:
   I'm in favor of gun control. I believe that guns are too dangerous for ordinary people to own and use . . .

10 | ON THE INTERNET

Do a search on **teen voting rights**. *Make notes about some of the arguments for and against lowering the voting age to 16. Discuss the arguments in small groups.*

   Example: This article says that teenagers take courses in history, government, and current events. That means they are educated enough to vote.

Grammar in Context

BEFORE YOU READ

🎧 *Do you always find excuses not to do certain things? If you answered "yes," you are a procrastinator. What types of things do you put off doing? Why do you procrastinate? Read the excerpt from a magazine article about procrastinating.*

STOP PROCRASTINATING—NOW!

It's a beautiful day. Eva doesn't **feel like spending** it at the library. She goes to the park instead. She **keeps telling** herself she'll work better the next day.

Todd **planned to make** an appointment with the dentist, but he **decided to wait** another week, or maybe two.

Procrastinating—putting off until tomorrow things you **need to do** today—is a universal problem. College students are famous **for procrastinating**, but we all do it sometimes. What **causes** people **to put off** important tasks? Read what the experts say.

UNPLEASANT TASKS • **It**'s not always fun **to do** a lot of the things on our To Do lists. Most people **prefer to do** enjoyable things.

POOR TIME MANAGEMENT • **Having** too little time for a task is discouraging. **It**'s hard **to get** started on a project when you feel that you can't finish it.

FEAR • An important test can make you feel so nervous that you **put off studying**.

PERFECTIONISM • The belief that you must do a perfect job can prevent you **from starting** or **finishing** a task.

As you can see, people often procrastinate because they **want to avoid** bad feelings. But procrastinators **end up feeling** even worse because of their procrastination. The only solution: **stop procrastinating**. Now!

Did you **finish writing** your paper on procrastination?

No. I'll do it tomorrow.

AFTER YOU READ

Check the reasons the article gives for procrastination.

☐ **1.** being lazy

☐ **2.** not enjoying the task

☐ **3.** feeling nervous about the task

☐ **4.** not having enough time

☐ **5.** not getting enough sleep

☐ **6.** feeling depressed

Grammar Presentation

GERUNDS AND INFINITIVES

Gerunds
Eva **enjoys going** to the park.
She **loves taking** long breaks.
She **stopped studying**.
Changing habits is hard.
She's worried **about finishing** her paper.

Infinitives
Eva **wants to go** to the park.
She **loves to take** long breaks.
She **stopped to study**.
It's hard **to change** habits.

GRAMMAR NOTES

1. Some **verbs**, like the ones below, are **followed by a gerund** (base form + *-ing*).

appreciate	avoid	can't stand
end up	feel like	keep
mind	recall	regret

2. Some **verbs**, like the ones below, are **followed by an infinitive** (*to* + base form).

afford	agree	decide
expect	need	offer
plan	want	would like

USAGE NOTE: We usually <u>do not repeat *to*</u> when there is more than one infinitive.

EXAMPLES

- Eva *avoids* **doing** her work.
- She *keeps* **making** excuses.
- She *regrets* **not studying** more.

- Todd doesn't *want* **to go** to the dentist.
- He'*d like* **to stay** home.
- He *decided* **not to keep** his appointment.

- He *plans* **to watch** TV, **read** the paper, and **call** his friends.
  NOT He plans to watch TV, ~~to~~ read the paper, and ~~to~~ call his friends.

(continued)

3. Some **verbs**, like the ones below, can be **followed by a gerund or an infinitive**.

| begin | continue | hate |
| like | love | prefer |

- Jeff *hates* **studying**.

OR

- Jeff *hates* **to study**.

4. BE CAREFUL! The verbs *stop*, *remember*, and *forget* can be followed by either the gerund or the infinitive, but they have very <u>different meanings</u>.

- Eva *stopped* **taking** breaks.
(She doesn't take breaks anymore.)
- Eva *stopped* **to take** a break.
(She stopped another activity in order to take a break.)

- Todd *remembered* **reading** the story.
(First he read the story. Then he remembered that he did it.)
- Todd *remembered* **to read** the story.
(First he remembered. Then he read the story. He didn't forget.)

- Jeff *forgot* **meeting** Dana.
(Jeff met Dana, but afterwards he didn't remember the event.)
- Jeff *forgot* **to meet** Dana.
(Jeff had plans to meet Dana, but he didn't meet her because he forgot about the plans.)

5. The **gerund** is the only verb form that can **follow a preposition**.

preposition
- Jeff is worried *about* **writing** his paper.

preposition
- He's looking forward *to* **finishing** it.

6. To make **general statements**, you can use:

- **gerund as subject**

OR

- *it* + **infinitive**

- **Writing** a paper is hard.

OR

- *It*'s hard **to write** a paper.

Reference Notes
For a more complete list of **verbs followed by a gerund,** see Appendix 13 on page A-7.
For a more complete list of **verbs followed by an infinitive,** see Appendix 14 on page A-7.
For a more complete list of **verbs followed by a gerund or an infinitive,** see Appendix 15 on page A-7.
For more on **gerunds after prepositions,** see Unit 28 on page 326, and Appendices 17 and 18 on pages A-7 and A-8.

Focused Practice

 | **DISCOVER THE GRAMMAR**

Read this paragraph. Circle the gerunds. Underline the infinitives.

Like many students, Eva is a procrastinator. She keeps (putting off) her school work. When she
studies, she often stops to go for a walk in the park. She wants to improve her study habits, but
she isn't sure how. Eva decided to make a list of things she needs to do every day. She always
remembers to make her list, but she often forgets to read it. It's very frustrating. Last night Eva
remembered reading an article in the school newspaper about a support group for procrastinators.
She thinks being in a group is a good idea. She likes sharing ideas with other students.

Now read these sentences. Write **T (True)** *or* **F (False)**.

_F_ **1.** Eva never does her school work.   _____ **5.** She always reads her list.

_____ **2.** She quit going for walks in the park.   _____ **6.** She read about a support group.

_____ **3.** She'd like to be a better student.   _____ **7.** She thinks it's good to be in a group.

_____ **4.** Eva makes a list every day.   _____ **8.** She likes to share ideas with others.

2 | **ARE YOU A PROCRASTINATOR?**   *Grammar Notes 1–3, 5*

Read this quiz. Circle the correct form of the verbs. In some cases, both forms are correct.

☐ When I don't feel like to do / (doing) something, I often put off to start / starting it.
                              1.   **2.**

☐ I sometimes start to study / studying the night before a test.
                         3.

☐ I sometimes start a job but then postpone to finish / finishing it.
                                           4.

☐ I often delay to make / making difficult decisions.
                     5.

☐ I find excuses for not to do / doing things I dislike.
                         6.

☐ When a task seems too difficult, I often avoid to work / working on it.
                                                7.

☐ I prefer to do / doing easy tasks first.
                    8.

☐ I often promise myself to work / working on a project but then fail to do / doing it.
                                 9.   **10.**

☐ I worry about to make / making mistakes or about not to be / being perfect.
                         11.   **12.**

☐ I often choose to do / doing other tasks instead of the most important one.
                         13.

☐ I want to improve / improving, but I keep to put / putting it off!
                     14.   **15.**

3 | FROM AN ADVICE COLUMN

Complete these tips. Use the correct form of the verbs in parentheses.

Some Tips for _____Stopping_____ *Procrastination*
1. (stop)

🕐 If you have a large project to work on, break it into small tasks. Finish _____
2. (do)

one small task before _____ the next.
3. (start)

🕐 Choose _____ the hardest task first. You'll get it out of the way, and you'll feel
4. (do)

better about yourself.

🕐 Promise _____ at least 15 minutes on a task even if you don't really feel like
5. (spend)

_____ it. You'll be surprised. You can get a lot done in 15 minutes—and you'll
6. (do)

often keep _____ even longer.
7. (work)

🕐 Stop _____ *short* breaks—but no more than 10 minutes.
8. (take)

🕐 Arrange _____ yourself a reward when you succeed in _____
9. (give)   **10. (finish)**

a task. Do something you enjoy _____.
11. (do)

🕐 Consider _____ a support group for procrastinators.
12. (join)

4 | SUPPORT GROUP

Read these conversations that took place at a procrastinators' support group meeting.
Complete the summary statements. Use the gerund or the infinitive.

1. **JEFF:** Hi, Todd. Did you bring the soda?

    TODD: Yes. Here it is.

    SUMMARY: Todd remembered _to bring the soda._ _____

2. **LEE:** Eva, do you remember Todd?

    EVA: Oh, yes. We met last year.

    SUMMARY: Eva remembers _____

3. **JEFF:** You take too many breaks.

    TODD: No, I don't!

    SUMMARY: Todd denied _____

4. EVA: What do you do in your free time, Kay?

    KAY: I listen to music a lot.

    SUMMARY: Kay enjoys _____

5. UTA: I'm tired. Let's go home.

    KAY: OK. Just five more minutes.

    SUMMARY: Uta wants _____

6. UTA: Eva, can we give you a ride home?

    EVA: Thanks, but I think I'll stay a little longer.

    SUMMARY: Uta offered _____

    Eva decided _____

7. PAT: Good night. Please drive carefully.

    UTA: Don't worry. I will.

    SUMMARY: Uta promised _____

5 | IN OTHER WORDS   *Grammar Note 6*

Eva and Todd are talking. They agree on everything. Read one person's opinion and write the other's. If the first person used the gerund, use the infinitive. If the first person used the infinitive, use the gerund.

1. EVA: It's hard to start a new project.

    TODD: I agree. *Starting a new project is hard.*

2. TODD: Taking short breaks is helpful.

    EVA: You're right. *It's helpful to take short breaks.*

3. EVA: It's difficult to work on a long project.

    TODD: That's true. _____

4. TODD: Completing a job on time feels great.

    EVA: You're right. _____

5. TODD: Rewarding yourself for finishing a project is a good idea.

    EVA: I agree. _____

6. EVA: Being in a support group is very helpful.

    TODD: Yes. _____

7. EVA: It's good to meet people with the same problem.

    TODD: I feel the same way. _____

6 | EDITING

Read Eva's journal entry. There are eight mistakes in the use of the gerund and infinitive. The first mistake is already corrected. Find and correct seven more.

> *going*
> For months I was thinking about ~~to go~~ to a support group for procrastinators,
> but I kept putting it off! Last night I finally decided going, and I'm glad I did. I'm not
> alone! There were a lot of people there with the same problem as me. I expected
> being bored, but it was really quite interesting—and helpful. I even knew some of the
> other students there. I remembered to meet a few of them at a school party last
> year. I really enjoyed to talk to Todd, and before I left I promised coming again.
>
>   I have a math test tomorrow, so I really should stop to write now and start
> studying. See, I've already learned something from to be in this group! I have to stop
> making excuses and start my work! Now!

Communication Practice

7 | LISTENING

🎧 *The school newspaper is interviewing Eva about her study habits. Read the list of activities. Listen to the interview. Then listen again and check the things Eva does and doesn't do now when she is studying for a test.*

	Things Eva Does	**Things Eva Doesn't Do**
1. clean her work area	✔	☐
2. start the night before the test	☐	☐
3. study the hardest thing first	☐	☐
4. make a To Do list	☐	☐
5. take long breaks	☐	☐
6. do relaxation exercises	☐	☐
7. reward herself for finishing	☐	☐

8 | TAKE A BREAK!

Taking short breaks can help you work more effectively. Work in groups. Brainstorm ideas for 10-minute work breaks. Share your ideas with the rest of your classmates.

Examples: I enjoy . . .
It's relaxing . . .
You could consider . . .
I recommend . . .
I like . . .
Try . . .

9 | STOP PUTTING THINGS OFF

Work in small groups. Discuss these questions:

1. Can you complete projects on time?

2. Do you follow any of the tips in Exercise 3?

Example: A: I sometimes put off writing a paper.
B: I always make a note on my calendar when the paper is due.

10 | QUOTABLE QUOTES

Read these quotes about procrastination. Discuss them with a partner. What do they mean? Do you agree with them?

Never put off till tomorrow what you can do today.

—*Lord Chesterfield (British politician, 1694–1773)*

Example: Lord Chesterfield advises doing things right away. I think that is not always possible because . . .

Procrastination is the art of keeping up with yesterday.

—*Don Marquis (U.S. author, 1878–1937)*

Procrastination is the thief of time.

—*Edward Young (British poet, 1683–1765)*

When there is a hill to climb, don't think that waiting will make it smaller.

—*Anonymous*

Putting off an easy thing makes it hard, and putting off a hard one makes it impossible.

—*George H. Lorimer (U.S. magazine editor, 1868–1937)*

Procrastination is like a credit card: It's a lot of fun until you get the bill.

—*Christopher Parker*

11 INFORMATION GAP: AT THE SUPPORT GROUP

Work in pairs (A and B). Student A, follow the instructions on this page. Student B, turn to page 366 and follow the instructions there.

1. Look at the picture below. Ask your partner questions to complete what people said at the support group meeting.

    Example: **A:** What does Eva remember doing?
    B: She remembers meeting Todd.

2. Answer your partner's questions.

    Example: **B:** What does Todd hope to do?
    A: He hopes to see Eva again.

When you are done, compare your pictures. Are they the same?

12 | WRITING

Writing a goals worksheet is a good way to help prevent procrastination. First, complete this worksheet. List three goals for this month in order of importance (1 = the most important goal).

This Month's Goals	
Goal 1:	Complete by:
Goal 2:	Complete by:
Goal 3:	Complete by:

Now, write three paragraphs (one for each goal) on how you plan to accomplish your goals.

Example: I want to finish writing my English paper by March 28. First, I plan to . . .

13 | ON THE INTERNET

*Do a search on **procrastination quiz**. Take the quiz and discuss the results with your classmates.*

INFORMATION GAP FOR STUDENT B

1. Look at the picture below. Answer your partner's questions.

Example: **A:** What does Eva remember doing?
B: She remembers meeting Todd.

2. Ask you partner questions to complete what people said at the support group meeting.

Example: **B:** What does Todd hope to do?
A: He hopes to see Eva again.

When you are done, compare your pictures. Are they the same?

From **Grammar** to **Writing**
Combining Sentences with **and, but, so, or**

You can combine two sentences with **and**, **but**, **so**, and **or**. The resulting longer sentence is made up of two main clauses.

Example: Commuting to school is hard. I prefer to live in the dorm. ⟶
            main clause   main clause
            Commuting to school is hard, **so** I prefer to live in the dorm.

The clause starting with **and**, **but**, **so**, or **or** always comes second. Note that a comma comes after the first clause.

1 | *Circle the correct words to complete this letter.*

Dear Dania,

I have just a little time before my next class, (so) / but this will be a short letter. This
                                              1.
semester has been difficult, but / or I'm enjoying it. I'm taking two English classes, and / so
                              2.   **3.**
I'm also on the Student Council. Being on the Council has taught me a lot, but / so it takes
                                                                            4.
up a lot of time.

Studying takes up most of my time, and / but I try to find time for sports too. I've got to
                                     5.
keep in shape! This weekend I'm going hiking with some classmates. Do you remember the

time we went hiking, and / so we couldn't find our way back?
                      6.
Your visit is in just two weeks! I'm really looking forward to seeing you, and / but I'm
                                                                            7.
sure we'll have a great time. You can stay in my dorm, and /or I can arrange for us both to
                                                        8.
stay with my parents. Which would you prefer to do? My parents don't live far from my dorm,

and / but I know they will want to see you.
9.
Let me know which train you're taking, so / but I can meet you at the station.
                                        10.
                        Love,

                        Monica

Note these different ways to close a personal letter:
• *Love,* for family and close friends
• *Warmly,* for friends
• *Best wishes,* for colleagues and acquaintances.

2 | Complete these rules for using **and**, **but**, **so**, and **or**. Look at the letter in Exercise 1 for help.

1. Use _____*and*_____ when the second sentence adds information.

2. Use _____ when the second sentence gives a choice.

3. Use _____ when the second sentence gives a contrasting idea.

4. Use _____ when the information in the second sentence is a result of the information in the first sentence.

3 | Complete these sentences with your own ideas.

1. It has started to rain, but_____

2. I don't really want to study tonight, so_____

3. This weekend my friends and I will go to a movie, or_____

4. I'm reading a lot of books in English, and _____

5. After class I'm going shopping, so _____

6. I used to go dancing a lot, but_____

7. I'm looking forward to graduating, and _____

8. Ed is too young to vote, but_____

9. We can take a train, or_____

10. Dan is tired of staying home evenings, so _____

4 | Before you write . . .

Talk to a partner about your life these days. Answer some of these questions.

- What are you doing these days?
- What do you enjoy doing?
- What can't you stand?
- What do you plan to do next semester?
- What are you looking forward to?

5 | Write a letter to a friend describing your present life. Use the letter in Exercise 1 as a model. Include some of the ideas you spoke about in Exercise 4. Use **and**, **but**, **so**, and **or**.

6 | Exchange letters with a new partner. Answer your partner's letter.

Review Test

I *Complete the conversation. Use the prepositions in the box and the gerund form of the verbs in parentheses.*

about	~~by~~	for	in	to	without

A: Carla, your English is just great. How did you learn so quickly?

B: _____ *By using* _____ some special strategies.
     1. (use)

A: Like what?

B: Well, first I got used _____ my time. I scheduled time
                              2. (plan)

_____ television and writing letters in English to my pen pal.
     3. (watch)

A: How did you practice speaking?

B: At first I was very nervous _____ English. I had to learn to talk
                                   4. (speak)

_____ about mistakes. I used deep breathing exercises and music to
     5. (worry)

calm myself down.

A: What else helped you relax?

B: Jokes. I got interested _____ jokes in English. That way I always had
                               6. (learn)

something to say, and I also learned a lot about American culture.

II *Complete each conversation with the correct phrase in parentheses.*

1. A: Let's go running.

  B: No. You always run _____ *too fast* _____ for me to keep up with you.
                            (too fast / fast enough)

  A: OK. Let's go swimming, then.

2. A: Why did you get an F on this paper?

  B: My handwriting was _____ for the teacher to read.
                            (messy enough / too messy)

  A: Then how did he know the answers were wrong?

                                                                        (continued)

3. A: Have you tried the coffee?

    B: I will in a minute. It's _____ to drink yet.
                         (too cool / not cool enough)

4. A: This steak is _____ to eat.
                        (too tough / tough enough)

    B: Send it back and ask for something else.

5. A: John's a good player. Why didn't he make the soccer team?

    B: He doesn't play _____ to win.
                      (too aggressively / aggressively enough)

6. A: What did the forecaster say about thunderstorms?

    B: I'm not sure. The radio wasn't _____ for me to hear.
                           (loud enough / too loud)

III   *Complete this text with the correct form of the verbs in the box. Choose between the gerund or the infinitive of purpose.*

drink	eat	feel	follow	give up	~~quit~~	read
reward	save	shop	smoke	take	tell	

Cigarettes. They're bad for your health. Your doctor recommends _____*quitting*_____.
                                                                 1.
Your friends keep _____ you to stop. Even your dry cleaner suggests that you stop
                              2.
_____. (He says you burned holes in your suit jacket.) You want to stop, but
    3.
_____ an old habit is difficult. _____ these suggestions can help.
    4.   **5.**

- List your reasons for quitting. Are you quitting _____ better?
                                          6.

  _____ money? Keep your list nearby _____ when you want
    7.   **8.**
  a cigarette.

- Stop _____ coffee and tea. Caffeine causes people to want a cigarette.
          9.

- When you feel the desire to light up, put it off for five minutes. Use the time

  _____ some deep breaths. The urge will pass quickly.
    10.

- Avoid _____ big meals for a few weeks.
    11.

- Save the money that you aren't spending on cigarettes. Go _____ for
                                                          12.

  something special _____ yourself for your success.
           13.

If you follow these suggestions, it shouldn't be too hard to give up this unhealthy habit.

IV *Complete the conversation by writing the words and phrases in parentheses in the correct order.*

A: Why are so many people starting home-based businesses?

B: In offices, work hours are often _____*too long for people to spend*_____ time with their
1. (people / to spend / too long / for)

families.

A: What are some keys to home business success?

B: Networking is one. _____ organizations. After you
2. (necessary / to / It's / join)

join, you must _____ a lot of people. But don't get
3. (enough / meet / participate / to)

_____ people who sound interested in your product.
4. (too / to / busy / call)

A: Do business owners really work fewer hours?

B: No, they are most likely to work more. But they can arrange their time. Their hours are

_____ family time too.
5. (to have / enough / for them / flexible)

A: What do you warn new business owners about?

B: I _____ their privacy. Remember, the business phone is
6. (them / to think about / advise)

always going to ring right in the middle of the family dinner. Also,

_____ the loneliness of working alone, especially when
7. (important / it's / to know about)

you're used to a big office.

A: Anything else?

B: In my seminars, I teach strategies for getting paid on time. Home business owners often find

that they don't get paid _____ their own bills.
8. (for / enough / to pay / soon / them)

A: What kind of home businesses are people starting?

B: Well, as I said, a lot of working people are _____ care
9. (take / to / too / busy)

of things like shopping and planning parties. Many home-based businesses supply these

services.

A: You mean, someone will pay me for shopping?

B: Sure. In fact, I _____ planning your own shopping
10. (you / to start / encourage)

business. My class for new business owners starts next week.

V   *Circle the letter of the correct answer to complete each sentence.*

1. Tom is late because he stopped _____ dinner.   A   B   C   (D)

   (**A**) buying   (**C**) and buy

   (**B**) buy   (**D**) to buy

2. My key was in my pocket, but I don't remember _____ it there.   A   B   C   D

   (**A**) to put   (**C**) I put

   (**B**) putting   (**D**) to put

3. Bob's 17 years old, so he's still _____ vote.   A   B   C   D

   (**A**) too young to   (**C**) too old to

   (**B**) young enough to   (**D**) too young for

4. I bought a camera phone _____ photos to my friends.   A   B   C   D

   (**A**) by sending   (**C**) to send

   (**B**) I sent   (**D**) send

5. Chris _____, so her grades are low this semester.   A   B   C   D

   (**A**) stopped studying (**C**) stopped to study

   (**B**) stopping to study (**D**) was stopping to study

6. As firefighters, women work _____ the job done.   A   B   C   D

   (**A**) hardly get   (**C**) not enough to get

   (**B**) too hard to get   (**D**) hard enough to get

7. He's used _____ a big breakfast.   A   B   C   D

   (**A**) ate   (**C**) to eating

   (**B**) to eat   (**D**) eats

8. I used to be very nervous _____, but I'm not anymore.   A   B   C   D

   (**A**) to drive   (**C**) to driving

   (**B**) for driving   (**D**) about driving

9. I didn't remember _____ my check, so I paid the rent twice!   A   B   C   D

   (**A**) mailed   (**C**) mailing

   (**B**) to mail   (**D**) I mail

10. Sal enjoyed _____ in Texas.   A   B   C   D

    (**A**) live   (**C**) living

    (**B**) to live   (**D**) lived

VI *Complete the interview with the gerund or infinitive form of the verbs in parentheses.*

INTERVIEWER: You're one of the best baseball players today, Anthony. Who taught you

_____ *to play* _____?
1. (play)

ANTHONY: I learned _____ a ball with my dad. We used to play together
2. (hit)
for hours on weekends.

INTERVIEWER: What was the most important thing he taught you?

ANTHONY: Dad believed in _____ fun. He always forgot about
3. (have)
_____ when he played. By _____ with him,
4. (win)   5. (play)
I developed the same attitude.

INTERVIEWER: When did you decide _____ a professional?
6. (become)

ANTHONY: Too early—in elementary school. That was a mistake. I was too young

_____ that decision.
7. (make)

INTERVIEWER: Why?

ANTHONY: My schoolwork suffered. I thought a lot about _____ a pro ball
8. (become)
player, and I didn't think much about _____ homework.
9. (do)

INTERVIEWER: Did anything happen to change your mind about school?

ANTHONY: Yes, I planned _____ to City High School, which had a great team.
10. (go)
Then I found out that my grades were probably too low for the school

_____ me.
11. (accept)

INTERVIEWER: But you graduated from City High School. Right?

ANTHONY: Yes, I did. My parents urged me _____ harder. I followed their advice
12. (study)
and I've never stopped _____.
13. (study)

INTERVIEWER: Well, thank you for _____ to this interview.
14. (agree)

ANTHONY: You're welcome. I enjoyed _____ your questions.
15. (answer)

VII *Each sentence has four underlined words or phrases. The four underlined parts of the sentence are marked A, B, C, or D. Circle the letter of the <u>one</u> underlined word or phrase that is NOT CORRECT.*

1. It's <u>difficult</u> <u>study</u> in a foreign country, so students <u>need</u> <u>to prepare</u>
        A   B   C   D

   for the experience.   A **Ⓑ** C D

2. Students <u>look forward</u> <u>to traveling</u>, but they <u>worry about</u> <u>don't make</u>   A B C D
              A   B   C   D

   a good impression.

3. They're afraid <u>of</u> <u>not understanding</u> the culture, and they <u>don't want</u>   A B C D
                  A   B   C

   <u>making</u> mistakes.
     D

4. Counselors can <u>advise</u> them <u>against wear</u> the wrong <u>clothing</u> and   A B C D
                       A   B   C

   <u>making</u> the wrong gestures.
     D

5. It's <u>natural</u> <u>to have</u> some problems because no one can <u>get used to</u>   A B C D
        A   B   C

   <u>live</u> in a new culture immediately.
     D

6. No one escapes <u>from</u> <u>feeling</u> some culture shock, and <u>it's important</u>   A B C D
                   A   B   C

   <u>realizing</u> this fact.
     D

7. Jan <u>stopped</u> <u>to feel</u> uncomfortable after she <u>started</u> <u>to make</u> new A B C D
        A   B   C   D

   friends.

8. Now she is <u>looking</u> <u>forward to</u> <u>stay</u> here and <u>getting</u> a job.   A B C D
             A   B   C   D

▶ *To check your answers, go to the Answer Key on page RT-4.*

PART

VIII

More Modals
and Similar Expressions

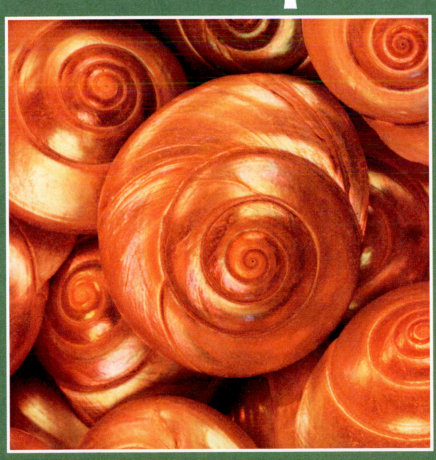

33 Preferences: *Prefer, Would prefer, Would rather*

Grammar in Context

BEFORE YOU READ

🎧 *Look at the bar graph. What is* leisure time? *Which leisure-time activity is most popular? Read the online questionnaire about leisure-time preferences.*

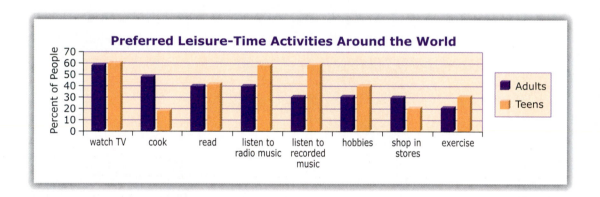

Preferred Leisure-Time Activities Around the World

Percent of People

70 60 50 40 30 20 10 0

watch TV | cook | read | listen to radio music | listen to recorded music | hobbies | shop in stores | exercise

■ Adults
■ Teens

Leisure-Time Activities ➡ **Market Survey, Inc.**

Click on the answer closest to your preference.

1 When you go to the movies, **would** you **rather see** a comedy or a thriller?
 ◯ I **prefer seeing** a thriller.   ◯ I'**d rather watch** a comedy.

2 When you choose a restaurant, do you look for interesting foods or big portions?
 ◯ I **prefer** big portions.   ◯ I'**d rather try** interesting foods.

3 Which **would** you **prefer**: tickets to a rock concert or tickets to a football game?
 ◯ I'**d prefer to go** to the game.   ◯ I'**d rather go** to the concert.

4 Which **do** you **prefer—eating out** or **cooking** at home?
 ◯ I almost always **prefer eating out**.   ◯ I'**d rather cook** at home.

5 How **do** you **prefer communicating** with friends?
 ◯ I **prefer to e-mail**.   ◯ I'**d rather talk** on the phone.

AFTER YOU READ

Look at the bar graph. Read the statements. Check **True** *or* **False***.*

		True	False
1.	Teens would rather watch TV than shop in stores.	☐	☐
2.	Adults would rather listen to radio music than recorded music.	☐	☐
3.	Adults and teens prefer hobbies to exercise.	☐	☐
4.	Adults and teens prefer reading to watching TV.	☐	☐
5.	Teens would prefer watching TV to all other activities.	☐	☐
6.	Adults would rather shop than cook.	☐	☐

Grammar Presentation

PREFERENCES: *PREFER, WOULD PREFER*

Statements		
Subject	***Prefer / Would prefer****	**Noun / Gerund / Infinitive**
I You We They	**prefer** **would prefer**	**TV news** (to newspapers). **watching** the news (to reading newspapers). **(not) to watch** the news.
He She	**prefers** **would prefer**	

Contraction
would prefer = **'d prefer**

*Like modals, *would prefer* does not have *-s* in the third-person singular.

Yes / No Questions			
Do / Would	**Subject**	***Prefer***	**Noun / Gerund / Infinitive**
Do **Would**	I you we they	**prefer**	**TV news**? **watching** the news? **to watch** the news?
Does **Would**	he she		

Short Answers						
Affirmative				**Negative**		
Yes,	you I / we you they	**do.** **would.**	**No,**	you I / we you they	**don't.** **wouldn't.**
	he she	**does.** **would.**		he she	**doesn't.** **wouldn't.**

PREFERENCES: *WOULD RATHER*

Statements			
Subject	***Would rather****	**Base Form of Verb**	
I You He She We They	**would rather**	**watch**	the news (than read newspapers).
		not read	newspapers.

Contraction
would rather = **'d rather**

*Like modals, *would rather* does not have *-s* in the third-person singular.

Yes / No Questions			
Would	**Subject**	***Rather***	**Base Form of Verb**
Would	you she	**rather**	**read?**

Short Answers				
Affirmative			**Negative**	
Yes,	I she	**would.**	I'**d** She'**d**	**rather not.**

GRAMMAR NOTES

1. Use *prefer*, *would prefer*, and *would rather* to talk about things or activities that you <u>like better</u> than other things or activities.

   USAGE NOTES:
   a. We usually use the **contraction** for *would* in speech and <u>informal</u> writing.

   b. We often use *prefer* to express a <u>general</u> preference.

   c. We use *would prefer* or *would rather* to talk about a preference in a <u>specific</u> situation.

   ▶ **BE CAREFUL!** Do not use *will* to talk about preferences.

EXAMPLES

- We usually **prefer** Italian food.
- I'**d prefer** to have Chinese food tonight.
- I'**d rather** cook at home.

- I'**d** rather go.
  NOT I ~~would rather~~ go.

- Which **do** you **prefer**—action movies or romantic comedies?

- I usually **prefer** action movies, but tonight I'**d prefer** a romantic comedy.
- I'**d rather go** to the rock concert next weekend.
  NOT I ~~will rather go~~ to the rock concert next weekend.

2. *Prefer* and *would prefer* may be followed by a <u>noun</u>, a <u>gerund</u>, or an <u>infinitive</u>.

noun
- Jeffrey usually **prefers** *comedies*.
- Right now, he**'d prefer** *a thriller*.

gerund
- **Does** Kyle **prefer** *reading* magazines?
- **Would** he **prefer** *watching* a movie?

infinitive
- Kathleen **prefers** *to read* magazines.
- She **would prefer** *to watch* TV tonight.

USAGE NOTE: *Would prefer* + infinitive is more common than *would prefer* + gerund.

---

3. *Would rather* can only be followed by the <u>base form</u> of the verb.

A: Would you like to eat out tonight?
base form
B: **I'd rather** *cook* dinner at home.

- **I'd rather not** *have* dessert.
  NOT ~~I wouldn't rather~~ have dessert.
  NOT ~~I'd not rather~~.

The <u>negative</u> of *I'd rather* is **I'd rather not**.

USAGE NOTE:
We often use **I'd rather not**, by itself, <u>to refuse</u> an offer, suggestion, or invitation.

A: Let's see the movie at the Film House.
B: **I'd rather not**. I hear it's terrible.

---

4. A **comparison with** *to* can follow *prefer / would prefer* + <u>noun</u>.

noun   noun
- Lani **prefers** comedies *to* thrillers.
noun   noun
- She**'d prefer** *Life to Crash*.

A **comparison with** *to* can also follow *prefer / would prefer* + <u>gerund</u>.

gerund   gerund
- I **prefer** visiting friends *to* going to parties.
gerund   gerund
- Tonight I**'d prefer** visiting Lani *to* going to the office party.

---

5. A **comparison with** *than* can follow *would rather* + <u>base form</u> of verb.

base form   base form
- They**'d rather** eat out *than* cook.
base form   base form
- I**'d rather** watch football *than* play it.

Focused Practice

1 | DISCOVER THE GRAMMAR

 Terry and Grace are spending the afternoon at the mall. Underline the sentences that talk about preferences.

TERRY: <u>Which would you rather do first, get stuff for your project or shop?</u>

GRACE: I think I'd rather get the things for my project first. There's ABC Crafts.

TERRY: Have you tried Franklin's? I really prefer them for science projects.

GRACE: So let's go there.

* * * *

GRACE: Do you want to look at computer games at Nerdly's?

TERRY: I'd prefer looking for DVDs at Goodly's. What about you?

GRACE: I'd rather do that too. Let's check out that group we saw at the concert last week.

* * * *

TERRY: There's Stella Blue. Do you want to buy new earrings for Sara's party?

GRACE: I've been thinking about it, and I'd rather not. I'll just wear some old ones.

* * * *

TERRY: Have you seen *The Racer* yet?

GRACE: No, but you know me. I always prefer romantic comedies to action movies.

TERRY: We can see *Breakfast in Bogotá* at 5:00. That's romantic.

GRACE: Sounds good. Are you hungry? Let's get a pizza.

TERRY: The line's awfully long. I'd rather just get a taco.

GRACE: You're right. The movie starts in about 10 minutes.

Now look at the Mall Directory. Check the places that Grace and Terry decide to go to.

MALL DIRECTORY

Computers & Electronics		Jewelry	
• Nerdly's Software	☐	• Gem Stones	☐
• Radio Hut	☐	• Stella Blue	☐
• Goodly's Music	☐	• Dupree's Diamonds	☐
Fashions		**Show Time Cinemas**	
• Fantastic Footwear	☐	• *The Racer* 4:30	☐
• Jan Tyler Dresses	☐	• *Breakfast in Bogotá* 5:00	☐
Food Court		**Toys and Hobbies**	
• Candy Man	☐	• ABC Crafts	☐
• Taco Bill's	☐	• Animal Farm Pets	☐
• Viva Pizza!	☐	• Franklin's	☑

2 | **MUSHROOMS OR PEPPERONI?**   *Grammar Notes 1, 3*

Emma and Kyle are discussing their evening plans. Complete their conversation. Use
would rather (not) *with one of the verbs from the box. Use short answers.*

cook	have	see	~~stay~~

EMMA: Would you like to go to a movie tonight?

KYLE: _____*I'd rather stay*_____ home and watch TV.
            1.

EMMA: Sounds good. Maybe we could make dinner later.

KYLE: _____ tonight. Let's order out for some pizza.
            2.

EMMA: OK. Mushrooms or anchovies?

KYLE: I'm in the mood for pepperoni. Let's get a pepperoni pizza.

EMMA: _____. Pepperoni gives me heartburn.
            3.

      _____ mushrooms than pepperoni, if that's OK.
            4.

KYLE: Mushrooms it is! Now, what should we watch on TV? How about the new Stephen King

      thriller?

EMMA: _____. His movies give me the creeps.
            5.

KYLE: Well . . . there's a comedy on at 8:00 and a documentary at 8:30.

EMMA: _____ the comedy. I need a laugh.
            6.

3 | DECISIONS

*Complete the questions with **prefer**, **would prefer**, or **would rather**. Use **prefer** to state general preferences.*

1. A: When we go to St. Louis next week, _____*would*_____ you _____*rather*_____ travel by train or by plane?

   B: Let's take the train. It's cheaper.

2. A: _____ Kyle usually _____ an aisle or a window seat?

   B: He always asks for an aisle seat. He says there's more room.

3. A: Look—we won the prize! We have two choices. _____ you _____ going to a World Series game or getting a new television set?

   B: Let's go to the baseball game. I've always wanted to go to a World Series game.

4. A: I'm looking for a movie.

   B: What do you like? _____ you _____ to watch comedies or thrillers?

5. A: Listen up, everyone! We're going on a field trip next week. You have a choice. _____ you _____ go to the museum or to the Capitol?

   B: The museum!

6. A: Waiter, this cigarette smoke is really bothering us.

   B: _____ you _____ a table in the non-smoking section?

4 | SPORTS PREFERENCES

*Complete this report about sports preferences around the world. Use the words in parentheses plus **to** or **than** to make a comparison. If there is a verb, choose the correct form.*

THE WIDE WORLD OF SPORTS

Soccer or Basketball?

You're going to play a sport today. Would you prefer _____*playing soccer to playing basketball*_____?
                                                         1. (play soccer / play basketball)

Your answer depends a lot on your age, your gender, and your nationality. Boys age 13 and older

prefer _____, but girls of the same age prefer
                    2. (soccer / basketball)

_____. Because of girls' preferences, teens as a group
       3. (shoot hoops / make goals)

would rather _____. In this age group, basketball is

               4. (play basketball / play soccer)

as popular in Colombia and Thailand as it is in the United States.

Play or Watch?

People of all ages prefer _____. Seventy percent of

                        5. (watch / play)

Latin Americans prefer _____, but Filipinos would

                   6. (soccer / other TV sports)

rather see a basketball game (85 percent watch regularly). Worldwide, cricket is not a popular

sport on TV, but in India, 80 percent prefer _____.

                           7. (it / basketball or soccer)

In general, people like to watch the sports they love to play.

No, Thanks.

This is not true of car racing, figure skating, and wrestling. For these sports, almost everyone

would rather _____.

               8. (watch a pro / participate)

5 | EDITING

*Read Kyle's report. There are six mistakes in the use of **prefer** and **would rather**. The first mistake is already corrected. Find and correct five more.*

> For my study, I interviewed 50 men and women. There was no real
> difference in men's and women's preferences for television. I found that
> everyone prefers watching television ~~than~~ *to* going to the movies.
>
> Men and women both enjoy news programs and entertainment specials.
> However, men would rather watching adventure programs and science
> fiction, while women prefer soap operas. Men also like to watch all kinds
> of sports, but women would rather see game shows to sports events.
>
> I found a big difference in reading preferences. Men prefer to reading
> newspapers while women would much rather read magazines and books.
> When men read books, they prefer read nonfiction and adventure stories.
> Women will prefer novels.

Communication Practice

6 | LISTENING

🎧 *Emma is ordering in a restaurant. Listen to her conversation with the server. Then listen again and circle the items on the menu that Emma wants.*

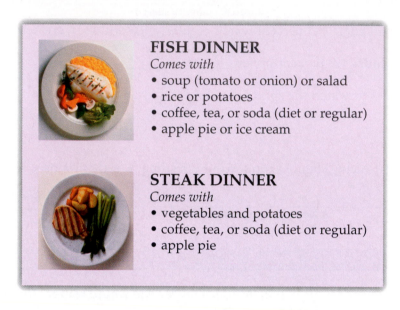

FISH DINNER
Comes with
- soup (tomato or onion) or salad
- rice or potatoes
- coffee, tea, or soda (diet or regular)
- apple pie or ice cream

STEAK DINNER
Comes with
- vegetables and potatoes
- coffee, tea, or soda (diet or regular)
- apple pie

7 | WHAT'S ON TV?

*Work in small groups. Look at the TV schedule and try to agree on something to watch at 8:00 P.M. Use **would rather** or **would prefer** to talk about your preferences.*

	8:00
2	**Hockey** Maple Leafs vs. Canucks
4	**Science Watch** Are we alone in the universe?
6	**Everybody Loves Raymond** The whole family goes to Italy.
CNN	**World News**
35	**Movie***** (2004) *Spiderman 2* Action film follows the adventures of the famous superhero. Entertaining and exciting. (127 min)
38	**Movie**** (1999) *Life* Comedy starring Eddie Murphy. Two criminals discover the value of life after going to prison. Funny with serious message. (108 min)
40	**Movie****** (2003) *Love Actually* Romantic comedy follows the lives of eight couples in London. Very sweet "feel-good" movie. (134 min)

Example: A: Let's watch the hockey game at 8:00.
        B: I don't really like hockey. I'd prefer to watch *Everybody Loves Raymond*.

8 | IF I HAD MY WAY

Read the choices below. In pairs, discuss your preferences. Give reasons for your choices.

- live in the city / live in the country
- work in an office / work at home
- be married / be single
- work for someone else / own your own business

Example: A: Would you rather live in the city or in the country?
B: I'd rather live in the city. There's a lot more to do.
A: Really? I'd prefer the country. It's quieter.

Now ask your partner about some other choices.

9 | INFORMATION GAP: PREFERRED SNACKS

Work in pairs (A and B). Student A, follow the instructions on this page. Student B, turn to page 387 and follow the instructions there.

1. Look at the bar graphs below. Ask your partner for the information you need to complete each graph. Draw the missing bar(s) on each graph.

Example: A: In the overall favorites: What percentage of people would rather eat chips than any other snack?
B: About 25 percent.

2. Answer your partner's questions.

Example: B: What percentage prefer eating cheese?
A: Fifteen percent prefer cheese to chips or popcorn.

When you are finished, compare graphs. Are they the same?

10 | CHOICES

Complete the leisure-time activities questionnaire on page 376. Discuss your answers with a partner. Give reasons for your choices.

> **Example:** **A:** I prefer seeing thrillers. They're more exciting.
> **B:** Not me. I prefer comedies. I'd rather laugh than be frightened.

11 | WRITING

Write a paragraph about one of the choices you discussed in Exercise 8. Give reasons and examples for your choice.

> **Example:** I prefer living in the city to living in the country. There are a lot more choices of things to do in the city. For example . . .

12 | ON THE INTERNET

*Do a search on **movies** playing in your city or town (or a city of your choice). Discuss the choices with a partner and decide on a movie to see. Also choose a day and time.*

> **Example:** **A:** Would you rather see a comedy or a thriller?
> **B:** I always prefer comedies. *The Purple Cow* is playing at the Cineplex. How about that?
> **A:** Sure. We could go Monday night.
> **B:** I'd rather go on the weekend . . .

INFORMATION GAP FOR STUDENT B

1. Look at the bar graphs below. Answer your partner's questions.

> **Example:** **A:** In the overall favorites: What percentage of people would rather eat chips than any other snack?
>
> **B:** About 25 percent.

2. Ask your partner for the information you need to complete each bar graph. Draw the missing bar(s) on each graph.

> **Example:** **B:** What percentage prefer eating cheese?
>
> **A:** Fifteen percent prefer cheese to chips or popcorn.

When you are finished, compare graphs. Are they the same?

Necessity: *Have (got) to, Must, Don't have to, Must not, Can't*

Grammar in Context

BEFORE YOU READ

🎧 *Have you ever traveled to a different country? How did you prepare for your trip? What did you need to know? Read the article about some rules for international travel.*

KNOW BEFORE YOU GO

What do international travelers **have to know** before they go? This week's column answers some questions from our readers.

Q: Do I **have to put** my computer and digital camera through the X-ray machine at airport security? I'm worried that the machine will damage them.

A: It probably won't, but you **don't have to put** them through the X-ray equipment. An agent **must inspect** them, though. Ask for an agent to inspect them by hand.

Q: My passport is going to expire in three months. Can I use it for a short trip to Asia next month?

A: For many countries, your passport **must be** valid for at least six months after you enter the country. Renew your passport before you leave, or you**'ll have to check** the rules of each country you plan to visit.

Q: I'm a French citizen. Last month I visited the U.S., and I brought some gifts for friends. Why did U.S. Customs take the cheese?

A: You **can't bring** most types of cheese into the U.S. without a special permit. Many governments have strict rules about bringing food into their countries. To avoid problems, don't bring gifts of fresh food and eat your snacks on the plane.

Q: I'm from Australia. My family and I are planning a trip to Europe and North America. We'd like to rent cars in a few places. **Do I have to get** an International Driver's Permit (IDP)?

A: Regulations differ: In Germany you **must not drive** without an IDP; in Canada you **don't have to have** one, but it's recommended. For an around-the-world tour, you really should get an IDP to avoid problems and disappointment.

KNOW BEFORE YOU GO

Q: I'm planning a trip from Toronto to New Delhi. There's a new nonstop flight, but it's more expensive, and it's about 14 hours long! What do you recommend?

A: Several airlines are now offering super-long flights. They provide more comfortable seats, wireless computers, and lots of entertainment. They cost a bit more, but you **won't have to make** as many connecting flights. That saves you time and hassles. But remember: To stay healthy on long flights you**'ve got to get up** and **move** around. You also **must drink** plenty of water. On a long flight these are "musts," not "shoulds"!

AFTER YOU READ

Read the statements. Check **True** *or* **False**.

	True	False
1. Passengers must put computers and cameras through security X-ray equipment.	☐	☐
2. An international visitor needs an IDP to drive in Germany.	☐	☐
3. Travelers are not permitted to bring cheese into the U.S.	☐	☐
4. Passengers are not permitted to move around on long flights.	☐	☐

Grammar Presentation

NECESSITY: *HAVE (GOT) TO, DON'T HAVE TO*

Affirmative Statements			
Subject	*Have to / Have got to*	**Base Form of Verb**	
I You We They	**have to** **have got to**	leave	now.
He She It	**has to** **has got to**		

Negative Statements				
Subject	*Do not*	*Have to*	**Base Form of Verb**	
I You We They	**don't**	**have to**	leave	now.
He She It	**doesn't**			

Contractions		
have got to	=	**'ve got to**
has got to	=	**'s got to**

Note: There are no contractions for *have to* and *has to*.

(continued)

Yes / No Questions				
Do	Subject	*Have to*	Base Form of Verb	
Do	I you we they	**have to**	**leave**	now?
Does	he she it			

Short Answers						
Affirmative			Negative			
Yes,	you I / we you they	**do**.	**No,**	you I / we you they	**don't**.
	he she it	**does**.		he she it	**doesn't**.

Wh- Questions					
Wh- Word	*Do*	Subject	*Have to*	Base Form of Verb	
When	**do**	I you we they	**have to**	**leave**?	
	does	he she it			

NECESSITY: *MUST, MUST NOT, CAN'T*

Must			
Subject	*Must** (*not*)	Base Form of Verb	
I You He She It We They	**must**	**leave**	early.
	must not	**arrive**	late.

Contraction
must not = **mustn't**

*Must is a modal. Modals have only one form.
They do not have *-s* in the third-person singular.

Can't			
Subject	*Can't*	Base Form of Verb	
You They	**can't**	**sit**	here.

GRAMMAR NOTES	EXAMPLES
1. Use *have to*, *have got to*, and *must* for **necessity**.	
a. *Have to* is the most common expression in <u>everyday speaking and writing</u>.	• You **have to carry** your passport for international travel.
b. *Have got to* is used in conversation and informal writing to express <u>strong feelings</u>.	• I**'ve got to apply** for a new passport right away!
c. *Must* is used in <u>writing</u>, including official forms, signs, and notices.	• Travelers **must show** their passports when they check in.
USAGE NOTE: *Must* is stronger than *have to*.	• Jess, you really **must pack** tonight.

2. Use the correct form of *have to* for **all tenses**.	• She **has to travel** a lot for her job. • He **had to travel** a lot last year. • We**'ll have to visit** them soon.
Use *have got to* and *must* only for the **present** and the **future**.	• You**'ve got to turn off** your cell phone on this flight. • Passengers **must arrive** one hour before the flight.

3. Use *have to* for most **questions**.	• **Did** you **have to get** an IDP? • **Do** you **have to leave** now?
USAGE NOTE: We almost never use *must* or *have got to* in questions.	

4. BE CAREFUL! *Have (got) to* and *must* have similar meanings. However, *don't have to* and *must not* have very <u>different meanings</u>.	
a. Use *don't have to* to show that something is <u>not necessary</u>. There is a choice.	• A tourist **doesn't have to have** an IDP in Canada.
b. Use *must not* for <u>prohibition</u>. There is no choice.	• Most tourists **must not drive** without an IDP in Spain.
USAGE NOTE: We often use *can't* instead of *must not* to express prohibition in <u>spoken English</u>.	• You **can't drive** without an IDP in Thailand.

Pronunciation Note
In informal speech, *have to* is often pronounced "hafta" and *got to* is often pronounced "gotta."

Reference Notes
For general information on **modals**, see Unit 11, Grammar Note 1, on page 126.
Have (got) to, *must*, and *can't* are also used to draw **conclusions** (see Unit 37).
Can't is also used to express **ability** (see Unit 11), refuse **permission** (see Unit 12) or **requests** (see Unit 13).
For a list of **modals and their functions**, see Appendix 19 on page A-8.

Focused Practice

1 | DISCOVER THE GRAMMAR

🎧 *Read Ben Leonard's telephone conversation with a clerk from the Italian consulate. Underline the words in the conversation that express something **necessary**, **not necessary**, or **prohibited**.*

BEN: Hello. I'm Australian, and I'm planning to spend several weeks in Europe with my family. I have some questions. First, do we have to get visas to visit Italy?

CLERK: Not for a short visit. But you can't stay for longer than 90 days without a visa. Australians also need a Permit to Stay for visits in Italy longer than eight days. You must apply for the permit at a local police station within eight days of your arrival.

BEN: Can my wife and I use our Australian driver's licenses in Italy?

CLERK: You have to carry your Australian license, but you must also have an International Driver's Permit. And you've got to be at least 18 years old.

BEN: When do we have to get the IDPs? Is it possible to apply for them when we get to Europe?

CLERK: No, you must apply before you leave. The Australian Automobile Association can help you. You'll also have to get an International Insurance Certificate to show you have insurance. But you'll be able to get that at the car rental agency.

BEN: We'll be in Italy in January. We don't have a set schedule, so we haven't made any reservations.

CLERK: Oh, you've got to have reservations, even in January—especially in major cities like Rome, Florence, or Venice.

BEN: OK. Thanks a lot. You've been very helpful.

Now check the appropriate box for each instruction.

	Necessary	Not Necessary	Prohibited
1. Get a visa for a two-week visit.	☐	✔	☐
2. Get a Permit to Stay for visits longer than eight days.	☐	☐	☐
3. Apply for a Permit to Stay ten days after arrival.	☐	☐	☐
4. Get a visa for a one-month visit.	☐	☐	☐
5. Use only an Australian driver's license.	☐	☐	☐
6. Apply for an IDP in Europe.	☐	☐	☐
7. Make hotel reservations.	☐	☐	☐

2 | **GETTING READY**   Grammar Notes 1 and 4

*The Leonards have checked off the things they've already done to get ready for their trip. Read the lists and write sentences about what the Leonards still **have to do** and what they **don't have to do**.*

BEN
✔ make copies of passports and IDPs
buy euros
give the house keys to Nora

ANN
buy phone cards online
✔ call Pet Care
buy batteries for the digital camera
✔ stop the mail for two weeks

Sean and Maya
✔ pack clothes
choose DVDs and CDs for the trip
say good-bye to friends

Ben doesn't have to make copies of passports and IDPs.

He has to buy euros, and he has to give the house keys to Nora.

Ann . . .

---

3 | **ARE WE THERE YET?**   Grammar Notes 1–4

*Ben's family is traveling from Australia to Italy. Complete the conversations with the correct form of **have to**, **have got to**, or **can't** and the verbs in parentheses. Use short answers.*

1. **BEN:** What time ____*do*____ we ____*have to leave*____ tomorrow?
                                          a. (leave)

    ANN: We _____ later than 5:30. We _____
                     b. (start)   **c. (check in)**
    with the airline by 7:00.

    SEAN: _____ we really _____ there so early? Our flight leaves at
                                  d. (get)
    10:00. We've got plenty of time.

    ANN: Yes, _____. It takes a long time to check in and get through
                        e.
    airport security these days.

    MAYA: And Mom _____ the car. That takes some time too!
                        f. (park)

    (continued)

2. **BEN:** Maya, this bag _____ over 70 pounds or we
   _____
   a. (weigh)

   _____ extra. _____ you _____
   b. (pay)   c. (bring)

   so many clothes?

   MAYA: Yes, _____. I _____ all my stuff!
                              d.   e. (have)

   We'll be gone for weeks.

   ANN: Put some in my bag. And hurry. We _____!
                                            f. (go)

3. **BEN:** We _____ never _____ this long to check in before.
                              a. (wait)

   ANN: I know. But we _____ much longer. We're next.
                           b. (wait)

4. **SEAN:** Look! They have computers and TV screens! I _____ Randy!
                                                        a. (call)

   BEN: We _____ our cell phone on the plane. Send an e-mail.
                b. (use)

5. **ANN:** We _____ around again. Come on, everybody, let's go.
                a. (walk)

   SEAN: Why _____ we _____ up all the time?
                          b. (get)

   BEN: Remember our rules? We _____ for more than three hours.
                                 c. (sit)

   It's unhealthy.

6. **MAYA:** Are we there yet? This flight is endless!

   ANN: We _____ in here much longer. We're landing in an hour.
                a. (not be)

4 | FOLLOWING THE RULES   *Grammar Notes 1, 4*

*Complete these rules for airline travel. Use **must** or **must not**.*

1. Passengers _____ *must* _____ arrive three hours before an international flight.

2. They _____ keep their bags with them at all times.

3. Carry-on bags _____ be bigger than 45 inches (115 cm).

4. They _____ fit under the seat or in the overhead compartment of the airplane.

5. They _____ contain knives, scissors, or other dangerous items.

6. Checked bags _____ have labels with the passenger's name.

7. They _____ weigh more than 70 pounds, or there will be additional charges.

8. Travelers _____ show identification when they check in with the airline.

9. Everyone _____ have a ticket in order to go through security.

10. On board, passengers _____ get up when the seat belt sign is on.

11. On many flights, passengers _____ use cell phones.

5 | AT THE POOL

Read the sign at the Casa Luciani swimming pool and complete each statement with
must not *or* **don't have to**.

Swimming Pool Rules and Regulations

Pool Hours 10:00 A.M. – 10:00 P.M.

Children under 12 years NOT ALLOWED

in pool without an adult.

Towels available at front desk.

- NO radio
- NO diving
- NO ball playing
- NO glass bottles
- NO alcoholic beverages

1. Children under age 12 _____must not swim_____
   (swim)
   without an adult.

2. You _____ your own towel.
   (bring)

3. You _____ ball in or around
   (play)
   the pool.

4. You _____ into the pool.
   (dive)

5. Teenagers _____ swimming
   (go)
   with an adult.

6. You _____ the swimming
   (leave)
   pool at 8:00 P.M.

7. You _____ in the pool past
   (stay)
   10:00 P.M.

6 | EDITING

*Read Sean's e-mail to his friend. There are seven mistakes in expressing necessity. The first
mistake is already corrected. Find and correct six more.*

Hi Randy,

                              had

We're on our way back to Australia. We ~~have~~ to leave the hotel at 5:30 this morning, and then we

had got to wait in line at the airport for hours. This flight is great. There are computers and TVs

at every seat and hundreds of movies to watch. But we can't sit for more than three hours at a

time because it's unhealthy, and we must to drink water every hour when we're not sleeping. This

flight is 14 hours long, so we have to taking care of ourselves. Thanks for the camping knife.

I used it a lot in Italy, but before we left, I has to put it in my suitcase. You don't have to bring

knives in carry-on bags. Well, I got to get up and walk around again.

E-mail me. We'll be on this plane for 10 more hours! —Sean

Communication Practice

7 | LISTENING

🎧 *Listen to the conversations. Then listen again and write the number of each conversation next to the appropriate sign.*

a. _____

b. _____

c. _____ (30)

d. _____

e. _____

f. _*1*_

8 | READING THE SIGNS

Work in pairs. Where can you find these signs? What do they mean? What do you have to do when you see each one? What can't you do? What do you think of these rules?

9 | INVENT A SIGN

Draw your own sign to illustrate something people **have to do** *or* **must not do**. *Show it to a classmate. See if he or she can guess the meaning. Decide where the sign belongs.*

10 | TAKING CARE OF BUSINESS

Make a list of your most important tasks for this week. Check off the things you've already done. Tell a partner what you still **have to do** *and what you* **don't have to do**. *Report to a group.*

Examples: I don't have to do English homework. I've already done it.
Hamed has to wash the car. He doesn't have to go shopping because he went on Monday.

11 | WRITING

Write about the application procedure for getting a driver's license, a passport, a work permit, citizenship, school admission, or a new job. What do you have to do? What don't you have to do? Use **have to**, **don't have to**, **must**, *and* **must not**.

Example: To get a driver's license in my state, you must be at least 16 years and 3 months old. Drivers under the age of 19 also have to take a driver's education course. Then they have to . . .

12 | ON THE INTERNET

Do a search on **driving rules** *in another country. Look for rules about some of the things below. Discuss the information in a group. Compare some of the rules.*

- cell phone use
- seat belts or air bags
- driver's license
- learner's permit
- speed limits
- side of the road
- car insurance
- helmets for motorcycle riders
- minimum and maximum age
- license plates

Example: In Japan, you have to drive on the left side of the road, but in Taiwan you can't drive on the left. You have to drive on the right.

Grammar in Context

BEFORE YOU READ

🎧 *What do you think the letter to Ms. Etiquette is about? What does* etiquette *mean?*
Read this page from Ms. Etiquette's book, The Right Thing.

Wedding Wisdom

Dear Ms. Etiquette:

What **is** the maid of honor **supposed to do** in a wedding ceremony? My best friend is getting married soon. She has invited me to be her maid of honor. I was planning to buy a new dress to wear, but someone told me that the bride **is supposed to select** my dress. This surprised me. I'm new in this country, and I'm not sure what my friend expects of me.

Dear Reader:

First of all, you should be very proud. In the past, the bride's sister **was supposed to serve** as her maid of honor, and the groom's brother **was supposed to be** his best man. Today, however, the bride and groom can ask anyone they want. Your friend's invitation means that she values your friendship very highly.

The maid of honor is the bride's assistant, and the best man is the groom's. Before the wedding, these two **are supposed to help** the couple prepare for the ceremony. You might help the bride choose the bridesmaids' dresses and send the wedding invitations, for example. The day of the wedding, the best man **is supposed to drive** the groom to the ceremony. During the ceremony, the maid of honor holds the bride's flowers. After the wedding, the maid of honor and the best man **are** both **supposed to sign** the marriage certificate as witnesses.

AFTER YOU READ

Check the maid of honor's responsibilities.

She has to _____.

- ☐ **1.** choose her own dress for the wedding
- ☐ **2.** help send wedding invitations
- ☐ **3.** choose the best man
- ☐ **4.** drive the groom to the ceremony
- ☐ **5.** hold the bride's flowers during the ceremony
- ☐ **6.** sign the marriage certificate as a witness

Grammar Presentation

EXPECTATIONS: *BE SUPPOSED TO*

Statements					
Subject	***Be***	***(not)***	***Supposed to***	**Base Form of Verb**	
I	**am** **was**	**(not)**	**supposed to**	**sign**	the marriage certificate.
You We They	**are** **were**				
He She	**is** **was**				
It				**be**	a small wedding.

Yes / No Questions			
Be	**Subject**	***Supposed to***	**Base Form of Verb**
Am **Was**	I	**supposed to**	**stand**?
Are **Were**	you		
Is **Was**	she		

Short Answers					
Affirmative			**Negative**		
Yes,	you	**are.** **were.**	**No,**	you	**aren't.** **weren't.**
	I	**am.** **was.**		I	**'m not.** **wasn't.**
	she	**is.** **was.**		she	**isn't.** **wasn't.**

(continued)

Wh- Questions				
Wh- Word	Be	Subject	Supposed to	Base Form of Verb
Where	am was	I	supposed to	stand?
	are were	you		
	is was	she		

GRAMMAR NOTES

EXAMPLES

1. Use *be supposed to* to talk about different kinds of <u>expectations</u>:

   a. rules
   - You**'re not supposed to park** over here. There's a No Parking sign.

   b. customs (usual ways of doing things)
   - The groom **is supposed to arrive** at the ceremony early. It's a custom.

   c. predictions
   - The weather forecast says it**'s supposed to rain** tomorrow.

   d. hearsay (what everyone says)
   - The beaches in Aruba **are supposed to be** beautiful. Everyone says so.

   e. plans or **arrangements**
   - Let's hurry. We**'re supposed to pick up** the Smiths at 6:00.

2. Use *be supposed to* only in the **simple present** or the **simple past**.

   a. Use the **simple present** for the <u>present</u> or the <u>future</u>.
   - The bride **is supposed to be** here *now*.
   - I**'m supposed to be** at the wedding rehearsal *tomorrow*.
     NOT I ~~will be~~ supposed to be . . .

   b. Use the **simple past** for <u>past</u> expectations.
   - They **were supposed to get** there by 6:00, so they took a taxi.

   USAGE NOTES:
   Was / were supposed to and *was / were going to* can have similar meanings.
   - The show **was supposed to start** at 8:00.
   - The show **was going to start** at 8:00.

   We often use *was / were supposed to* or *was / were going to* when something we expected to happen <u>did not happen</u>.
   - Carl **was supposed to get** here at noon, *but* his train was late.
   - Carl **was going to get** here at noon, *but* his train was late.

Focused Practice

1 | **DISCOVER THE GRAMMAR**

Read the article and underline the phrases that express expectations.

It wasn't <u>supposed to be</u> a big wedding.

BY MATT PEDDLER

PROVIDENCE, July 19—The Stricklands wanted a small, quiet wedding—that's why they eloped to Block Island, off the Atlantic Coast of the United States.

The ferry they took to their wedding site doesn't carry cars, so the Stricklands packed their bikes for the trip.

The couple found a lonely hill overlooking the ocean. The weather was supposed to be beautiful, so they asked the town mayor to marry them on the hill the next afternoon. They were going to have a small, private ceremony in this romantic setting.

"When we got there, we found a crowd of cyclists admiring the view," laughed Beth Strickland.

When Bill kissed his bride, the audience burst into loud applause and rang their bicycle bells. "We weren't supposed to have 50 wedding guests, but we love biking, and we're not sorry," Bill said.

When they packed to leave the island the next day, Beth left her wedding bouquet at the hotel. She remembered it minutes before the ferry was going to leave. Bill jumped on his bike, recovered the flowers, and made it back to the ferry before it departed.

"Cyclists are supposed to stay fast and fit," he said. "Now I know why."

*Read the article again. Check **True** or **False** for each statement.*

	True	False
1. The Stricklands planned a big wedding.	☐	☑
2. The weather forecaster predicted rain.	☐	☐
3. The Stricklands wanted an outdoor wedding.	☐	☐
4. They didn't expect 50 guests.	☐	☐
5. Beth remembered her bouquet after the ferry left.	☐	☐
6. People believe that cyclists are in good shape.	☐	☐

2 | GETTING READY

Complete the conversations with the verbs in parentheses and a form of **be supposed to**.

1. A: Netta, Gary called while you were out.

  B: ___Am___ I _____*supposed to call*_____ him back?

  a. (call)

  A: No, he'll call you later in the afternoon.

2. A: The dress store called too. They delivered your wedding dress to your office this morning.

  _____ they _____ that?

  a. (do)

  B: No, they weren't! They _____ it here. That's why I

  b. (deliver)

  stayed home today.

3. A: Let's get in line. The rehearsal _____ in a few minutes.

  a. (start)

  B: We're bridesmaids. Where _____ we _____?

  b. (stand)

  A: Right here, behind Netta.

4. A: Hi. Where's Netta?

  B: Gary! You _____ here!

  a. (not be)

  A: Why not?

  B: The groom _____ the bride on the day of the wedding

  b. (not see)

  until the ceremony. It's bad luck.

5. A: Sophie, could I borrow your handkerchief, please?

  B: Sure, but why?

  A: I _____ something old, something new, something

  a. (wear)

  borrowed, and something blue. I don't have anything borrowed.

  B: It _____ this afternoon. Maybe I should lend you my

  b. (rain)

  umbrella instead.

6. A: Where are Gary and Netta going on their honeymoon?

  B: Aruba.

  A: Oh, that _____ a really nice island.

  a. (be)

7. A: How long are they going to be away?

  B: They _____ ten days, but they decided to stay two weeks.

  a. (stay)

3 | PLANS CHANGE

Grammar Note 2

Look at the list of wedding plans. There have been a lot of changes. Write sentences with
was / were going to.

TASK	WHO	COMPLETED
1. choose the bridesmaids' dresses	Netta *and Sophie*	☑
2. mail ~~180~~ *210* invitations	Netta's parents	☑
3. order a ~~vanilla~~ *chocolate!* cake	Netta	☑
4. hire a ~~rock~~ *jazz* band	Gary's parents	☑
5. give the bridal shower May ~~10~~ *20*	Sophie	☑
6. plan the rehearsal dinner	~~Gary~~ *Gary's parents*	☑
7. find a photographer	~~Netta~~ *Jack*	☑
8. rent a ~~limo~~ *red sports car*	Jack	☑
9. order flowers by ~~April 1~~ *April 15*	Sophie	☑
10. Buy ~~candles~~ *clocks* as bridesmaids' gifts	Netta's parents	☑
11. Send the wedding announcement to the newspaper	~~Gary~~ *Jack*	☑

1. *Netta was going to choose the bridesmaids' dresses, but Netta and Sophie chose them.*

2. _____

3. _____

4. _____

5. _____

6. _____

7. _____

8. _____

9. _____

10. _____

11. _____

4 | EDITING

Read Jack's e-mail to a friend. There are eight mistakes in the use of **be supposed to** *and*
was / were going to. *The first mistake is already corrected. Find and correct seven more.*

Hi!

Remember my old college roommate Gary? He's getting married tomorrow, and I'm the best man!

He and his fiancée *were* supposed to have a small wedding, but they ended up inviting more than 200

people! As best man, I have some important responsibilities. For one thing, I'm supposing to make

sure Gary gets to the wedding ceremony on time—not an easy job for me. At first we was going to

hire a limousine and driver, but I decided to drive him there myself in a rented red sports car. I'm

also supposed to hold the wedding rings during the ceremony. Then, at the end of the reception

party, I'm supposed to helping the newlyweds leave quickly for their honeymoon. They're going

straight to the airport (I'm also suppose to hold the plane tickets for them). They are going to go

to Hawaii, but they changed their minds and are going to Aruba instead. Oh! I just looked at the

clock. I'd better sign off now, or I'll be late for the rehearsal dinner. I going to leave five minutes

ago! By the way, Sophie, the maid of honor, will be there too. I've never met her, but she supposes

to be very nice. I'll let you know how it goes! —Jack

Communication Practice

5 | LISTENING

 *It's the day of the wedding. Listen to the conversations. Then listen again and circle
the correct words.*

1. Netta is / isn't supposed to be at the church by 2:00.

2. Netta was / wasn't going to walk to the wedding.

3. The photographer is / isn't supposed to take pictures during the ceremony.

4. Members of the bride's family are / aren't supposed to sit on the right.

5. The bridesmaids were / weren't going to wear pink.

6. The maid of honor is / isn't supposed to walk behind the bride.

7. Guests are / aren't supposed to say "congratulations" to the groom.

8. Guests are / aren't supposed to throw rice at the bride and groom.

6 | **A CHANGE OF PLANS**

Work with a partner. Discuss important plans that you had that changed.
Use **was / were supposed to** *and* **was / were going to**.

Example: A: My family and I were supposed to move to Mexico City, but my mother got a
better job in Guadalajara, so we moved there instead.
B: When were you going to move to Mexico City?

7 | **INTERNATIONAL CUSTOMS**

Work in small groups. Discuss these important events. What are people in your culture
supposed to do and say at these times? Are people expected to give certain gifts? Report
to the class.

- a wedding

- an important birthday

- a graduation ceremony

- an engagement to be married

- an anniversary

- a birth

- a funeral

Example: In traditional Japanese weddings,
the bride and groom are supposed
to wear kimonos.

8 | **WRITING**

Write a short essay about one of the events listed in Exercise 7. Use **be supposed to** *to*
describe customs.

9 | **ON THE INTERNET**

Do a search on **international etiquette**. *Choose a country that interests you. Write*
about some things that you are supposed to do and some things you are not supposed to
do in that country.

Example: In Turkey you're supposed to shake hands firmly when you meet someone.
You're not supposed to show the bottom of your shoes when you're sitting.
You're . . .

Grammar in Context

BEFORE YOU READ

🎧 *Look at the weather map. Are the temperatures in Celsius or Fahrenheit? How warm might it get in Ankara? How cool? What's the weather prediction for Madrid? Read this transcript of a weather report on British TV.*

WEATHER WATCH

CAROL: Good morning. I'm Carol Johnson, and here's the local forecast. The cold front that has been affecting much of northern Europe is moving toward Great Britain. Temperatures **may drop** as much as 11 degrees by late tomorrow afternoon. In London, expect a high of only 2 and a low of –4 degrees. We **might** even **see** some snow flurries later on in the day. By evening, winds **could reach** 40 miles per hour. So, bundle up; it's going to be a cold one! And now it's time for our travelers' forecast with Ethan Harvey. Ethan?

ETHAN: Thanks, Carol. Take your umbrella if you're traveling to Paris. Stormy conditions **may move** into France by tomorrow morning. Rain **could turn** into snow by evening when temperatures fall to near or below freezing. On a warmer note— you **may not need** your coat at all if you plan to be in Rome. Expect to see partly cloudy skies with early morning highs around 10. Temperatures **could climb** to above 20 as skies clear up in the afternoon. It looks like it will turn out to be a beautiful, sunny day in central Italy.

CAROL: Italy sounds great! Will you join me on a Roman holiday?

ETHAN: I **might**!

Map labels:

Stockholm $\frac{1}{-3}$
Moscow $\frac{3}{-4}$
London $\frac{2}{-4}$
Berlin $\frac{6}{3}$
Warsaw $\frac{9}{3}$
Paris $\frac{5}{2}$
Budapest $\frac{15}{1}$
Madrid $\frac{19}{6}$
Rome $\frac{20}{10}$
Ankara $\frac{16}{4}$
Athens $\frac{22}{18}$

AFTER YOU READ

Read the statements. Check **True** *or* **False**.

	True	False
1. Temperatures will definitely drop 11 degrees in Great Britain.	☐	☐
2. Snow is possible in London.	☐	☐
3. There will definitely be stormy weather in France.	☐	☐
4. Snow is possible in Paris.	☐	☐
5. Temperatures will definitely be above 20°C in Rome.	☐	☐

Grammar Presentation

FUTURE POSSIBILITY: *MAY, MIGHT, COULD*

Statements			
Subject	*May / Might / Could**	**Base Form of Verb**	
You It They	**may (not)** **might (not)** **could**	**get**	cold.

*May, *might*, and *could* are modals. Modals have only one form. They do not have *-s* in the third-person singular.

Yes / No Questions		
Are you going to fly to Paris? Are you leaving on Monday?		
Are you going to Will you Is it possible you'll	**be**	there long?

Short Answers		
I	**may (not).** **might (not).** **could.**	
We	**may** **might** **could**	**be.**

Note: *May not* and *might not* are not contracted.

Wh- Questions
When are you **going** to Paris?
How long are you going to **be** there?

Answers			
I We	**may** **might** **could**	**go**	next week.
		be	there a week.

GRAMMAR NOTES	**EXAMPLES**
1. Use *may*, *might*, and *could* to talk about **future possibility**.	• It **may be** windy *later*. • It **might get** cold *tonight*. • It **could rain** *tomorrow*.
▶ BE CAREFUL! *May be* and *maybe* both express possibility. Notice these differences: • *May be* is a <u>modal + be</u>. It is always two words. • *Maybe* is not a modal. It is an <u>adverb</u>. It is always one word, and it comes at the beginning of the sentence.	• He **may be** late today. • *Maybe* he'll take the train. NOT He ~~maybe take~~ the train.

2. Use *may not* and **might not** to express the <u>possibility</u> that something <u>will not happen</u>.	• There are a lot of clouds, but it **might not rain**.
Use **couldn't** to express the idea that something is <u>impossible</u>.	A: Why don't you ask John for a ride? B: I **couldn't do** that. He's too busy.
▶ BE CAREFUL! We usually <u>do not contract</u> **might not**, and we never contract **may not**.	• You **may not** need a coat. NOT You ~~mayn't~~ need a coat.

3. Questions about possibility usually do not use *may*, *might*, or *could*. Instead, they use the future (*will*, *be going to*, the present progressive) or phrases such as ***Do you think . . . ?*** or ***Is it possible that . . . ?***	A: When *will* it *start* snowing? B: It **might start** around lunchtime. A: *Are* you *going to drive* to work? B: I don't know. I **might take** the bus.
The **answers** to these questions often use *may*, *might*, or *could*.	A: When *are* you *leaving*? B: I **may leave** now. A: *Do you think* it'll snow tomorrow? B: It **could stop** tonight.
In **short answers** to *yes / no* questions, use *may*, *might*, or *could* alone.	A: Will your office close early? B: It **might**.
USAGE NOTE: If *be* is the main verb, it is common to include *be* in the short answer.	A: Will our flight *be* on time? B: It **might be**.

Reference Notes

For general information on **modals**, see Unit 11, Grammar Note 1 on page 126.
May is also used to ask and give **permission** (see Unit 12).
Might is also used to draw **conclusions** (see Unit 37).
Could is also used to talk about **ability** (see Unit 11), ask and give **permission** (see Unit 12), make **requests** (see Unit 13), make **suggestions** (see Unit 15), and draw **conclusions** (see Unit 37).
For a list of **modals and their functions**, see Appendix 19 on page A-8.

Focused Practice

1   DISCOVER THE GRAMMAR

🎧 *Anna is a college student who works part-time; Cody is her boyfriend. Read their conversation. Underline the words that express future possibility.*

ANNA: Are you going to drive to work tomorrow?

CODY: I <u>might</u>. Why?

ANNA: I just heard the weather report. It may snow tonight.

CODY: Then I might take the 7:30 train instead. I have a 9:00 meeting, and I don't want to miss it. Do you have a class tomorrow morning?

ANNA: No, but I'm going to the library to work on my paper. Maybe I'll take the train with you.

CODY: Could we have lunch together after you go to the library?

ANNA: Oh, I'm sorry. I have a class at noon every day this week.

CODY: Cut class tomorrow. One day won't make any difference.

ANNA: I couldn't do that. I'll meet you at 6:00 at the train station, OK? I'm going to take the 6:30 train home.

CODY: I might not catch the 6:30 train. My boss said something about working late tomorrow. I'll call you and let you know what I'm doing.

ANNA: OK. I'll get some takeout on the way home. Do you mind eating late?

CODY: No. I definitely want to have dinner together. Maybe I'll rent a movie.

ANNA: There might be something good on TV.

CODY: Let's decide tomorrow.

Read the conversation again. Check the appropriate box for each activity.

CODY'S SCHEDULE	Certain	Possible	Impossible
1. shovel snow	☐	✔	☐
2. take 7:30 A.M. train	☐	☐	☐
3. 9:00 A.M. meeting	☐	☐	☐
4. meet Anna for lunch	☐	☐	☐
5. call Anna	☐	☐	☐
6. work until 8:00 P.M.	☐	☐	☐
7. dinner with Anna	☐	☐	☐
8. rent a movie	☐	☐	☐

ANNA'S SCHEDULE	Certain	Possible	Impossible
1. ride train with Cody	☐	☐	☐
2. go to library	☐	☐	☐
3. go to class	☐	☐	☐
4. lunch with Cody	☐	☐	☐
5. 6:00 P.M.—meet Cody	☐	☐	☐
6. take 6:30 train home	☐	☐	☐
7. buy takeout for dinner	☐	☐	☐
8. dinner with Cody	☐	☐	☐

2 | MAKING PLANS

Anna is graduating from college with a degree in early childhood education. Complete this paragraph from her diary. Choose the appropriate words in parentheses.

I just got the notice from my school. I _____*'m going to*_____ graduate in June, but I still don't

1. (might not / 'm going to)

have plans. Some day-care centers hire students before they graduate, so I _____

2. (could / couldn't)

apply for a job now. On the other hand, I _____ apply to a graduate school and get

3. (might / might not)

my master's degree. I'm just not sure, though—these past two years have been really hard, and

I _____ be ready to study for two more years. At least I *am* sure about my career.

4. (may / may not)

I _____ work with children—that's certain. I made an appointment to discuss my

5. ('m going to / might)

grades with my teacher, Mrs. Humphrey, tomorrow. I _____ talk about my plans

6. (maybe / may)

with her. She _____ have an idea about what I should do.

7. (won't / might)

3 | I MIGHT

*Look at Anna's schedule for Monday. She put a question mark (?) next to each item she wasn't sure about. Write sentences about Anna's plans for Monday. Use **may** or **might** (for things that are possible) and **be going to** (for things that are certain).*

MONDAY
1. call Cody at 9:00
2. buy some notebooks before class ?
3. go to the meeting with Mrs. Humphrey at 11:00
4. have coffee with Sue after class ?
5. go to work at 1:00
6. go shopping after work ?
7. take the 7:00 train ?

1. *Anna is going to call Cody at 9:00.* _____

2. _____

3. _____

4. _____

5. _____

6. _____

7. _____

4 | STORM WARNING

*For each question, write a short answer with **could** or **couldn't**. Use **be** when necessary.*

1. A: Do you think the roads will be dangerous? It's snowing really hard.

   B: _____*They could be*_____. It's a big storm.

2. A: Will the schools stay open?

   B: Oh, no. _____. It's too dangerous for school buses in a storm as bad as this one.

3. A: Will it be very windy?

   B: _____. The winds are very strong already.

4. A: Will it get very cold?

   B: _____. The temperature in Centerville is below zero.

5. A: Is it possible that the storm will be over by Monday?

   B: _____. It's moving pretty quickly now.

6. A: Do you think it will be warmer on Tuesday?

   B: _____. It has stopped snowing in Centerville already.

5 | EDITING

*Read this student's report about El Niño. There are seven mistakes in the use of **may**, **might**, and **could**. The first mistake is already corrected. Find and correct six more.*

> Every few years, the ocean near Peru becomes warmer. This change is called El Niño. An El Niño
> *may*
> ~~maybe~~ cause big weather changes all over the world. The west coasts of North and South America
> might have very heavy rains. On the other side of the Pacific, New Guinea might becomes very dry.
> Northern areas could have warmer, wetter winters, and southern areas maybe become much
> colder. These weather changes affect plants and animals. Some fish mayn't survive in warmer
> waters. They may die or swim to colder places. In addition, dry conditions could causing crops to
> die. When that happens, food may get very expensive. El Niño does not happen regularly. It may
> happen every two years, or it could not come for seven years. Will El Niños get worse in the future?
> They could be. Pollution might increase the effects of El Niño, but no one is sure yet.

Communication Practice

6 | LISTENING

🎧 *Listen to the weather forecast. Then listen again and check* **Certain** *or* **Possible** *for each forecast.*

Friday	Certain	Possible
Dry	☐	☑
Sunny	☐	☐
Low 50s	☐	☐

Saturday	Certain	Possible
Sunny	☐	☐
60°	☐	☐
Windy	☐	☐

Sunday	Certain	Possible
Cold	☐	☐
Windy	☐	☐
Snow flurries	☐	☐

7 | POSSIBILITIES

Look at these student profiles from a school newspaper. Work in a group. Talk about what these students might do in the future. Use the information in the box on the next page or your own ideas.

About Your Classmates

Name: Anna Lane
Major: Early Childhood Education
Activities: Students' Association, school newspaper
Likes: adventure, meeting new people
Dislikes: snow, boring routines
Plans: teach in a preschool
Dreams: travel around the world

Name: Nick Vanek
Major: Information Systems
Activities: Computer Club, Runners' Club
Likes: learning something new
Dislikes: crowded places
Plans: go to a four-year college
Dreams: become an inventor

FUTURE POSSIBILITIES		
Occupations	**Hobbies**	**Achievements**
• computer programmer	• dancing	• fly on space shuttle
• teacher	• skiing	• teach in Alaska
• manager, day-care center	• creative writing	• develop a computer program

Example: A: Anna is on the school newspaper. She might do creative writing as a hobby.

B: Nick hates crowded places. He couldn't work on the space shuttle.

Now write your own profile. Discuss your future possibilities with your group.

8 | WRITING

Write a paragraph about your future plans. Use **will** *and* **be going to** *for the things you are certain about. Use* **may**, **might**, *and* **could** *for the things you think are possible.*

Example: I'm going to graduate in a few months, and suddenly I'm facing a lot of choices. I might look for a job and work for a few years to get experience . . .

9 | ON THE INTERNET

 Do a search on **weather** *in your area. Write about the weather for the next two days. Include modals of future possibility.*

Example: Monday will be warm and sunny in Miami, but there might be some thunderstorms in the afternoon . . .

BEFORE YOU READ

Who is Sherlock Holmes? What kind of a story is this? Read an excerpt from a Sherlock Holmes story called "The Red-Headed League."

When Dr. Watson arrived, Sherlock Holmes was with a visitor.

"Dr. Watson, this is Mr. Jabez Wilson," said Holmes. Watson shook hands with a fat, red-haired man.

"Mr. Wilson **must write** a lot," Dr. Watson said.

Holmes smiled. "You **could be** right. But why do you think so?"

"His right shirt cuff looks very old and worn. And he has a small hole in the left elbow of his jacket. He probably rests his left elbow on the desk when he writes."

Wilson looked amazed. "Dr. Watson is correct," he told Holmes. "Your methods **may be** useful after all."

"Please tell Dr. Watson your story," said Holmes.

"I have a small shop," began the red-haired man. "I don't have many customers, so I was very interested in this advertisement. My clerk, Vincent, showed it to me." He handed Watson a piece of newspaper:

An American millionaire started the Red-Headed League to help red-headed men.
The League now has one position open. The salary is £4 per week for four hours of work every day.
The job is to copy the encyclopedia in our offices.

"They **couldn't pay** someone just for having red hair and copying the encyclopedia," Watson laughed. "This **has to be** a joke."

"It **might not be**," said Holmes. "Listen to Wilson tell the rest of his story."

"I got the job, and I worked at the League for two months. Then this morning I found a note on the door." Wilson gave Holmes the note . . .

AFTER YOU READ

Read the statements. Check **True** *or* **False**.

	True	False
1. Dr. Watson is almost certain that Mr. Wilson writes a lot.	☐	☐
2. Holmes thinks Dr. Watson is wrong about Mr. Wilson.	☐	☐
3. Mr. Wilson is certain that Holmes's methods will be useful.	☐	☐
4. Dr. Watson is sure that the newspaper job is a joke.	☐	☐
5. Holmes is sure that it isn't a joke.	☐	☐

Grammar Presentation

CONCLUSIONS: *MUST, HAVE (GOT) TO, MAY, MIGHT, COULD, CAN'T*

Affirmative Statements

Subject	Must / May / Might / Could*	Base Form of Verb	
I You He She It We You They	must may might could	be	wrong.

*Must, *may*, *might*, and *could* are modals. Modals have only one form. They do not have *-s* in the third-person singular.

Negative Statements

Subject	Must / May / Might / Could / Can	Not	Base Form of Verb	
I You He She It We You They	must may might could can	not	be	right.

Contractions

could not	=	**couldn't**
cannot OR can not	=	**can't**

Note: We usually do not contract *must not*, *may not*, and *might not* when we draw conclusions.

Affirmative Statements with *Have (got) to*

Subject	Have (got) to	Base Form	
I You We They	**have (got) to**	**be**	right.
He She It	**has (got) to**		

Yes / No Questions

Can / Could	Subject	Base Form	
Could **Can**	he	**know**	that?

Do	Subject	Base Form	
Does	he	**know**	that?

Short Answers

Subject	Modal
He	**must (not).** **may (not).** **might (not).** **could(n't).** **has (got) to.** **can't.**

Yes / No Questions with *Be*

Can / Could	Subject	Be	
Could **Can**	he	**be**	a detective?

Be	Subject	
Is	he	a detective?

Short Answers

Subject	Modal	Be
He	**must (not)** **may (not)** **might (not)** **could(n't)** **has (got) to** **can't**	**be.**

Wh- Questions with *Can* and *Could*

Wh- Word	Can / Could	Subject	Base Form
Who What	**can** **could**	it they	**be**? **want**?

GRAMMAR NOTES

EXAMPLES

---

1. We often make guesses and draw **conclusions** about present situations using the information we have.

We use **modals** to show how certain or uncertain we are about our conclusions.

100% certain

AFFIRMATIVE	NEGATIVE
must	**can't, couldn't**
have (got) to	**must not**
may	**may not**
might, could	**might not**

0% certain

---

2. When we are almost 100 percent certain, we use ***must***, ***have to***, or ***have got to*** to state **affirmative conclusions**.

USAGE NOTE: We often use ***have got to*** instead of *have to* in informal speech and writing. We usually contract *have* or *has*.

FACT	CONCLUSION
Wilson has only one clerk.	• His shop **must be** quite small.
Wilson applied for a job.	• He **has to need** money.
They pay men for having red hair.	• It**'s got to be** a joke.

Pronunciation Note

In informal speech, ***have to*** is usually pronounced "hafta" and ***got to*** is usually pronounced "gotta." Do not write "hafta" or "gotta."

---

3. When we are less certain about our conclusion, we use ***may***, ***might***, or ***could*** to express that something is **possible**.

FACT	CONCLUSION
Wilson has a hole in his sleeve.	• He **may write** a lot.
Watson knows a lot about medicine.	• He **might be** a doctor.
Vincent knows a lot about cameras.	• He **could be** a photographer.

---

4. To express **negative conclusions**, use the following modals:

- Use ***can't*** and ***couldn't*** when you are almost 100 percent certain that something is **impossible**.

- Use ***must not*** when you are slightly less certain.

- Use ***may not*** and ***might not*** when you are even less certain.

▶ **BE CAREFUL!** Do not use *have to* and *have got to* to draw negative conclusions.

- He **can't be** dead! I just saw him!
- Vincent **couldn't be** dishonest! I trust him completely!

- He **must not have** enough money. He never buys new clothes.

- He **may not know** about the plan. His boss doesn't tell him everything.

- It **can't be** true! NOT It ~~doesn't have to be~~ true!

(continued)

5. Use *can* and *could* in **questions**.	• Someone's coming. Who **can** it **be**? • **Could** Vincent **be** in the shop?

6. In **short answers**, use a <u>modal alone</u>.	**A:** Does she still work at Wilson's? **B:** She **may not**. I saw a new clerk there.
▶ **BE CAREFUL!** Use *be* in short answers to questions that include *be*.	**A:** *Is* Ron still with City Bank? **B:** I'm not sure. He **might not** *be*.

Reference Notes

May, *can*, and *could* are also used to express **permission** (see Unit 12).
Must, *have to*, and *have got to* are also used to express **necessity** (see Unit 34).
May, *might*, and *could* are also used to express **future possibility** (see Unit 36).
For a list of **modals and their functions**, see Appendix 19 on page A-8.

Focused Practice

1 | DISCOVER THE GRAMMAR

 Read the next part of "The Red-Headed League." Underline the phrases that draw conclusions.

Sherlock Holmes studied the note: *The Red-Headed League does not exist anymore.*
"This <u>could be serious</u>," Holmes told Wilson. "What can you tell us about your clerk Vincent?"

"Vincent couldn't be dishonest," replied Wilson. "In fact, he took this job for half-pay because he wanted to learn the business. His only fault is photography."

"Photography?" Holmes and Watson asked together.

"Yes," replied Wilson. "He's always running down to the basement to work with his cameras."

Wilson left soon after that.

"Wilson's clerk might be the key to this mystery," Holmes told Watson. "Let's go see him." An hour later, Holmes and Watson walked into Wilson's shop. The clerk was a man of about 30, with a scar on his forehead. Holmes asked him for directions. Then he and Watson left the shop.

"My dear Watson," Holmes began. "It's very unusual for a 30-year-old man to work for half-pay. This clerk has to have a very special reason for working here."

"Something to do with the Red-Headed League?" Watson asked.

"Yes. Perhaps the clerk placed that ad in the newspaper. He may want to be alone in the shop. Did you look at his legs?"

"No, I didn't."

"He has holes in his trouser knees. He must spend his time digging a tunnel from Wilson's basement. But where is it?"

Holmes hit the ground sharply with his walking stick. "The ground isn't hollow, so the tunnel must not be here in front of the shop. Let's walk to the street in back of Wilson's shop."

Read the second part of the story again. What does Holmes believe about each of the following statements? Check **Possible** *or* **Almost Certain** *for each statement.*

	Possible	**Almost Certain**
1. Something serious is happening.	✓	☐
2. The clerk is the key to the mystery.	☐	☐
3. The clerk has a special reason for working in Wilson's shop.	☐	☐
4. He wants to be alone in the shop.	☐	☐
5. He's digging a tunnel from Wilson's basement.	☐	☐
6. The tunnel isn't in front of the shop.	☐	☐

2 | PICTURE THIS   *Grammar Notes 1–4*

Look at the picture. Think about it in connection to the story, "The Red-Headed League." Draw conclusions and circle the appropriate words.

1. It (must) / could be nighttime.

2. Number 27 might / can't be a bank.

3. The delivery couldn't / might be for the bank.

4. The box could / must not contain gold.

5. The two men on the sidewalk must not / could notice the delivery.

6. The manager might not / must want people to know about this delivery.

7. He couldn't / may worry about robbers.

3 | DRAWING CONCLUSIONS

Grammar Notes 1, 2, 4

*Look at the poster and the map of Wilson's neighborhood. Use the evidence and the words in parentheses to write sentences with **must** and **must not**.*

1. Wilson's clerk is the man on the poster.

   He must be a criminal.
   (He / be a criminal)

2. The man on the poster is named John Clay.

   _____
   (Vincent / be the clerk's real name)

3. Mr. Wilson trusts Vincent.

   _____
   (He / know about the poster)

4. John Clay has committed a lot of crimes, but the police haven't caught him.

   _____
   (He / be very clever)

5. The address of the bank on the map and the address in the picture for Exercise 2 are the same.

   _____
   (Number 27 Carlisle Street / be City Bank)

6. The hat shop and the drugstore don't make much money.

   _____
   (Vincent's tunnel / lead to those shops)

7. There's a lot of money in the bank, and it's very close to Wilson's shop.

   _____
   (Vincent's tunnel / lead to the bank)

8. The bank is expecting a shipment of gold.

   _____
   (The tunnel / be almost finished)

4 | IT'S GOT TO BE

Ann and Marie are buying hats in the shop on Carlisle Street. Read the conversation and rewrite the underlined sentences another way. Use **have got to** *or* **can't** *and the word in parentheses.*

ANN: Look at this hat, Marie. What do you think?

MARIE: Oh, come on. <u>That's got to be a joke.</u>

You can't be serious.
_____
1. (serious)

Anyway, it's much too expensive. Look at the price tag.

ANN: It's $100! <u>That can't be right.</u>

_____
2. (wrong)

MARIE: I know. <u>It can't cost more than $50.</u>

_____
3. (less)

Anyway, let's talk about it over lunch. I'm getting hungry.

ANN: It's too early for lunch. <u>It has to be before 11:00.</u>

_____
4. (after)

MARIE: Look at my watch. It's already 12:30.

ANN: Then let's go to Café Au Lait. It's on Jones Street. <u>It can't be far.</u>

_____
5. (nearby)

MARIE: Let's go home after lunch. I don't feel well.

ANN: Oh, come on. <u>You're fine.</u> You must be hungry.

_____
6. (sick)

5 | BEST GUESSES

Write a short answer to each question. Use **might (not)** *or* **must (not)** *and include* **be** *where necessary.*

A: You sound terrible. Are you sick?

B: I _____*must be*_____. I have a headache and my throat is starting to hurt.
     1.

A: This bottle is empty. Are we all out of cough syrup?

B: We _____. I think that was the last bottle.
   2.

(continued)

A: I'll go get you some cough medicine. Does that nighttime cough medicine work?

B: It _____ . It's worth a try.
3.

A: I forgot to cash a check today. Do you have any money?

B: I _____ . Look in my wallet. It's on the table downstairs.
4.

A: I found it. It's 9:30. Is Drake Drugstore still open?

B: It _____ . Their advertisement says "Open 'til 11."
5.

A: Do you think they sell chicken soup? Some drugstores carry food.

B: They _____ . It's a very small store.
6.

A: What about Quickshop? Do they have soup?

B: They _____ . They've got everything.
7.

6 | MAYBE IT'S THE CAT   *Grammar Notes 3–6*

🎧 *Mr. and Mrs. Wilson are trying to get to sleep. Write questions and answers with* **could be, couldn't be,** *or* **can't be**. *Choose between affirmative and negative forms.*

MRS. WILSON: Shh! I hear someone at the door. It's 9:30.

Who _____*could*_____ it _____*be*_____ ?
1.

MR. WILSON: It _____ a late customer.
2.

MRS. WILSON: No, it _____ . It's much too late. Maybe it's the cat.
3.

MR. WILSON: It _____ . I put the cat out before we went to bed.
4.

MRS. WILSON: _____ it _____ Vincent? He's always down in the
5.

basement with his camera.

MR. WILSON: No, Vincent went out an hour ago. He _____ back this early.
6.

Wait a minute. It _____ Holmes and Dr. Watson. They said they
7.

wanted to talk to me.

MRS. WILSON: _____ they really _____ here so late?
8.

MR. WILSON: No. You're right. It _____ them.
9.

MRS. WILSON: What _____ it _____ then?
10.

MR. WILSON: That door rattles whenever the wind blows. It _____ the wind.
11.

MRS. WILSON: That must be it. Let's go to sleep.

7 | **EDITING**

Read this student's reading journal for a mystery novel. There are six mistakes in the use of **must**, **have (got) to**, **may**, **might**, **could**, *and* **can't**. *The first mistake is already corrected. Find and correct five more.*

> The main character, Molly Smith, is a college ESL teacher. She is trying to find her dead grandparents' first home in the United States. It may ~~being~~ be in a nearby town. The townspeople there seem scared. They could be have a secret, or they must just hate strangers. Molly has some old letters that might lead her to the place. They are in Armenian, but one of her students mights translate them for her. They hafta be important because the author mentions them right away. The letters must contain family secrets. I'm sure of it. Who is the bad guy? It couldn't be the student because he wants to help. It might to be the newspaper editor in the town.

Communication Practice

8 | **LISTENING**

🎧 *Holmes, Dr. Watson, and a police captain meet in front of City Bank. Listen to their conversation. Then listen again and check* **Possible** *or* **Almost Certain** *for each statement.*

	Possible	Almost Certain
1. It's 10:00.	☐	✔
2. They have a long wait.	☐	☐
3. John Clay knows about the gold.	☐	☐
4. Clay's tunnel is finished.	☐	☐
5. The tunnel is under the bank floor.	☐	☐
6. John Clay is dangerous.	☐	☐
7. Clay is waiting for Wilson to go to sleep.	☐	☐
8. There's someone in the tunnel.	☐	☐
9. The man is John Clay.	☐	☐

9 | TELL-TALE SIGNS

Look at the pictures of Sandra Diaz and some things that she and her family own.
Make guesses about the Diaz family. Give reasons for your guesses.

Example: A: Sandra might be a construction worker. She's wearing a hard hat.
B: Or she could be an architect.

10 | POSSIBLE EXPLANATIONS

Read the following situations. In pairs, discuss possible explanations for each situation.
Then come to a conclusion. Discuss your explanations with the rest of the class. Use your
imagination!

1. You've been calling your sister on the phone for three days. No one has answered.

Example: A: She might be at the library. She always studies hard for her exams.
B: I don't think so. She's already finished her exams.
A: You could have the wrong number.
B: This is the number I always call. I think she's been on vacation this week.
A: Then she must be away.

2. You are on the street. You have asked a woman three times for the time. She hasn't answered.

3. You go to dinner with a good friend. Your friend hardly says a word all evening.

4. You went on a picnic in the park. You ate strawberries and cheese. Now you are sneezing and your eyes are watering.

5. You're at a party, and no one is talking to you.

11 | WRITING

Agatha James, the mystery writer, starts a new novel by writing story outlines about each one of her characters. Read about the murder suspect's activities on the day of the crime.

MARCH 1	MURDER SUSPECT'S ACTIVITIES
7:00-8:00	gym-aerobics class—<u>talks</u> to exercise instructor!
9:30	calls Dr. Lorenzo
11:00-1:00	hairdresser—changes hair color
1:30	pharmacy—picks up prescription
2:00	bank—withdraws #10,000
3:00	Mr. Jordan
4:30	calls travel agency—vegetarian meal?

Work in small groups to speculate about the story and the characters. Consider questions like these:

- Is the murder suspect a man or a woman?
- Who is Dr. Lorenzo?
- Who is Mr. Jordan? What is his relationship with the suspect?
- Why does the suspect need $10,000?

Example: **A:** The suspect must be a woman. She's going to the hairdresser.
              B: It could be a man. Men go to hairdressers too.

Now write possibilities and conclusions about the story and the characters.

12 | ON THE INTERNET

🕑 *Do a search on* **mystery pictures**. *Print out one picture. Then work in a group. Show your picture and discuss what it might be with your classmates. Do the same with your classmates' pictures.*

Example: **A:** It could be part of a plant.
              B: I don't think so. It must be from outer space.

From **Grammar** to **Writing**
Combining Sentences with because, although, even though

You can combine two sentences with *because*, *although*, and *even though*. In the new sentence, the clause that begins with *because*, *although*, or *even though* is the dependent clause. The other clause is the main clause.

Example: It was my mistake. I think the cashier was rude. ⟶

           dependent clause   main clause

           Even though it was my mistake, I think the cashier was rude.

The dependent clause can come first or second. When it comes first, a comma separates the two clauses.

1 Circle the correct words to complete this business letter. Underline the main clauses once and the dependent clauses twice.

---

                                                 23 Creek Road
                                                 Provo, UT 84001
                                                 September 10, 2005

Customer Service Representative
Hardly's Restaurant
12345 Beafy Court
Provo, UT 84004

Dear Customer Service Representative:

     I am writing this letter of complaint although / (because) one of your cashiers treated me rudely.

Because / Even though I was sure I paid her with a $20 bill, I only received change for $10. I told her

that there was a mistake. She said, "You're wrong." Later the manager called. He said the cashier was

right although / because the money in the cash drawer was correct.

     Because / Even though the mistake was mine, I believe the cashier behaved extremely rudely.

Although / Because I like Hardly's, I also value polite service. I hope I won't have to change restaurants

although / because I can't get it there.

Sincerely,

Ken Nelson
Ken Nelson

---

2 | *Look at the letter in Exercise 1. Circle the correct words in the sentences below to complete these rules about dependent clauses and business letters.*

1. Use *because* to give a reason / contrasting idea.

2. Use *although* or *even though* to give a reason / contrasting idea.

3. When you begin a sentence with a dependent clause, use a colon / comma after it.

4. When a sentence has a dependent clause, it must also / doesn't have to have a main clause.

5. When a sentence has a main clause, it must also / doesn't have to have a dependent clause.

6. In a business letter, the sender's / receiver's address comes first.

7. The date comes before / after the receiver's address.

8. Use a colon / comma after the receiver's name.

3 | *Before you write . . .*

1. Work with a partner. Complete these complaints with dependent clauses and the correct punctuation. Use your own ideas.

   a. _____ I will not bring my car to your mechanic again.

   b. The server brought me a hamburger _____.

   c. _____ I missed my plane.

   d. My neighbor still won't turn down the TV _____.

2. Choose one of the above situations. Plan a role play about the conflict. Act out your role play for another pair of students.

3. Discuss what to write in a letter of complaint.

4 | *Write a letter of complaint. Use information from your role play in Exercise 3.*

5 | *Exchange letters with a different partner. Complete the chart.*

Did the writer _____?	Yes	No
1. use subordinate clauses correctly	☐	☐
2. use modals correctly	☐	☐
3. give enough information about the complaint	☐	☐
4. use correct business-letter form	☐	☐

6 | *Work with your partner. Discuss each other's editing questions from Exercise 5. Then rewrite your own letter and make any necessary corrections.*

I *Circle the letter of the appropriate response to each question.*

1. Are we supposed to bring a gift?
   a. Yes, we are.
   b. Yes, we were.

2. Do you think Fred has the report?
   a. Yes, he may. It's OK with me.
   b. He might. Let's ask him.

3. Will the weather improve tomorrow?
   a. It might.
   b. It might be.

4. Do you have to practice every day?
   a. Yes, I have.
   b. Yes, I do.

5. Do we have any more orange juice?
   a. We might.
   b. We might have.

6. Would you prefer to go out or stay home?
   a. Yes, I would.
   b. Let's stay home.

7. Should I turn left at the corner?
   a. You can't turn left. It says, Do Not Enter.
   b. You don't have to turn left. It says, Do Not Enter.

8. Is it going to rain?
   a. It might.
   b. It can.

9. Was I supposed to call you?
   a. No, you weren't.
   b. Yes, I was.

10. There's someone at the door. Who can it be?
    a. It can be Melissa.
    b. It could be Melissa.

11. I'd rather stay home. What about you?
    a. So had I.
    b. So would I.

12. Lena isn't here yet. Was she going to take the 7:00 train?
    a. Yes. Maybe she missed it.
    b. Yes, she is.

13. Do I have to wear a suit to the wedding?
    a. Yes, you have.
    b. Yes, you do.

14. Would you rather walk or drive?
    a. I'd rather not.
    b. I'd rather walk.

II *Read each sentence. Write its function. Use the words in the box. You will use some words more than once.*

| conclusion | expectation | future possibility | necessity | preference | prohibition |

1. She might arrive around noon. ___*future possibility*___

2. You must fill out the entire form. _____

3. I'd rather not see that movie. _____

4. He might be sick. _____

5. We're supposed to take the test on Friday. _____

6. You can't drive without a license. _____

7. Because of the cold front, the temperature could fall below freezing. _____

8. There is only one Maple Street, so this has to be the correct street. _____

9. That new restaurant is supposed to be very good. _____

10. She must be very happy about her promotion. _____

11. Please hurry. We've got to be home by 11:00. _____

12. You must not ride your bike without a helmet. _____

III *Circle the letter of the correct answer to complete each sentence.*

1. I'd rather _____ the movie. It's supposed to be good.　　　Ⓐ B C D
   - (**A**) watch
   - (**B**) to watch
   - (**C**) watching
   - (**D**) not watch

2. Take your umbrella. It _____ rain.　　　A B C D
   - (**A**) might not
   - (**B**) must
   - (**C**) 's supposed to
   - (**D**) going to

3. There are two umbrellas. This one is definitely mine, so the
   other one _____ be yours.　　　A B C D
   - (**A**) must not
   - (**B**) might not
   - (**C**) might
   - (**D**) must

4. Don't forget your sweater. The movie theater _____ be cold.　　　A B C D
   - (**A**) might
   - (**B**) has to
   - (**C**) couldn't
   - (**D**) must

5. We _____ bring a gift, but we can if we want to.　　　A B C D
   - (**A**) have to
   - (**B**) don't have to
   - (**C**) must
   - (**D**) must not

6. I _____ have dessert. I'm trying to lose some weight.　　　A B C D
   - (**A**) 'd rather
   - (**B**) 'd rather not
   - (**C**) 'd prefer
   - (**D**) 'd prefer not

7. That's a beautiful gold watch. It _____ be expensive.　　　A B C D
   - (**A**) couldn't
   - (**B**) doesn't have to
   - (**C**) must
   - (**D**) maybe

8. Hurry up. We _____ be home by 11:00.　　　A B C D
   - (**A**) have to
   - (**B**) might
   - (**C**) must not
   - (**D**) prefer

9. We _____ be late, or we'll get into trouble.　　　A B C D
   - (**A**) don't have to
   - (**B**) can't
   - (**C**) couldn't
   - (**D**) might

10. We _____ to drive, but we took the train instead.　　　A B C D
   - (**A**) were going
   - (**B**) are going
   - (**C**) might
   - (**D**) 've got to

IV | *Write a sentence about each situation. Use the negative or affirmative form of the modal and the words in parentheses.*

1. John gets headaches. At school, he can't see the board unless he sits in the front row.

   He might need glasses.
   _____
   (might / need glasses)

2. Your sister won't go see *Visitor from Another Planet* with you, and she turns off the TV when *Star Ship* starts.

   _____
   (prefer / watch science fiction)

3. Carmen is looking at some jewelry. It's beautiful and it's made of gold.

   _____
   (must / be expensive)

4. In Thai culture it's impolite to open a gift in front of the giver. Somchai felt embarrassed when Linda opened his birthday gift.

   _____
   (be supposed to / open it in front of him)

5. You've called your friend at work several times today. He doesn't answer, and he hasn't returned your messages.

   _____
   (must / be at work today)

6. You've invited some friends to dinner, and you've served curry. Everyone except Sue has had two servings. Sue hasn't even finished the first one.

   _____
   (might / like curry)

7. In the United States, international travelers must arrive at the airport three hours before their flight. Your flight from New York to Los Angeles leaves at 3:00 P.M.

   _____
   (have to / arrive at the airport by noon)

8. Marc invited his sister to his graduation. She accepted the invitation, but she got sick, so she didn't go.

   _____
   (be going to / go to his graduation)

9. Carl has just left for a trip to Hong Kong. You've seen him off at the airport. A few minutes after you get home, the doorbell rings.

   _____
   (could / be Carl)

10. You just bought a painting for $10 at a garage sale. Your friend Tim thinks it looks a lot like a Picasso. First you laughed, but then you looked at some art books.

   _____
   (could / be very valuable)

V *Read this journal entry. There are eight mistakes in the use of modals and similar expressions. The first mistake is already corrected. Find and correct seven more.*

Thursday
     I'm

+ supposed to take my road test tomorrow. I'm a little nervous because I heard that there might be a storm. I'd not rather drive in the rain! My instructor, John, is supposed to pick me up at 8:00 and drive me to the test area. Then he have to wait for me while I take the test. He doesn't have to be in the car with me during the test-it's not allowed. I like John. I don't know much about him. He says he's been driving for more than 40 years, so I guess he got to be at least 60. He maybe even older than that.

     Well, it's getting late, and I should go to bed. I'd rather watching some TV, but I hafta get up early tomorrow.

▶ *To check your answers, go to the Answer Key on page RT-5.*

APPENDICES

1 | Irregular Verbs

Base Form	Simple Past	Past Participle	Base Form	Simple Past	Past Participle
arise	arose	arisen	give	gave	given
awake	awoke	awoken	go	went	gone
be	was/were	been	grind	ground	ground
beat	beat	beaten/beat	grow	grew	grown
become	became	become	hang	hung	hung
begin	began	begun	have	had	had
bend	bent	bent	hear	heard	heard
bet	bet	bet	hide	hid	hidden
bite	bit	bitten	hit	hit	hit
bleed	bled	bled	hold	held	held
blow	blew	blown	hurt	hurt	hurt
break	broke	broken	keep	kept	kept
bring	brought	brought	kneel	knelt/kneeled	knelt/kneeled
build	built	built	knit	knit/knitted	knit/knitted
burn	burned/burnt	burned/burnt	know	knew	known
burst	burst	burst	lay	laid	laid
buy	bought	bought	lead	led	led
catch	caught	caught	leap	leaped/leapt	leaped/leapt
choose	chose	chosen	leave	left	left
cling	clung	clung	lend	lent	lent
come	came	come	let	let	let
cost	cost	cost	lie *(lie down)*	lay	lain
creep	crept	crept	light	lit/lighted	lit/lighted
cut	cut	cut	lose	lost	lost
deal	dealt	dealt	make	made	made
dig	dug	dug	mean	meant	meant
dive	dived/dove	dived	meet	met	met
do	did	done	pay	paid	paid
draw	drew	drawn	prove	proved	proved/proven
dream	dreamed/dreamt	dreamed/dreamt	put	put	put
drink	drank	drunk	quit	quit	quit
drive	drove	driven	read /rid/	read /rɛd/	read /rɛd/
eat	ate	eaten	ride	rode	ridden
fall	fell	fallen	ring	rang	rung
feed	fed	fed	rise	rose	risen
feel	felt	felt	run	ran	run
fight	fought	fought	say	said	said
find	found	found	see	saw	seen
fit	fit/fitted	fit	seek	sought	sought
flee	fled	fled	sell	sold	sold
fling	flung	flung	send	sent	sent
fly	flew	flown	set	set	set
forbid	forbade/forbid	forbidden	sew	sewed	sewn/sewed
forget	forgot	forgotten	shake	shook	shaken
forgive	forgave	forgiven	shave	shaved	shaved/shaven
freeze	froze	frozen	shine *(intransitive)*	shone/shined	shone/shined
get	got	gotten/got	shoot	shot	shot

(continued)

Base Form	Simple Past	Past Participle
show	showed	shown
shrink	shrank/shrunk	shrunk/shrunken
shut	shut	shut
sing	sang	sung
sink	sank/sunk	sunk
sit	sat	sat
sleep	slept	slept
slide	slid	slid
speak	spoke	spoken
speed	sped/speeded	sped/speeded
spend	spent	spent
spill	spilled/spilt	spilled/spilt
spin	spun	spun
spit	spit/spat	spat
split	split	split
spread	spread	spread
spring	sprang	sprung
stand	stood	stood
steal	stole	stolen
stick	stuck	stuck
sting	stung	stung
stink	stank/stunk	stunk

Base Form	Simple Past	Past Participle
strike	struck	struck/stricken
swear	swore	sworn
sweep	swept	swept
swim	swam	swum
swing	swung	swung
take	took	taken
teach	taught	taught
tear	tore	torn
tell	told	told
think	thought	thought
throw	threw	thrown
understand	understood	understood
upset	upset	upset
wake	woke	woken
wear	wore	worn
weave	wove/weaved	woven/weaved
weep	wept	wept
win	won	won
wind	wound	wound
withdraw	withdrew	withdrawn
wring	wrung	wrung
write	wrote	written

2 | Non-action Verbs

APPEARANCE
appear
be
look *(seem)*
represent
resemble
seem
signify

VALUE
cost
equal
weigh

EMOTIONS
admire
adore
appreciate
care
detest
dislike
doubt
envy
fear
hate
like
love
miss
regret
respect
trust

MENTAL STATES
agree
assume
believe
consider
disagree
disbelieve
estimate
expect
feel *(believe)*
find *(believe)*
guess
hesitate
hope
imagine
know
mean
mind
presume
realize
recognize
remember
see *(understand)*
suppose
suspect
think *(believe)*
understand
wonder

POSSESSION AND RELATIONSHIP
belong
contain
have
own
possess

SENSES AND PERCEPTIONS
feel
hear
notice
observe
perceive
see
smell
sound
taste

WANTS AND PREFERENCES
desire
hope
need
prefer
want
wish

3 | Verbs and Expressions Used Reflexively

allow yourself
amuse yourself
ask yourself
avail yourself of
be hard on yourself
be yourself
be pleased with yourself
be proud of yourself

behave yourself
believe in yourself
blame yourself
cut yourself
deprive yourself of
dry yourself
enjoy yourself
feel sorry for yourself

forgive yourself
help yourself
hurt yourself
imagine yourself
introduce yourself
kill yourself
look at yourself
prepare yourself

pride yourself on
push yourself
remind yourself
see yourself
take care of yourself
talk to yourself
teach yourself
tell yourself

(s.o. = someone   s.t. = something)

PHRASAL VERB	MEANING
ask s.o. **over**	invite to one's home
blow s.t. **out**	stop burning by blowing air on it
blow s.t. **up**	make explode
bring s.o. or s.t. **back**	return
bring s.o. **up**	raise (a child)
bring s.t. **up**	bring attention to
burn s.t. **down**	burn completely
call s.o. **back**	return a phone call
call s.t. **off**	cancel
call s.o. **up**	contact by phone
carry s.t. **out**	complete (a plan)
clean s.o. or s.t. **up**	clean completely
clear s.t. **up**	explain
close s.t. **down**	close by force
cover s.o. or s.t. **up**	cover completely
cross s.t. **out**	draw a line through
do s.t. **over**	do again
drink s.t. **up**	drink completely
drop s.o. or s.t. **off**	take someplace in a car and leave there
empty s.t. **out**	empty completely
figure s.o. **out**	understand (the behavior)
figure s.t. **out**	solve, understand after thinking about it
fill s.t. **in**	complete with information
fill s.t. **out**	complete (a form)
find s.t. **out**	learn information
give s.t. **back**	return
give s.t. **up**	quit, abandon
hand s.t. **in**	give work (to a boss/teacher), submit
hand s.t. **out**	distribute
hand s.t. **over**	give
help s.o. **out**	assist
keep s.o. or s.t. **away**	cause to stay at a distance
keep s.t. **on**	not remove (a piece of clothing/ jewelry)
keep s.o. or s.t. **out**	not allow to enter
lay s.o. **off**	end employment
leave s.t. **on**	1. not turn off (a light/radio) 2. not remove (a piece of clothing/ jewelry)
leave s.t. **out**	not include, omit
let s.o. **down**	disappoint
let s.o. or s.t. **in**	allow to enter
let s.o. **off**	allow to leave (from a bus/car)
light s.t. **up**	illuminate
look s.o. or s.t. **over**	examine
look s.t. **up**	try to find (in a book/on the Internet)

PHRASAL VERB	MEANING
make s.t. **up**	create
pass s.t. **on**	give to
pass s.t. **out**	distribute
pass s.o. or s.t. **over**	decide not to use
pass s.o. or s.t. **up**	decide not to use, reject
pay s.o. or s.t. **back**	repay
pick s.o. or s.t. **out**	choose
pick s.o. or s.t. **up**	1. lift 2. go get someone or something
pick s.t. **up**	1. get (an idea/a new book) 2. answer the phone
point s.o. or s.t. **out**	indicate
put s.t. **away**	put in an appropriate place
put s.t. **back**	return to its original place
put s.o. or s.t. **down**	stop holding
put s.t. **off**	delay
put s.t. **on**	cover the body (with clothes/lotion)
put s.t. **together**	assemble
put s.t. **up**	erect
set s.t. **up**	1. prepare for use 2. establish (a business)
shut s.t. **off**	stop (a machine/light)
straighten s.t. **up**	make neat
switch s.t. **on**	start (a machine/light)
take s.o. or s.t. **back**	return
take s.t. **off**	remove
talk s.o. **into**	persuade
talk s.t. **over**	discuss
tear s.t. **down**	destroy
tear s.t. **off**	remove by tearing
tear s.t. **up**	tear into small pieces
think s.t. **over**	consider
think s.t. **up**	invent
throw s.t. **away/out**	put in the trash, discard
try s.t. **on**	put clothing on to see if it fits
try s.t. **out**	use to see if it works
turn s.o. or s.t. **down**	reject
turn s.t. **down**	lower the volume (a TV/radio)
turn s.t. **in**	give work (to a boss/teacher), submit
turn s.o. or s.t. **into**	change from one form to another
turn s.o. **off**	[slang] destroy interest in
turn s.t. **off**	stop (a machine/light), extinguish
turn s.t. **on**	start (a machine/light)
turn s.t. **up**	make louder (a TV/radio)
use s.t. **up**	use completely, consume
wake s.o. **up**	awaken
work s.t. **out**	solve, find a solution to a problem
write s.t. **down**	write on a piece of paper
write s.t. **up**	write in a finished form

Intransitive Phrasal Verbs

Phrasal Verb	Meaning
blow up	explode
break down	stop working (a machine)
burn down	burn completely
call back	return a phone call
clear up	become clear
close down	stop operating
come about	happen
come along	come with, accompany
come back	return
come in	enter
come off	become unattached
come out	appear
come up	arise
dress up	wear special clothes
drop in	visit by surprise
drop out	quit
eat out	eat in a restaurant
empty out	empty completely
find out	learn information

Phrasal Verb	Meaning
follow through	complete
fool around	act playful
get ahead	make progress, succeed
get along	have a good relationship
get back	return
get by	survive
get through	finish
get together	meet
get up	get out of bed
give up	quit
go on	continue
grow up	become an adult
hang up	end a phone call
keep away	stay at a distance
keep on	continue
keep out	not enter
keep up	go as fast
lie down	recline
light up	illuminate

Phrasal Verb	Meaning
look out	be careful
make up	end a disagreement, reconcile
play around	have fun
run out	not have enough
set out	begin a project
show up	appear
sign up	register
sit down	take a seat
slip up	make a mistake
stand up	rise
start over	start again
stay up	remain awake
straighten up	make neat
take off	depart (a plane)
turn up	appear
wake up	stop sleeping
watch out	be careful
work out	1. be resolved 2. exercise

 Irregular Plural Nouns

Singular	Plural
half	halves
knife	knives
leaf	leaves
life	lives
loaf	loaves
shelf	shelves
wife	wives

Singular	Plural
man	men
woman	women
child	children
foot	feet
tooth	teeth
goose	geese
mouse	mice

Singular	Plural
deer	deer
fish	fish
sheep	sheep
person	people

7 | Non-count Nouns

Remember: Non-count nouns are singular.

Activities	Food		Ideas and Feelings	Liquids and Gases	School Subjects	Very Small Things
baseball	bread	ice cream	anger	air	art	dust
biking	butter	lettuce	beauty	gasoline	English	pepper
football	cake	meat	fear	milk	math	rice
golf	cheese	pasta	freedom	oil	music	salt
hiking	chicken	pizza	friendship	oxygen	photography	sand
running	chocolate	salad	happiness	water	science	sugar
sailing	coffee	soup	hate			
soccer	cream	spaghetti	hope	**Materials**		**Weather**
swimming	fat	tea	loneliness	cotton		fog
tennis	fish	yogurt	love	glass		ice
				gold		rain
				leather		snow
				paper		wind
				wood		
				wool		

NAMES OF CATEGORIES

equipment	(BUT: computers, phones, TVs . . .)
food	(BUT: bananas, eggs, vegetables . . .)
furniture	(BUT: beds, chairs, lamps, tables . . .)
homework	(BUT: assignments, pages, problems . . .)
jewelry	(BUT: bracelets, earrings, necklaces . . .)
mail	(BUT: letters, packages, postcards . . .)
money	(BUT: dinars, dollars, euros, pounds . . .)
work	(BUT: jobs, projects, tasks . . .)

OTHER

(Some non-count nouns don't fit into any list. You must memorize these non-count nouns.)

advice
garbage/trash
information
traffic
news

 8 | ## Proper Nouns

REMEMBER: Write proper nouns with a capital letter.

PEOPLE

• first names	Anne, Eduardo, Mehmet, Olga, Shao-fen
• family names	Chen, García, Haddad, Smith
• titles	Doctor, Grandma, Professor
• title + names	Mr. García, Professor Smith, Uncle Steve

PLACES

• continents	Africa, Asia, Australia, Europe, South America
• countries	Argentina, China, France, Nigeria, Turkey, the United States
• provinces/states	Brittany, Ontario, Szechwan, Texas
• cities	Beijing, Istanbul, Rio de Janeiro, Toronto
• streets	Adalbertstrasse, the Champs-Elysées, Fifth Avenue
• structures	Harrods, the Louvre, the Petronas Towers, the Golden Gate Bridge
• schools	Midwood High School, Oxford University
• parks	Central Park, the Tivoli Gardens
• mountains	the Andes, the Himalayas, the Pyrenees, the Rocky Mountains
• oceans	the Arctic, the Atlantic, the Indian Ocean, the Pacific
• rivers	the Amazon, the Ganges, the Seine
• lakes	Baikal, Erie, Tanganyika, Titicaca
• deserts	the Gobi, the Kalahari, the Sahara

LANGUAGES
Arabic, Chinese, Portuguese, Russian, Spanish

NATIONALITIES
Brazilian, Japanese, Mexican, Saudi, Turkish

RELIGIONS
Buddhism, Christianity, Hinduism, Islam, Judaism

COURSES
Introduction to Computer Sciences, Math 201

PRODUCT BRANDS
Adidas, Dell, Kleenex, Mercedes, Samsung

TIME

• months	January, March, December
• days	Monday, Wednesday, Saturday
• holidays	Bastille Day, Buddha Day, Christmas, Hanukah, New Year's Day, Ramadan

9 | ## Adjectives That Form the Comparative and Superlative in Two Ways

ADJECTIVE	COMPARATIVE	SUPERLATIVE
cruel	crueler/more cruel	cruelest/most cruel
deadly	deadlier/more deadly	deadliest/most deadly
friendly	friendlier/more friendly	friendliest/most friendly
handsome	handsomer/more handsome	handsomest/most handsome
happy	happier/more happy	happiest/most happy
likely	likelier/more likely	likeliest/most likely
lively	livelier/more lively	liveliest/most lively
lonely	lonelier/more lonely	loneliest/most lonely
lovely	lovelier/more lovely	loveliest/most lovely
narrow	narrower/more narrow	narrowest/most narrow
pleasant	pleasanter/more pleasant	pleasantest/most pleasant
polite	politer/more polite	politest/most polite
quiet	quieter/more quiet	quietest/most quiet
shallow	shallower/more shallow	shallowest/most shallow
sincere	sincerer/more sincere	sincerest/most sincere
stupid	stupider/more stupid	stupidest/most stupid
true	truer/more true	truest/most true

10 | Irregular Comparisons of Adjectives, Adverbs, and Quantifiers

ADJECTIVE	ADVERB	COMPARATIVE	SUPERLATIVE
bad	badly	worse	the worst
far	far	farther/further	the farthest/furthest
good	well	better	the best
little	little	less	the least
many/a lot of	—	more	the most
much*/a lot of	much*/a lot	more	the most

*Much is usually only used in questions and negative statements.

11 | Participial Adjectives

-ed	-ing	-ed	-ing	-ed	-ing
alarmed	alarming	disturbed	disturbing	moved	moving
amazed	amazing	embarrassed	embarrassing	paralyzed	paralyzing
amused	amusing	entertained	entertaining	pleased	pleasing
annoyed	annoying	excited	exciting	relaxed	relaxing
astonished	astonishing	exhausted	exhausting	satisfied	satisfying
bored	boring	fascinated	fascinating	shocked	shocking
charmed	charming	frightened	frightening	surprised	surprising
confused	confusing	horrified	horrifying	terrified	terrifying
depressed	depressing	inspired	inspiring	tired	tiring
disappointed	disappointing	interested	interesting	touched	touching
disgusted	disgusting	irritated	irritating	troubled	troubling

12 | Order of Adjectives before a Noun

REMEMBER: We do not usually use more than three adjectives before a noun.

1. Order of Adjectives from Different Categories

Adjectives from different categories usually go in the following order. Do not use a comma between these adjectives.

Opinion	Size*	Age	Shape	Color	Origin	Material	Nouns used as Adjectives	
beautiful	enormous	antique	flat	blue	Asian	cotton	college	
comfortable	huge	modern	oval	gray	European	gold	flower	
cozy	little	new	rectangular	green	Greek	plastic	kitchen	+ NOUN
easy	tall	old	round	purple	Pacific	stone	mountain	
expensive	tiny	young	square	red	Southern	wooden	vacation	

*EXCEPTION: Big and small usually go first in a series of adjectives: a **small** comfortable apartment

EXAMPLES: I bought an **antique Greek flower** vase.   NOT a ~~Greek antique~~ flower vase
She took some **easy college** courses.   NOT some ~~college easy~~ courses
We sat at an **enormous round wooden** table.   NOT a ~~wooden enormous~~ round table

2. Order of Adjectives from the Same Category

Adjectives from the same category do not follow a specific order. Use a comma between these adjectives.

EXAMPLES: We rented a **beautiful, comfortable, cozy** apartment. OR
We rented a **cozy, comfortable, beautiful** apartment. OR
We rented a **comfortable, cozy, beautiful** apartment.

13 | Verbs Followed by the Gerund (Base Form of Verb + -ing)

acknowledge	celebrate	dislike	forgive	miss	recommend	support
admit	consider	endure	give up (stop)	postpone	regret	tolerate
advise	delay	enjoy	imagine	practice	report	understand
appreciate	deny	escape	justify	prevent	resent	
avoid	detest	explain	keep (continue)	prohibit	resist	
can't help	discontinue	feel like	mention	quit	risk	
can't stand	discuss	finish	mind (object to)	recall	suggest	

14 | Verbs Followed by the Infinitive (To + Base Form of Verb)

agree	can't wait	fail	learn	pay	refuse	wait
appear	choose	help	manage	plan	request	want
arrange	consent	hesitate	mean (intend)	prepare	rush	wish
ask	decide	hope	need	pretend	seem	would like
attempt	deserve	hurry	neglect	promise	volunteer	
can't afford	expect	intend	offer			

15 | Verbs Followed by the Gerund or the Infinitive

begin	continue	hate	love	remember*	stop*
can't stand	forget*	like	prefer	start	try

*These verbs can be followed by either the gerund or the infinitive, but there is a big difference in meaning (see Unit 32).

16 | Verbs Followed by Object + Infinitive

advise	convince	get	need*	persuade	require	want*
allow	encourage	help*	order	promise*	teach	warn
ask*	expect*	hire	pay*	remind	tell	wish
cause	forbid	invite	permit	request	urge	would like*
choose*	force					

*These verbs can also be followed by an infinitive without an object (example: ask to leave or ask someone to leave).

17 | Adjective + Preposition Combinations

accustomed to	bad at	different from	interested in	safe from	surprised
afraid of	bored with/by	excited about	nervous about	satisfied with	at/about/by
amazed at/by	capable of	famous for	opposed to	shocked at/by	terrible at
angry at	careful of	fond of	pleased about	sick of	tired of
ashamed of	concerned about	glad about	ready for	slow at/in	used to
aware of	content with	good at	responsible for	sorry for/about	worried about
awful at	curious about	happy about	sad about		

18 | Verb + Preposition Combinations

admit to
advise against
apologize for
approve of

believe in
choose between
complain about
count on

deal with
dream about/of
feel like
insist on

look forward to
object to
pay for
plan on

rely on
resort to
succeed in
talk about

thank someone for
think about
wonder about

19 | Modals and Their Functions

FUNCTION	MODAL OR EXPRESSION	TIME	EXAMPLES
Ability	can can't	Present	• Sam **can swim**. • He **can't skate**.
	could couldn't	Past	• We **could swim** last year. • We **couldn't skate**.
	be able to* not be able to*	All verb forms	• Lea **is able to run** fast. • She **wasn't able to run** fast last year.
Permission	can	Present or Future	• **Can** I **sit** here? • **Can** I **call** tomorrow? • Yes, you **can**.
	can't		• No, you **can't**. Sorry.
	could		• **Could** he **leave** now?
	may		• **May** I **borrow** your pen? • Yes, you **may**.
	may not		• No, you **may not**. Sorry.
Requests	can	Present or Future	• **Can** you **close** the door, please? • Sure, I **can**.
	can't		• Sorry, I **can't**.
	could		• **Could** you please **answer** the phone?
	will		• **Will** you **wash** the dishes, please?
	would		• **Would** you please **mail** this letter?
Advice	should	Present or Future	• You **should study** more.
	shouldn't		• You **shouldn't miss** class.
	ought to**		• We **ought to leave**.
	had better**		• We**'d better go**.
	had better not**		• We**'d better not stay**.
Necessity	have to*	All verb forms	• He **has to go** now. • I **had to go** yesterday. • I **will have to go** soon.
	not have to*		• He **doesn't have to go** yet.
	have got to*	Present or Future	• He**'s got to leave**!
	must		• You **must use** a pen for the test.
Prohibition	must not	Present or Future	• You **must not drive** without a license.
	can't		• You **can't drive** without a license.

*The meaning of this expression is similar to the meaning of a modal. Unlike a modal, it has -s for third-person singular.
**The meaning of this expression is similar to the meaning of a modal. Like a modal, it has no -s for third-person singular.

FUNCTION	MODAL OR EXPRESSION	TIME	EXAMPLES
Possibility	must must not have to* have got to*	Present	• This **must be** her house. Her name is on the door. • She **must not be** home. I don't see her car. • She **has to know** him. They went to school together. • He's **got to be** guilty. We saw him do it.
	may may not might might not could	Present or Future	• She **may be** home now. • It **may not rain** tomorrow. • Lee **might be sick** today. • He **might not come** to class. • They **could be** at the library. • It **could rain** tomorrow.
Impossibility	can't couldn't	Present or Future	• That **can't be** Ana. She left for France yesterday. • It **can't snow** tomorrow. It's going to be too warm. • He **couldn't be** guilty. He wasn't in town when the crime occurred. • The teacher **couldn't give** the test tomorrow. Tomorrow's Saturday.

*The meaning of this expression is similar to the meaning of a modal. Unlike a modal, it has -s for third-person singular.

20 Spelling Rules for the Simple Present: Third-Person Singular (he, she, it)

1. Add -s for most verbs.

work	work**s**
buy	buy**s**
ride	ride**s**
return	return**s**

2. Add -es for verbs that end in **-ch**, **-s**, **-sh**, **-x**, or **-z**.

watch	watch**es**
pass	pass**es**
rush	rush**es**
relax	relax**es**
buzz	buzz**es**

3. Change the **y** to **i** and add -es when the base form ends in **consonant + y.**

study	stud**ies**
hurry	hurr**ies**
dry	dr**ies**

Do not change the **y** when the base form ends in **vowel + y.** Add -s.

play	play**s**
enjoy	enjoy**s**

4. A few verbs have **irregular forms.**

be	**is**
do	**does**
go	**goes**
have	**has**

21 | Spelling Rules for Base Form of Verb + -ing (Progressive and Gerund)

1. Add -*ing* to the base form of the verb.

read	read**ing**
stand	stand**ing**

2. If the verb ends in a **silent -e**, drop the final -*e* and add -*ing*.

leave	leav**ing**
take	tak**ing**

3. In **one-syllable** verbs, if the last three letters are a consonant-vowel-consonant combination (CVC), double the last consonant and add -*ing*.

   C V C
   ↓ ↓ ↓
   s i t sit**ting**

   C V C
   ↓ ↓ ↓
   p l a n plan**ning**

   Do not double the last consonant in verbs that end in -*w*, -*x*, or -*y*.

sew	sew**ing**
fix	fix**ing**
play	play**ing**

4. In verbs of **two or more syllables** that end in a consonant-vowel-consonant combination, double the last consonant only if the last syllable is stressed.

admít	admit**ting**	*(The last syllable is stressed.)*
whísper	whisper**ing**	*(The last syllable is not stressed, so don't double the -**r**.)*

5. If the verb ends in -*ie*, change the *ie* to *y* before adding -*ing*.

die	d**ying**

   STRESS
   ′ shows main stress.
   ---

22 | Spelling Rules for Base Form of Verb + -ed (Simple Past and Past Participle of Regular Verbs)

1. If the verb ends in a **consonant**, add -*ed*.

return	return**ed**
help	help**ed**

2. If the verb ends in -*e*, add -*d*.

live	live**d**
create	create**d**
die	die**d**

3. In **one-syllable** verbs, if the last three letters are a consonant-vowel-consonant combination (CVC), double the last consonant and add -*ed*.

   C V C
   ↓ ↓ ↓
   h o p hop**ped**

   C V C
   ↓ ↓ ↓
   g r a b grab**bed**

   Do not double the last consonant in verbs that end in -*w*, -*x*, or -*y*.

bow	bow**ed**
mix	mix**ed**
play	play**ed**

4. In verbs of **two or more syllables** that end in a consonant-vowel-consonant combination, double the last consonant only if the last syllable is stressed.

prefér	prefer**red**	*(The last syllable is stressed.)*
vísit	visit**ed**	*(The last syllable is not stressed, so don't double the -**t**.)*

5. If the verb ends in **consonant + y**, change the *y* to *i* and add -*ed*.

worry	worr**ied**
carry	carr**ied**

6. If the verb ends in **vowel + y**, add -*ed*. (Do not change the *y* to *i*.)

play	play**ed**
annoy	annoy**ed**

   EXCEPTIONS:

lay	la**id**
pay	pa**id**
say	sa**id**

23 | Spelling Rules for the Comparative (-er) and Superlative (-est) of Adjectives

1. With **one-syllable** adjectives, add **-er** to form the comparative. Add **-est** to form the superlative.

cheap	cheap**er**	cheap**est**
bright	bright**er**	bright**est**

2. If the adjective ends in **-e**, add **-r** or **-st**.

nice	nice**r**	nice**st**

3. If the adjective ends in **consonant + y**, change **y** to **i** before you add **-er** or **-est**.

pretty	pett**ier**	pett**iest**

   EXCEPTION:

shy	shy**er**	shy**est**

4. If a one-syllable adjective ends in a consonant-vowel-consonant combination (CVC), double the last consonant before adding **-er** or **-est**.

   C V C
   ↓ ↓ ↓
   b i g   big**ger**   big**gest**

   Do not double the consonant in adjectives ending in **-w** or **-y.**

slow	slow**er**	slow**est**
gray	gray**er**	gray**est**

24 | Spelling Rules for Adverbs Ending in -ly

1. Add **-ly** to the corresponding adjective.

nice	nice**ly**
quiet	quiet**ly**
beautiful	beautiful**ly**

2. If the adjective ends in **consonant + y**, change the **y** to **i** before adding **-ly**.

easy	eas**ily**

3. If the adjective ends in **-le**, drop the **e** and add **-y**.

possible	possibl**y**

   Do not drop the **e** for other adjectives ending in **-e.**

extreme	extreme**ly**

   EXCEPTION:

true	tru**ly**

4. If the adjective ends in **-ic**, add **-ally**.

basic	basic**ally**
fantastic	fantastic**ally**

25 | Spelling Rules for Regular Plural Nouns

1. Add **-s** to most nouns.

book	book**s**
table	table**s**
cup	cup**s**

2. Add **-es** to nouns that end in **-ch, -s, -sh,** or **-x.**

watch	watch**es**
bus	bus**es**
dish	dish**es**
box	box**es**

3. Add **-s** to nouns that end in **vowel + y.**

day	day**s**
key	key**s**

4. Change the **y** to **i** and add **-es** to nouns that end in **consonant + y.**

baby	bab**ies**
city	cit**ies**
strawberry	strawberr**ies**

5. Add **-s** to nouns that end in **vowel + o.**

radio	radio**s**
video	video**s**
zoo	zoo**s**

6. Add **-es** to nouns that end in **consonant + o.**

potato	potato**es**
tomato	tomato**es**

   EXCEPTIONS: kilo—kilos, photo—photos, piano—pianos

1. **SIMPLE PRESENT, PRESENT PROGRESSIVE, AND IMPERATIVE**

Contractions with *Be*

I am	=	**I'm**
you are	=	**you're**
he is	=	**he's**
she is	=	**she's**
it is	=	**it's**
we are	=	**we're**
you are	=	**you're**
they are	=	**they're**

SIMPLE PRESENT	PRESENT PROGRESSIVE
I'm a student.	**I'm** studying here.
He's my teacher.	**He's** teaching verbs.
We're from Canada.	**We're** living here.

I am not	=	**I'm not**		
you are not	=	**you're not**	OR	you **aren't**
he is not	=	**he's not**	OR	he **isn't**
she is not	=	**she's not**	OR	she **isn't**
it is not	=	**it's not**	OR	it **isn't**
we are not	=	**we're not**	OR	we **aren't**
you are not	=	**you're not**	OR	you **aren't**
they are not	=	**they're not**	OR	they **aren't**

SIMPLE PRESENT	PRESENT PROGRESSIVE
She's **not** sick.	She's **not** reading.
He **isn't** late.	He **isn't** coming.
We **aren't** twins.	We **aren't** leaving.
They**'re not** here.	They**'re not** playing.

Contractions with *Do*

do not	=	**don't**
does not	=	**doesn't**

SIMPLE PRESENT	IMPERATIVE
They **don't live** here.	**Don't run!**
It **doesn't snow** much.	

2. **SIMPLE PAST AND PAST PROGRESSIVE**

Contractions with *Be*

was not	=	**wasn't**
were not	=	**weren't**

SIMPLE PAST	PAST PROGRESSIVE
He **wasn't** a poet.	He **wasn't** singing.
They **weren't** twins.	They **weren't** sleeping.
We **didn't see** her.	

Contractions with *Do*

did not	=	**didn't**

3. **FUTURE**

Contractions with *Will*

I will	=	**I'll**
you will	=	**you'll**
he will	=	**he'll**
she will	=	**she'll**
it will	=	**it'll**
we will	=	**we'll**
you will	=	**you'll**
they will	=	**they'll**

will not	=	**won't**

FUTURE WITH *WILL*
I'll take the train.
It**'ll be** faster that way.
We'll go together.
He **won't come** with us.
They **won't miss** the train.

Contractions with *Be going to*

I am going to	=	**I'm** going to
you are going to	=	**you're** going to
he is going to	=	**he's** going to
she is going to	=	**she's** going to
it is going to	=	**it's** going to
we are going to	=	**we're** going to
you are going to	=	**you're** going to
they are going to	=	**they're** going to

FUTURE WITH *BE GOING TO*
I'm going to buy tickets tomorrow.
She**'s going to call** you.
It**'s going to rain** soon.
We**'re going to drive** to Boston.
They**'re going to crash**!

4. Present Perfect and Present Perfect Progressive

Contractions with *Have*

I have	=	I've
you have	=	you've
he has	=	he's
she has	=	she's
it has	=	it's
we have	=	we've
you have	=	you've
they have	=	they've
have not	=	haven't
has not	=	hasn't

> You've already **read** that page.
> We've **been writing** for an hour.
> She's **been** to Africa three times.
> It's **been raining** since yesterday.
> We **haven't seen** any elephants yet.
> They **haven't been living** here long.

5. Modals and Similar Expressions

cannot or can not	=	can't
could not	=	couldn't
should not	=	shouldn't
had better	=	'd better
would prefer	=	'd prefer
would rather	=	'd rather

> She **can't dance**.
> We **shouldn't go**.
> They'**d better decide**.
> I'**d prefer** coffee.
> I'**d rather take** the bus.

27 | Capitalization and Punctuation Rules

	USE FOR . . .	EXAMPLES
capital letter	• the pronoun *I* • proper nouns • the first word of a sentence	• Tomorrow **I** will be here at 2:00. • His name is **Karl**. He lives in **Germany**. • **When** does the train leave? **At** 2:00.
apostrophe (')	• possessive nouns • contractions	• Is that **Marta's** coat? • **That's** not hers. **It's** mine.
comma (,)	• after items in a list • before sentence connectors *and*, *but*, *or*, and *so* • after the first part of a sentence that begins with *because* • after the first part of a sentence that begins with a preposition • after the first part of a sentence that begins with a time clause or an *if* clause	• He bought **apples**, **pears**, **oranges**, and **bananas**. • They watched TV, **and** she played video games. • *Because* it's raining, we're not walking to the office. • *Across from* the post office, there's a good restaurant. • *After he arrived*, we ate dinner. • *If it rains*, we won't go.
exclamation mark (!)	• at the end of a sentence to show surprise or a strong feeling	• You're here! That's great! • Stop! A car is coming!
period (.)	• at the end of a statement	• Today is Wednesday.
question mark (?)	• at the end of a question	• What day is today?

28 | Pronunciation Table

🎧 These are the pronunciation symbols used in this text. Listen to the pronunciation of the key words.

	VOWELS				CONSONANTS		
Symbol	**Key Word**	**Symbol**	**Key Word**	**Symbol**	**Key Word**	**Symbol**	**Key Word**
i	beat, feed	ə	banana, among	p	pack, happy	ʃ	ship, machine, station, special, discussion
ɪ	bit, did	ɚ	shirt, murder	b	back, rubber		
eɪ	date, paid	aɪ	bite, cry, buy, eye	t	tie	ʒ	measure, vision
ɛ	bet, bed	aʊ	about, how	d	die	h	hot, who
æ	bat, bad	ɔɪ	voice, boy	k	came, key, quick	m	men
ɑ	box, odd, father	ɪr	beer	g	game, guest	n	sun, know, pneumonia
ɔ	bought, dog	ɛr	bare	tʃ	church, nature, watch	ŋ	sung, ringing
oʊ	boat, road	ɑr	bar	dʒ	judge, general, major	w	wet, white
ʊ	book, good	ɔr	door	f	fan, photograph	l	light, long
u	boot, food, student	ʊr	tour	v	van	r	right, wrong
ʌ	but, mud, mother			θ	thing, breath	y	yes, use, music
				ð	then, breathe	t̮	butter, bottle
				s	sip, city, psychology		
				z	zip, please, goes		

> **STRESS**
> ′ shows main stress.

29 | Pronunciation Rules for the Simple Present: Third-Person Singular (he, she, it)

1. The third-person singular in the simple present always ends in the letter -s. There are, however, three different pronunciations for the final sound of the third-person singular.

/s/	/z/	/ɪz/
talks	loves	dances

2. The final sound is pronounced /s/ after the voiceless sounds /p/, /t/, /k/, and /f/.

top	tops
get	gets
take	takes
laugh	laughs

3. The final sound is pronounced /z/ after the voiced sounds /b/, /d/, /g/, /v/, /m/, /n/, /ŋ/, /l/, /r/, and /ð/.

describe	describes
spend	spends
hug	hugs
live	lives
seem	seems
remain	remains
sing	sings
tell	tells
lower	lowers
bathe	bathes

4. The final sound is pronounced /z/ after all **vowel sounds**.

agree	agrees
try	tries
stay	stays
know	knows

5. The final sound is pronounced /ɪz/ after the sounds /s/, /z/, /ʃ/, /ʒ/, /tʃ/, and /dʒ/. /ɪz/ adds a syllable to the verb.

miss	misses
freeze	freezes
rush	rushes
massage	massages
watch	watches
judge	judges

6. *Do* and *say* have a change in vowel sound.

do	/du/	does	/dʌz/
say	/seɪ/	says	/sɛz/

1. The regular simple past and past participle always end in the letter *-d*. There are three different pronunciations for the final sound of the regular simple past and past participle.

/**t**/	/**d**/	/**ɪd**/
ra**c**e**d**	live**d**	attend**ed**

2. The final sound is pronounced /**t**/ after the voiceless sounds /**p**/, /**k**/, /**f**/, /**s**/, /ʃ/, and /tʃ/.

hop	ho**pped**
work	wor**ked**
laugh	lau**ghed**
address	addre**ssed**
publish	publi**shed**
watch	wa**tched**

3. The final sound is pronounced /**d**/ after the voiced sounds /**b**/, /**g**/, /**v**/, /**z**/, /ʒ/, /dʒ/, /**m**/, /**n**/, /ŋ/, /l/, /**r**/, and /ð/.

rub	ru**bbed**
hug	hu**gged**
live	live**d**
surprise	surpri**sed**
massage	massa**ged**
change	chan**ged**
rhyme	rhy**med**
return	retur**ned**
bang	ba**nged**
enroll	enro**lled**
appear	appea**red**
bathe	ba**thed**

4. The final sound is pronounced /**d**/ after all **vowel sounds**.

agree	agr**eed**
die	di**ed**
play	pla**yed**
enjoy	enj**oyed**
snow	sn**owed**

5. The final sound is pronounced /**ɪd**/ after /**t**/ and /**d**/. /**ɪd**/ adds a syllable to the verb.

start	star**ted**
decide	deci**ded**

GLOSSARY OF GRAMMAR TERMS

action verb a verb that describes an action.
- *Alicia **ran** home.*

adjective a word that describes a noun or pronoun.
- *That's a **great** idea.*
- *It's **wonderful**.*

adverb a word that describes a verb, an adjective, or another adverb.
- *She drives **carefully**.*
- *She's a **very** good driver.*
- *She drives **really** well.*

adverb of frequency an adverb that describes how often something happens.
- *We **always** watch that program.*

adverb of manner an adverb that describes how someone does something or how something happens. It usually ends in *-ly*.
- *He sings **beautifully**.*

adverb of time an adverb that describes when something happens.
- *We'll see you **soon**.*

affirmative a statement or answer meaning *Yes*.
- *He **works**.* (affirmative statement)
- ***Yes**, he **does**.* (affirmative short answer)

article a word that goes before a noun.
The indefinite articles are *a* and *an*.
- *I ate **a** sandwich and **an** apple.*
The definite article is *the*.
- *I didn't like **the** sandwich. **The** apple was good.*

auxiliary verb (also called **helping verb**) a verb used with a main verb. *Be*, *do*, and *have* are often auxiliary verbs. Modals (*can*, *should*, *may . . .*) are also auxiliary verbs.
- *I **am** exercising right now.*
- ***Does** he exercise every day?*
- *She **should** exercise every day.*

base form the simple form of a verb without any endings (*-s*, *-ed*, *-ing*) or other changes.
- ***be**, **have**, **go**, **drive***

capital letter the large form of a letter. The capital letters are: *A, B, C, D, . . .*
- ***A**licia lives in the **U**nited **S**tates.*

clause a group of words that has a subject and a verb. A sentence can have one or more clauses.
- ***We are leaving now.*** (one clause)
- ***When he calls, we'll leave.*** (two clauses)

common noun a word for a person, place, or thing (but not the name of the person, place, or thing).
- *Teresa lives in a **house** near the **beach**.*

comparative the form of an adjective or adverb that shows the difference between two people, places, or things.
- *Alain is **shorter** than Brendan.* (adjective)
- *Brendan runs **faster** than Alain.* (adverb)

comparison a statement that shows the difference between two people, places, or things. A comparison can use comparative adjectives and comparative adverbs. It can also use *as . . . as.*
- *Alain is **shorter than** Brendan.*
- *Alain isn't **as tall as** Brendan.*
- *He runs **faster than** Brendan.*

consonant a letter of the alphabet. The consonants are:
- ***b, c, d, f, g, h, j, k, l, m, n, p, q, r, s, t, v, w, x, y, z***

continuous See **progressive**.

contraction a short form of a word or words. An apostrophe (') replaces the missing letter or letters.
- ***she's** = she is*
- ***hasn't** = has not*
- ***can't** = cannot*
- ***won't** = will not*

count noun   a noun that you can count. It has a singular and a plural form.

- one **book**, two **books**

definite article   *the*.
This article goes before a noun that refers to a specific person, place, or thing.

- *Please bring me **the book** on the table. I'm almost finished reading it.*

dependent clause   (also called **subordinate clause**) a clause that needs a main clause for its meaning.

- ***When I get home**, I'll call you.*

direct object   a noun or pronoun that receives the action of a verb.

- *Marta kicked **the ball**. I saw **her**.*

formal   language used in business situations or with adults you do not know.

- *Good afternoon, Mr. Rivera. Please have a seat.*

gerund   a noun formed with verb + *-ing*.
It can be the subject or object of a sentence.

- ***Swimming** is great exercise.*
- *I enjoy **swimming**.*

helping verb   See **auxiliary verb**.

imperative   a sentence that gives a command or instructions.

- ***Hurry!***
- ***Don't touch that!***

indefinite article   *a* or *an*.
These articles go before a noun that does not refer to a specific person, place, or thing.

- *Can you bring me **a book**? I'm looking for something to read.*

indefinite past   past time, but not a specific time. It is often used with the present perfect.

- *I**'ve** already **seen** that movie.*

indefinite pronoun   a pronoun such as *someone, something, anyone, anything, anywhere, no one, nothing, everyone*, and *everything*. An indefinite pronoun does not refer to a specific person, place, or thing.

- ***Someone** called you last night.*
- *Did **anything** happen?*

indirect object   a noun or pronoun (often a person) that receives something as the result of the action of the verb.

- *I told **John** the story.*
- *He gave **me** some good advice.*

infinitive   *to* + base form of the verb.

- *I want **to leave** now.*

infinitive of purpose   *(in order) to* + base form. This form gives the reason for an action.

- *I go to school **in order to learn** English.*

informal   language used with family, friends, and children.

- *Hi, Pete. Sit down.*

information question   See ***wh-* question**.

inseparable phrasal verb   a phrasal verb whose parts must stay together.

- *We **ran into** Tomás at the supermarket.*

intransitive verb   a verb that does not have an object.

- *We **fell**.*

irregular   a word that does not change its form in the usual way.

- ***good → well***
- ***bad → worse***

irregular verb   a verb that does not form its past with *-ed*.

- ***leave → left***

main clause   a clause that can stand alone as a sentence.

- *When I get home, **I'll call you**.*

main verb   a verb that describes an action or state. It is often used with an auxiliary verb.

- *Jared is **calling**.*
- *He'll **call** again later.*
- *Does he **call** every day?*

modal   a type of auxiliary verb. It goes before a main verb and expresses ideas such as ability, advice, obligation, permission, and possibility. *Can, could, will, would, may, might, should*, and *must* are modals.

- ***Can** you swim?*
- *You really **should** learn to swim.*

negative   a statement or answer meaning *No.*
- He **doesn't** work. (negative statement)
- **No**, he **doesn't**. (negative short answer)

non-action verb (also called **stative verb**)
a verb that does not describe an action. It describes such things as thoughts, feelings, and senses.
- I **remember** that word.
- Chris **loves** ice cream.
- It **tastes** great.

non-count noun   a noun that you usually do not count (*air*, *water*, *rice*, *love*, . . .). It has only a singular form.
- The **rice** is delicious.

noun   a word for a person, place, or thing.
- My **sister**, **Anne**, works in an **office**.
- She uses a **computer**.

object   a noun or pronoun that receives the action of a verb. Sometimes a verb has two objects.
- She wrote **a letter to Tom**.
- She wrote **him a letter**.

object pronoun   a pronoun (*me, you, him, her, it, us, them*) that receives the action of a verb.
- I gave **her** a book.
- I gave **it** to **her**.

paragraph   a group of sentences, usually about one topic.

participial adjective   an adjective that ends in *-ing* or *-ed*. It comes from a verb.
- That's an **interesting** book.
- She's **interested** in the book.

particle   a word that looks like a preposition and combines with a main verb to form a phrasal verb. It often changes the meaning of the main verb.
- He looked the word **up**.
  (He looked for the meaning in the dictionary.)
- I ran **into** my teacher.
  (I met my teacher accidentally.)

past participle   a verb form (verb + *-ed*). It can also be irregular. It is used to form the present perfect. It can also be an adjective.
- We've **lived** here since April.
- She's **interested** in math.

phrasal verb   (also called **two-word verb**)
a verb that has two parts (verb + particle). The meaning is often different from the meaning of its separate parts.
- He **grew up** in Texas. (became an adult)
- His parents **brought** him **up** to be honest. (raised)

phrase   a group of words that forms a unit but does not have a main verb. Many phrases give information about time or place.
- **Last year**, we were living **in Canada**.

plural   two or more.
- There **are** three **people** in the restaurant.
- **They are** eating dinner.
- **We** saw **them**.

possessive   nouns, pronouns, or adjectives that show a relationship or show that someone owns something.
- Zach is **Megan's** brother. (possessive noun)
- Is that car **his**? (possessive pronoun)
- That's **his** car. (possessive adjective)

predicate   the part of a sentence that has the main verb. It tells what the subject is doing or describes the subject.
- My sister **works for a travel agency**.

preposition   a word that goes before a noun or a pronoun to show time, place, or direction.
- I went **to** the bank **on** Monday. It's **next to** my office.

Prepositions also go before nouns, pronouns, and gerunds in expressions with verbs and adjectives.
- We rely **on** him.
- She's accustomed **to** getting up early.

progressive   (also called **continuous**)
the verb form *be* + verb + *-ing*. It focuses on the continuation (not the completion) of an action.
- She**'s reading** the paper.
- We **were watching** TV when you called.

pronoun   a word used in place of a noun.
- That's my brother. You met **him** at my party.

proper noun   a noun that is the name of a person, place, or thing. It begins with a capital letter.
- **Maria** goes to **Central High School**.
- It's on **High Street**.

punctuation   marks used in writing (period, comma, . . .). They make the meaning clear. For example, a period (**.**) shows the end of a sentence. It also shows that the sentence is a statement, not a question.

quantifier   a word or phrase that shows an amount (but not an exact amount). It often comes before a noun.

- Josh bought **a lot of** books last year, but he only read **a few**.
- He doesn't have **much** time.

question   See **yes/no question** and **wh- question**.

question word   See **wh- word**.

reciprocal pronoun   a pronoun (*each other* or *one another*) that shows that the subject and object of a sentence refer to the same people and that these people have a two-way relationship.

- Megan and Jason have known **each other** since high school.
- All the students worked with **one another** on the project.

reflexive pronoun   a pronoun (*myself, yourself, himself, herself, itself, ourselves, yourselves, themselves*) that shows that the subject and the object of the sentence refer to the same people or things.

- He looked at **himself** in the mirror.
- They enjoyed **themselves** at the party.

regular   a word that changes its form in the usual way.

- **play** → play**ed**
- **fast** → fast**er**
- **quick** → quick**ly**

sentence   a group of words that has a subject and a main verb. It begins with a capital letter and ends with a period (**.**), question mark (**?**), or exclamation point (**!**).

- **Computers are** very useful.

EXCEPTION: In imperative sentences, the subject is *you*. We do not usually say or write the subject in imperative sentences.

- **Call** her now!

separable phrasal verb   a phrasal verb whose parts can separate.

- Tom **looked** the word **up** in a dictionary.
- He **looked** it **up**.

short answer   an answer to a *yes/no* question.

A: *Did you call me last night?*
B: *No, I didn't.* OR *No.*

singular   one.

- They have **a sister**.
- **She** works in **a hospital**.

statement   a sentence that gives information. In writing, it ends in a period.

- Today is Monday.

stative verb   See **non-action verb**.

subject   the person, place, or thing that the sentence is about.

- **Ms. Chen** teaches English.
- **Her class** is interesting.

subject pronoun   a pronoun that shows the person or thing *(I, you, he, she, it, we, they)* that the sentence is about.

- **I** read a lot.
- **She** reads a lot too.

subordinate clause   See **dependent clause**.

superlative   the form of an adjective or adverb that is used to compare a person, place, or thing to a group of people, places, or things.

- Cindi is **the best** dancer in the group. (adjective)
- She dances **the most gracefully**. (adverb)

tense   the form of a verb that shows the time of the action.

- **simple present**: *Fabio* **talks** *to his friend every day.*
- **simple past**: *Fabio* **talked** *to his teacher yesterday.*

third-person singular   the pronouns *he, she*, and *it* or a singular noun. In the simple present, the third-person-singular verb ends in *-s*.

- Tomás **works** in an office. (Tomás = he)

time clause   a clause that begins with a time word such as *when, before, after, while*, or *as soon as*.

- I'll call you **when I get home**.

time expression   a phrase that describes when something happened or will happen.

- We saw Tomás **last week**.
- He'll graduate **next year**.

transitive verb   a verb that has an object.

- She **paints** beautiful pictures.

two-word verb   See **phrasal verb**.

verb   a word that describes what the subject of the sentence does, thinks, feels, senses, or owns.

- They **run** two miles every day.
- She **loved** that movie.
- He **has** a new camera.

vowel   a letter of the alphabet. The vowels are:

- *a, e, i, o, u.*

wh- question   (also called **information question**) a question that begins with a *wh-* word. You answer a *wh-* question with information.

A: Where *are you going?*

B: *To the store.*

wh- word   (also called **question word**) a word such as *who, what, when, where, which, why, how,* and *how much.* It can begin a *wh-* question.

- **Who** *is that?*
- **What** *did you see?*
- **When** *does the movie usually start?*
- **How** *long is it?*

yes/no question   a question that begins with a form of *be* or an auxiliary verb. You can answer a *yes/no* question with *yes* or *no.*

A: Are *you a student?*

B: Yes, *I am.* OR **No,** *I'm not.*

A: Do *you come here often?*

B: Yes, *I do.* OR **No,** *I don't.*

REVIEW TESTS ANSWER KEY

Note: In this answer key, where the contracted verb form is given, it is the preferred form, though the full form is also acceptable. Where the full verb form is given, it is the preferred form, though the contracted form is also acceptable.

PART I

I (Unit 1)
2. breathe
3. 's going
4. goes
5. rains
6. 's raining
7. 're dancing
8. dance

II (Unit 1)
1. c. 'm brushing
   d. Is . . . getting
   e. think
   f. 's looking
2. a. smells
   b. are . . . cooking
   c. do . . . have
   d. don't
   e. Do . . . know
   f. 're keeping OR keep
   g. 'm standing
   h. don't see
3. a. tastes
   b. 'm packing
   c. Is
   d. don't want
   e. 'm not
   f. look
   g. Do . . . feel OR Are . . . feeling
   h. do OR am
   i. hear
   j. 're leaving

III (Unit 2)
2. don't walk
3. lock
4. don't forget
5. Don't put
6. Put
7. Call
8. don't call
9. Have . . . enjoy

IV (Unit 3)
2. moved
3. did . . . live
4. was
5. taught
6. Did . . . like
7. did
8. Did . . . appear
9. did

10. wasn't
11. didn't seem
12. was
13. went
14. Were
15. wasn't
16. began
17. Did . . . expect
18. didn't

V (Units 3 and 5)
2. cook
3. Were
4. used to
5. go
6. went
7. Did
8. didn't have

VI (Unit 4)
2. was mowing
3. rang
4. had
5. wasn't
6. wasn't driving
7. hit
8. did . . . do
9. was trying
10. wasn't paying
11. Did . . . call
12. happened
13. appeared
14. got
15. left
16. called

VII (Unit 6)
2. 'll be
3. 'll
4. does
5. 's going to
6. 'll have
7. 's going to
8. are we going to
9. Will
10. are

VIII (Unit 7)
2. a. get
   b. 'll see
3. a. 'll stay
   b. finish
4. a. graduates
   b. 'll live
5. a. 'll read
   b. eat
6. a. 'll buy
   b. save
7. a. will call
   b. leaves
8. a. turn
   b. 'll be

IX (Unit 8)
1. b. Who went
   c. What did you see
2. a. What happened
   b. What did you get
   c. Who(m) did you study

PART II

I (Unit 9)

2. herself	9. them
3. their	10. yourself
4. themselves	11. yourself
5. yourself	12. you
6. themselves	13. them
7. them	14. each other's
8. one another	

II (Unit 10)

2. turned into	8. pass over
3. found out	9. get back
4. set up	10. went on
5. help out	11. get by
6. look up	12. hand . . . over
7. pick out	

III (Unit 10)

2. wrote it down	5. help him out
3. pick her up	6. picked it out
4. put it on	7. write them up

IV (Units 9 and 10)

2. B	5. A	8. A
3. A	6. C	9. A
4. D	7. C	10. A

V (Units 9 and 10)

I have three older brothers, but my role model is my next oldest brother, Orlando. Orlando was

always there for ~~myself~~ *me* when we were growing up. I was very small, and he always kept the bullies

away. When I couldn't figure ~~up~~ *out* homework

problems by myself, he helped ~~out me~~ *me out*. Orlando never gave up when he had problems. Once, in

high school, my baseball team passed ~~myself~~ *me* up for pitcher. I wanted to quit the team, but he talked me

~~over~~ *into* playing. In fact, he woke *up* early every morning ~~up~~ to practice with me. When they chose me for pitcher the following year, we were really

proud of ~~ourselves~~ *each other* —he was proud of me for

succeeding, and I was proud of ~~himself~~ *him* for being such a great coach.

PART III

I (Units 11–15)

2. b	6. a
3. a	7. a
4. a	8. a
5. b	9. a

II (Units 11–15)

2. request	9. request
3. suggestion	10. request
4. permission	11. ability
5. ability	12. suggestion
6. permission	13. advice
7. suggestion	14. ability
8. advice	

III (Units 11–15)

1. b. should we	2. a. Let's
c. could	b. Could
d. Why not	c. be able to
e. 'd better	d. Do you mind if
f. How about	e. Not at all.
g. should	f. could
h. Let's	g. 'd better
i. We should	3. a. Why don't
	b. Could
	c. could
	d. Would you mind

IV (Units 11–15)

2. D	6. D	10. A
3. C	7. D	11. C
4. A	8. A	
5. D	9. B	

V (Units 11–15)

2. A: When you were a child, were you able to skate?

B: Yes. In fact, I once ~~could~~ *was able to* win a competition in my school.

3. **A:** Could ~~please you~~ *you please* help me?
   OR *Could you help me, please?*

   B: Sure. What seems to be the problem?

4. **A:** Would you mind giving me a ride home?

   Not at all. OR *No, I wouldn't.*

   B: ~~Yes, I would~~. When would you like to leave?

5. **A:** You really ought ^*to* update your virus protection.

   B: OK. I'll do it today.

6. **A:** We ~~would~~ *'d* better hurry, or we'll be late.

   B: Don't worry. We can still get there on time.

7. **A:** Could I borrow the car tonight?

   can't

   B: Sorry, but you ~~couldn't~~. I need it myself.

8. **A:** Do you mind if my friend ~~coming~~ *comes* to the party with me?

   B: Not at all. There's always room for one more!

PART IV

I (Unit 16)
2. have . . . been
3. has . . . gotten
4. 've . . . paid
5. Have . . . written
6. hasn't read
7. have . . . won
8. haven't told
9. Has . . . come
10. 've had
11. Have . . . chosen

II (Unit 16)
2. Since, for
3. for
4. since
5. for
6. Since
7. since
8. for

III (Units 17 and 18)
2. C   5. B   8. A
3. D   6. C   9. A
4. A   7. B   10. A

IV (Unit 20)
2. D   6. B   10. C
3. A   7. C   11. D
4. D   8. A
5. C   9. C

V (Units 16–20)
1. **b.** saw
2. **a.** drank (OR 's drunk)
   b. haven't drunk
   c. 've been drinking
3. **a.** has written
   b. Did . . . write
   c. wrote
4. **a.** 've been cooking
   b. cooked (OR 've cooked)
   c. 've cooked
5. **a.** 've been having (OR 've had)
   b. haven't had
   c. 've had
   d. had
   e. didn't have
6. **a.** looked
   b. 's been looking
   c. Has . . . looked (OR Did . . . look)
   d. looked

VI (Units 16–20)
2. I have been working as a bookkeeper in this company ~~since~~ *for* OR *since four years ago.* four years.
3. I have ~~did~~ *done* a good job.
4. I have already ~~been getting~~ *gotten* a promotion.
5. I ~~has~~ *have* gained a lot of experience in retail sales.
6. In addition, I have ~~took~~ *taken* several accounting courses.
7. Since February my boss ~~like~~ *has liked* my work a lot.
8. She has ~~gave~~ *given* me more and more responsibility.
9. I have already ~~show~~ *shown* my accounting skills.
10. This has been ~~being~~ a very good experience for me.

PART V

I (Unit 21)
1. **b.** many letters
2. **a.** it doesn't
3. **a.** 's
   b. several
   c. computers
4. **a.** It's
5. **a.** too much salt
   b. It tastes
6. **a.** it
7. **a.** a lot of
   b. many bags
8. **a.** much
   b. some
9. **a.** it

II (Unit 21)

2. enough
3. a lot of
4. How much
5. a little
6. a few
7. some
8. How many
9. any
10. much
11. a lot of
12. a few

III (Unit 22)

2. a, a, an
3. the
4. The
5. the, the
6. the
7. an
8. a
9. the, an

IV (Unit 22)

3. the
4. Money
5. Travel, Staying
6. The
7. Vegetables

V (Unit 22)

1. b. some
   c. a
   d. an
   e. The
   f. The
2. a. some
   b. some
   c. the
   d. some
   e. The
   f. the

VI (Units 21 and 22)

2. B
3. C
4. A
5. A
6. C
7. A

PART VI

I (Unit 23)

1. b. cozy
   c. Cheap
   d. perfect
2. a. incredibly
   b. new
   c. hardly
   d. terrific
3. a. good
   b. beautiful
   c. well
   d. obedient
   e. quickly

II (Units 25 and 26)

2. A
3. C
4. A
5. B
6. C
7. D
8. B
9. A
10. C
11. D
12. B
13. D

III (Unit 23)

2. C
3. D
4. B
5. C
6. B
7. A
8. B
9. B
10. C
11. C
12. B

IV (Units 25 and 26)

2. faster, more confused
3. later, sillier
4. harder, more fluently
5. more often, bigger
6. louder, faster
7. more frequently, worse

V (Units 24 and 26)

2. is as large as Apartment 22-G.
3. isn't as far (away) as Tony's pizzeria.
4. is as expensive as Tony's pizza.
5. play (OR are playing OR have played) as well as the Shock.
6. doesn't run as fast as (OR isn't as fast as) Jennifer.

VI (Units 25 and 26)

1. b. longest
   c. hardest
   d. the
   e. of
   f. best
2. a. big
   b. than
   c. much
   d. exciting
   e. Sooner
   f. as

VII (Units 23–26)

   I think today has been the ~~bad~~ *worst* day of my life. My car broke down on the expressway during rush hour this morning—~~a~~ *the* busiest time of day. I sat there for an hour waiting for a tow truck. The longer I waited, the *more* nervous I became. I was a wreck when I got to work. Of course, this was the day we were closing *the* biggest deal of the year. My boss called me five times about one letter. And *the* more frequently he called, the worse I typed. My next worry is the repair bill for the car. I hope it isn't as high *as* the last time.

   I'm going to try to relax now. There's an *interesting* ~~interested~~ movie on cable TV tonight. Jan saw it last week and says it's the ~~better~~ *best* film she's seen in a long time. After the movie, I'll take a ~~hotter~~ *hot* bath and go to bed. I'm looking forward to tomorrow. It can't be as ~~badly~~ *bad* as today!

PART VII

I (Unit 28)
2. to planning
3. for watching
4. about speaking
5. without worrying
6. in learning

II (Unit 31)
2. too messy
3. not cool enough
4. too tough
5. aggressively enough
6. loud enough

III (Units 27 and 30)
2. telling
3. smoking
4. giving up
5. Following
6. to feel
7. To save
8. to read
9. drinking
10. to take
11. eating
12. shopping
13. to reward

IV (Unit 29)
2. It's necessary to join
3. participate enough to meet
4. too busy to call
5. flexible enough for them to have
6. advise them to think about
7. it's important to know about
8. soon enough for them to pay
9. too busy to take
10. encourage you to start

V (Units 27–32)
2. B   5. A   8. D
3. A   6. D   9. C
4. C   7. C   10. C

VI (Units 27–32)
2. to hit
3. having
4. winning
5. playing
6. to become
7. to make
8. becoming
9. doing
10. to go
11. to accept
12. to study
13. studying
14. agreeing
15. answering

VII (Units 27–32)
2. D   4. B   6. D   8. C
3. D   5. D   7. B

PART VIII

I (Units 33–37)
2. b   6. b   9. a   12. a
3. a   7. a   10. b   13. b
4. b   8. a   11. b   14. b
5. a

II (Units 33–37)
2. necessity
3. preference
4. conclusion
5. expectation
6. prohibition
7. future possibility
8. conclusion
9. expectation
10. conclusion
11. necessity
12. prohibition

III (Units 33–37)
2. C   5. B   8. A
3. D   6. B   9. B
4. A   7. C   10. A

IV (Units 33–37)
2. She prefers not to watch science fiction.
3. It must be expensive.
4. She (OR Linda) wasn't supposed to open it in front of him (OR Somchai).
5. He must not be at work today.
6. She (OR Sue) might not like curry.
7. You (OR I) have to arrive at the airport by noon.
8. She (OR His sister) was going to go to his graduation.
9. It couldn't be Carl.
10. It could be very valuable.

V (Units 33–37)

I ['m] supposed to take my road test tomorrow. I'm a little nervous because I heard that there might be a storm. I'd ~~not rather~~ [rather not] drive in the rain! My instructor, John, is supposed to pick me up at 8:00 and drive me to the test area. Then he ~~have~~ [has] to wait for me while I take the test. He ~~doesn't have to~~ [must not OR can't] be in the car with me during the test—it's not allowed. I like John. I don't know much about him. He says he's been driving for more than 40 years, so I guess he [']s got to be at least 60. He ~~maybe~~ [may be] even older than that.

Well, it's getting late, and I should go to bed. I'd rather ~~watching~~ [watch] some TV, but I ~~hafta~~ [have to] get up early tomorrow.

INDEX

This Index is for the full and split editions. All entries are in the full book. Entries for Volume A of the split edition are in black. Entries for Volume B are in color.

Notes

Notes

Notes

NOTES

Notes

NOTES

Notes